Covert Investigation

Fifth Edition

Clive Harfield

MSc, LLM, MA, MPhil, PhD

and

Karen Harfield

BSc (Hons)

D1333839

OXFORD
UNIVERSITY PRESS

OXFORD

UNIVERSITY PRESS

Great Clarendon Street, Oxford, OX2 6DP,
United Kingdom

Oxford University Press is a department of the University of Oxford.
It furthers the University's objective of excellence in research, scholarship,
and education by publishing worldwide. Oxford is a registered trade mark of
Oxford University Press in the UK and in certain other countries

First Edition published in 2005
Fifth Edition published in 2018
Impression: 4

Published in the United States of America by Oxford University Press
198 Madison Avenue, New York, NY 10016, United States of America

British Library Cataloguing in Publication Data
Data available

Library of Congress Control Number: 2018941698

ISBN 978–0–19–882853–2

Printed in Great Britain by
Ashford Colour Press Ltd, Gosport, Hampshire

For Bryn

Foreword to the Fifth Edition

"Good Hunting!" Thirteen years ago, in the foreword to the first edition of this book, I wrote those words, Now I find myself writing them yet again in the fifth edition of this remarkable addition to the police hunter/gatherer's toolkit. It covers the difficult arena of police intelligence techniques and the balancing of democratic individual privacy and the state's duty to supply protection against criminals as they prey on communities. It is not, as some have claimed, only about terrorism and organized crime. It is about investigative strategy and decision making to solve problems. As I have argued on many occasions, would that I had this book long ago; my life and decision making, indeed my thinking and my understanding in this complicated field, would have been much enhanced. I am still answering questions about decisions I made twenty years ago.

To my knowledge there are very few handbooks, text books, or practical guides by police officers, serving or retired, that run to five editions.

There are at least eight reasons why this book is such a rare and valuable example of its kind. The first is that it is an intensely practical guide for police officers, especially investigators and their supervisors in these challenging times. Never have the police, in my more than fifty years of involvement with them either as a practitioner or academic and adviser/mentor, been under such scrutiny and pressure: political, media, community, legal, financial. This is one area of policing of widespread democratic concern and this book contains blueprints of the best ways of how to act.

This is related to the second reason: that it epitomizes the imperative, nay the duty, that the skilled practitioners in every age have to try to understand the extraordinary, complex environment in which they operate. This was articulated by John Steinbeck and Ed Ricketts long ago (in 1941 in 'The Log from the Sea of Cortez', Penguin Classics, 1995 edition of the narrative portion of 'The Sea of Cortez' page 92).

Third, through understanding what the legislators and the CJS require, the authors add to our detailed knowledge in what is a changing, politically highly charged, and critical environment. This book illustrates the difference between mere professional competence and high professional expertise. In an age of austerity and cuts it explains for example how to argue best value with sometimes expensive resources.

Fourth, it maps the expanding legal minefield that the legislation creates for police decision makers. This book describes in detail the processes and products that are needed to avoid the traps that can be set to undermine the investigator's and prosecutor's case. It epitomises the requirements of 'creative due process' and the 'lawfully audacious' requirement of being proportionate, legal, accountable, necessary, ethical, and acting on the best evidence available in covert response to crimes and criminals.

Fifth, it recounts the moral dimensions the decision making requires. This early inclusion of professional ethics has become increasingly valuable and relevant in the intervening decade and a bit.

Sixth, it is very thoughtful and empathetic of the difficulties of fulfilling all the requirements needed for surviving the white knuckle ride in the witness box to justify decisions, by analysing and assessing possibly fast changing situations and the problems they can create at an operational , tactical and strategic level.

Seventh, it demonstrates years of police officers digesting and learning as complex case law and political and legal thinking catches up with fast changing technical developments in the digital age. I was a member, two years ago, of the Deputy Prime Ministers Royal United Services Institute panel that reviewed aspects of our surveillance capability post the Snowden revelation. That learning helped me realise quite how far surveillance and counter surveillance had moved on in the thirteen years since the first edition of this book.

Eighth, and last for me, the demand from the book's many users from many disciplines for yet another update is a further tribute to the value it has for so many. The sheer numbers of practitioners I know at every rank, many using it operationally, others exploring the depths and issues on courses in academia and in police training, are remarkable. There may be many more reasons, but these I think put the lie to the lazy political shorthand that suggests that the legislation and its application by practitioners is a 'snoopers' charter'.

Since the first edition, my wish to see this book used in many a setting, dog eared and sprouting Times Law Reports, being used to bring offenders to justice has been fulfilled. Karen and Clive's work has lived up to and exceeded all my expectations. "Good Hunting" once again.

John G.D. Grieve CBE QPM BA(Hons) MPhil HonDL
Emeritus Professor London Metropolitan University
Former Deputy Assistant Commissioner Metropolitan Police Service
June 2018

Foreword to the Fourth Edition

I am truly honoured to write a yet another foreword for Clive and Karen, this time to the unprecedented fourth updated edition of this highly important book that promotes excellence in the use of intelligence. I quoted the earlier editions extensively as a member of the panel at the recent (July 2015) Royal United Services Institute (RUSI) Review ('A Democratic Licence to Operate') of digital surveillance law, theory and practice in the UK following the Edward Snowden revelations and debates.

Karen and Clive have helpfully revised the format of the book into two parts. In Part 1 they have focused on sound leadership, command and management techniques, and the moral bedrock of covert investigation in turn as a contributing foundation block for the integrity of criminal justice systems. Part 2 covers the law and procedure of covert investigation.

There are a number of significant developments wider than the investigation of 'digital footprints'. I will emphasize two where this volume is massively helpful in dealing with current concerns about intelligence: the concepts of 'legally audacious' and 'accountability' (more recently, 'lifetime accountability').

In the first foreword I called for investigators to be 'legally audacious' in what has been called a 'moral minefield' (see the new Chapter 1 here). It remains a justified and philosophically sound moral call to arms, I still believe, but there is a need for care and a rationale of what it can mean in specific contexts for practitioners who need to fully understand their accountability. Common practitioner and media parlance has sometimes translated this into a shorthand of 'lawfully audacious'. Strict adherence to the processes of checks and balances provided by Parliament and deep thought about the moral issues extensively explained in this book are a key part of being 'legally audacious' and are as important to successful covert investigation as knowledge of the law.

An important message is promoted with this fourth edition: 'It may be lawful, but is it moral?' is a key question that may be tested in the courts. As RUSI discussed, it is about policing and intelligence legitimacy, as well as legality; proportionality, as well as necessity; accountability which has become lifetime; and acting ethically on the best information available which is not limited to the law. All of these are helpfully explored and expanded in the toolkits in this new volume.

'Legally audacious', as opposed to unjustified and unreasonable risk-taking without taking into account the checks and balances of a democratic licence to operate, was never intended to be mere 'law enforcement audacious'. It did mean never straying across the line into 'unlawful' but considered ethically getting as close to the line as possible, recognizing that proportionality underpins legitimate audacity. It means a moral philosophy version of ethics proposed by practitioners themselves as opposed to imposed professional standards by the courts or politicians or even discipline codes. It is about moral autonomy— 'what does the good investigator do/how do they live their lives?' Even long after they have retired, that is what 'lifetime accountability' means.

In a recent review of a 16-year-old intelligence-related case, I reconstructed (albeit post facto though hinted at in surviving documents) over twenty issues that were on my mind/known to me at the time of the decision in respect of the operational, tactical context, and strategic environment. The reviewer still criticized my decisions as unreasonable and unjustified despite saying it was not unlawful and done for the best of reasons. And despite there being no criminal misfeasance and no disciplinary action. Another colleague has explained a series of decisions seventeen years ago with similar issues whilst also embroiled in 'lifetime accountability' (see BBC News website Magazine section 05.01.2016 for some of my thinking on this concept on another case over forty years old). Old challenges continue to bring new problems. Would that we had this excellent book then. It helps thinking, and not just with its useful checklists and toolkits. And it helps excellence in the hunters to bring the raptors and greedy to justice. Good hunting.

John G D Grieve CBE QPM
Former Deputy Commissioner Metropolitan Police
Professor Emeritus
London Metropolitan University
Senior Research Fellow
University of Portsmouth
January 2016

Foreword to the Third Edition

The value of this practical handbook, by my colleague and former colleagues Clive and Karen Harfield, is indicated by my title. This is the third edition, an unprecedented achievement in my experience of the writings for serving police officers and former police academics. Despite being on the other side of the globe their contribution to all that is best, in the application of the British Policing model in the complex shifting moral minefields of covert investigation, continues to be immense. Beyond the achievements and usage I listed in my foreword to the first and second editions I have seen this volume used on training courses, reviews of prosecutions and investigations, in arguments for more robust investigation tactics including in historic cases, in the creation of new tactics and thinking about strategy. For example their work has informed some of the thinking and concepts behind Her Majesty's Chief Inspector of Constabulary's (HMCIC) recent assessment of national policing units concerned with uncovering and preventing criminality associated with public protest (HMCIC 2012, *A review of national police units which provide intelligence on criminality associated with protest*, London, Home Office) following considerable public concern and debate. A lively public debate, which was not least, about the morality of decisions made during, and the ethics of, covert policing.

Whether the reader is a postgraduate serving officer student writing her dissertation, a Chief Officer under pressure to make a decision in a complicated investigation, or a Senior Investigating Officer in search of different investigative strategies in a serious crime case, all will benefit. As ever it is the investigative hunter-gatherers who are closest to my heart, there are many criminals who cannot prey on the vulnerable nor pursue their greed because of the advice obtained by the hunter-gatherers from this book. Good hunting to you all.

John G D Grieve CBE QPM
Senior Research Fellow University of Portsmouth
Professor Emeritus London Metropolitan University

Foreword to the Second Edition

This updated valuable guide now contains within the text the recent complex numerous cases and amendments that, as I predicted in the Foreword to the previous edition, were soon to be found in Times Law Reports sprouting from copies of the book, published only three years ago. As I anticipated, I have come across this book in bookshelves and on desks, dog-eared in vehicles and coffee-stained in canteens. What I had not predicted would be the welcome and praise from solicitors and barristers (see for example [2006] 6 EHRLR 759–60). To that number I add the CPS, for whom it has become a set text. I commend it to those either tasked with reducing or complaining about the police paperwork and bureaucracy involved (see for example *The Guardian* (London, 12.08.09, p 14); it will halve the time of even the slowest keyboard operator!). As a hunter/gatherer's and leader's craft box, as a practical, moral, legal, conceptual map of complexity, it is a great intelligence instrument. Would that I had had it long ago. Good hunting, it is again an honour to write this new foreword.

John G D Grieve CBE QPM
Professor Emeritus London Metropolitan University
Senior Research Fellow University of Portsmouth
August 2008

Foreword to the First Edition

As a Detective Sergeant in 1974, I was part of the team that reviewed the cases of Mealey and Sheridan. As a Detective Inspector in 1978, I inherited a team of investigators who had been involved in the Malone case. By the time that case reached the European Court of Human Rights in 1984, I was a Detective Chief Inspector member of the team that reorganized covert policing and, in particular, wrote the first editions of the *Informants Handling Guidelines*, which are now called *Covert Human Intelligence Sources*. A decade later, as Director of Intelligence at New Scotland Yard, I was again involved in the reorganisation of the intelligence function and its covert arm in particular. Another decade on, I am a recipient of all the dedicated, hard-developed products of RIPA as an independent Commissioner on the Independent Monitoring Commission in Belfast and Dublin. In any one of those task arenas, and in many others, I would have welcomed this valuable book into my toolkit.

Clive and Karen Harfield have done a remarkable job in distilling a vast amount of complex law and practice into this guide. Modestly, they told me their target readers were not the experienced SIOs on the specialist squads, but the practitioners in everyday policing. There are many who will benefit from the material gathered here.

The next generation of investigators gaining their initial experiences, the new teams leaders and those tasked with wider leadership and decision making are other groups where sensitive reasoning is required to acquire the resources needed for a successful investigation and the survival of that investigation in a court or courts of trial and appeal. Who would not benefit from over 80 cases described by the authors before facing a team of barristers who each have their chosen specialist field in the covert arena and are out to challenge every twist and turn of the investigation?

It is not just the police investigators who face that white-knuckle ride in the witness box. Besides the 43 police services, another 900 agencies and authorities are now beneficiaries of the act, there have been 30 statutory instruments directly connected to RIPA since 2000, supplementing the act which has been amended 89 times since then. The Police Act 1997 has itself been amended 92 times but not all relate to Part III. Here is a complex world described.

It is as much a neglect of duty not to use every lawful endeavour, not to be legally audacious in seeking every investigative tool to bring offenders to justice. In years to come, I hope to see heavily annotated copies of this book in offices, from crime squads to ACPO, on desks, hidden under the seats in surveillance vehicles, in briefcases and in any number of locations for ready reference, sprouting updating Times Law Reports. It is a valuable addition to the hunter/gatherer's toolkit. It is an honour to write this foreword. Good hunting.

John G D Grieve CBE QPM
Centre for Policing and Community Safety
Buckinghamshire Chilterns University College
September 2005

Acknowledgements

This fifth edition would not have been possible without the foundations laid in the first edition, and therefore those acknowledged previously deserve continued mention. The authors wish to express their appreciation to colleagues in a number of organizations, investigations and discussions with whom informed the writing of this book, and many of whom subsequently commented on early drafts. Others have provided material for study. In particular we thank: Cara Airey, Yvonne Ball, Sue Biddle, Simon Bronitt, Jackie Griffin, Glynis Hooper, Tony Hutchings, Kingsley Hyland, Mick Ives, Allyson MacVean, Simon McKay, Trevor Pearce, Louise Pierpoint, Phil Swinburne, Debbie Tedds, Simon Watkin, Dave Whordley, Katie Whiting, and Tim Wright. For this current edition additionally we thank Chris Dowen and Richard Lewis.

Organizations as well as individuals have provided practical assistance and access to information, as well as permission to reproduce copyright material: Bramshill Police Library (formerly part of the NPIA), the House of Commons Information Office, the former National Specialist Law Enforcement Centre (NPIA), University of Warwick Library, and Griffith University Library.

At Oxford University Press we thank Amy Baker and Rosie Chambers.

Professor Emeritus John Grieve CBE QPM (former Deputy Assistant Commissioner, Metropolitan Police Service and currently Independent Monitoring Commissioner for Northern Ireland) has, as ever, been a pillar of strength and support and a source of inspiration.

Contents

Abbreviations

AC	Appeal Court
ACPO	Association of Chief Police Officers
All ER	All England Law Reports
ANPR	Automatic Number Plate Recognition
AO	authorizing officer
BCU	basic command unit
CCTV	closed circuit television
CHIS	covert human intelligence source
CHIS Code	Covert Human Intelligence Sources Code of Practice
CMA	Competition and Markets Authority
CMLR	Common Market Law Reports
Communications Data Code	Acquisition and Disclosure of Communications Data Code of Practice
CPIA	Criminal Procedure and Investigations Act 1996
CPS	Crown Prosecution Service
Cr App R	Criminal Appeal Reports
Crim LR	Criminal Law Review
CSP	communications service provider
CSPI Code	Covert Surveillance and Property Interference Code of Practice
DPA	Data Protection Act 1998
DSO	Designated Senior Officer
ECHR	European Convention on Human Rights 1959
ECtHR	European Court of Human Rights, Strasbourg
EHRLR	European Human Rights Law Review
EHRR	European Human Rights Reports
EWHC	England and Wales High Court
GCHQ	Government Communications Headquarters
Hansard HC	Official Record of the House of Commons
Hansard HL	Official Record of the House of Lords
HMIC	Her Majesty's Inspectorate of Constabulary
HMRC	Her Majesty's Revenue and Customs (formerly
HMCE	Her Majesty's Customs and Excise)
HRA	Human Rights Act 1998
IPEI Code	Investigation of Protected Electronic Information Code of Practice
IOCA	Interception of Communications Act 1985 (repealed)

IOCCO	Interception of Communications Commissioner's Office
IPA2016	Investigatory Powers Act 2016
IPT	Investigatory Powers Tribunal
IPC	Investigatory Powers Commissioner
IPCO	Investigatory Powers Commissioner's Office
ISP	internet service provider
JIT	joint investigation team
MI5	Security Service
MI6	Secret Intelligence Service
MLA	mutual legal assistance
MOD	Ministry of Defence
NAFN	National Anti-Fraud Network
NCA	National Crime Agency
NCIS	National Criminal Intelligence Service
NCS	National Crime Squad
NHS	National Health Service
NGO	non-governmental organization
NOMS	National Offender Management Service
NPIA	National Policing Improvement Agency
NTAC	National Technical Advisory Centre
OFT	Office of Fair Trading
PA97	Police Act 1997
PACE	Police and Criminal Evidence Act 1984
PEI	protected electronic information
PII	public interest immunity
QB	Queen's Bench
RIPA2000	Regulation of Investigatory Powers Act 2000
RIP(S)A	Regulation of Investigatory Powers (Scotland) Act 2000
SDS	Special Demonstration Squad
SI	Statutory Instrument (secondary legislation supplementing Acts)
SOCA	Serious Organised Crime Agency
SPOC	Single Point of Contact
TPO	test purchase operative
UCO	undercover officer
UKCA	UK Central Authority (department of the Home Office)
WLR	Weekly Law Reports
WTA	Wireless Telegraphy Act 2006

Introduction

This book is written primarily to assist investigators and investigation managers in England and Wales, both criminal and regulatory, plan for and utilize those covert investigation methods for which specific statutory authority is required when statutory human rights are engaged by the proposed actions. In this context 'covert investigation' is legally specific. The term does not merely describe an inquiry of which the person under investigation is not yet aware. Rather, the term labels circumstances in which the privilege against self-incrimination—a founding principle of criminal justice in a liberal democratic society—is compromised. A suspect under arrest is advised of the legally protected due process rights that would enable them to act as they deem fit in their own best interests when confronted with the power and authority of the state and its agents acting against them. Covert investigation infringes legally protected human rights without giving the person under investigation the option to exercise any legally protected due process rights: the principle of the privilege against self-incrimination effectively is over-ridden. In the interests of preserving the characteristics of liberal democracy within the criminal justice system, recourse to such tactics should be exceptional rather than routine: a philosophy reinforced by the prerequisites of legality, legitimate purpose, necessity, and proportionality, which statutory tests must be satisfied if covert investigation is to be lawful.

This revised and updated fifth edition is occasioned by the enacting of the Investigatory Powers Act 2016 (IPA2016), which is not to be confused with the Regulation of Investigatory Powers Act 2000 (RIPA2000) (although with such similar titles, confusion should probably be anticipated). There are now two distinct elements to the covert investigation statutory regime in England and Wales: the new IPA2016 deals with interception of telecommunications and acquisition of telecommunications data; RIPA2000 now deals with visual surveillance, audio surveillance (other than of live telecommunications), and interactive surveillance through the deployment of informers and/or undercover investigators. The IPA2016 perpetuates the policy principle that intercepted communications content cannot be used in evidence at criminal trial. For crime investigators, interception product therefore remains an intelligence tool by means of which to identify conventional evidential opportunities.

This book concerns itself with the law and covert investigation management, not practitioner tradecraft; with requisite underpinning knowledge, not functional skills. The first edition was conceived in a context (2005) in which some police forces offered little or nothing in the way of covert investigation law and procedure training. A decade on, and the training lacuna is still evident from formal inspections (see, for example, the final Annual Report of the Chief Surveillance Commissioner, *OSC Annual Report* 2016–17 paras 4.3, 13.2, 15.3; also, the 2014 HMIC report *An Inspection of Undercover Policing in England and Wales*, Executive Summary, para 117, chapter paras 5.36, 5.72, 7.69, 7.74, 8.51). Publication logistics dictate that this volume must be regarded as a summary introduction rather than an all-inclusive, comprehensive encyclopaedia. This book helps to address the lacuna but does not purport to fill the void. The statutes, the accompanying Codes of Practice, and guidance previously published by the then Office of the Surveillance Commissioners (OSC) (some of it contained in the public annual reports but much of it restricted to those agencies that were subject to OSC inspection) remain the authoritative sources of information. It remains to be seen whether the newly created Investigatory Powers Commissioner, which role has superseded the former office of Chief Surveillance Commissioner under IPA2016, will follow OSC practice in issuing guidance, restricted or otherwise. This present volume identifies for practitioners ways of thinking and the issues to be considered.

We are grateful for the continued positive feedback from readers and reviewers, and for the content suggestions that are offered. To the extent consistent and feasible with the purpose of the book, such suggestions are incorporated. Often content suggestions relate to tradecraft matters and whilst tradecraft might consequentially come to be placed in the public domain through trial scrutiny, it is not the purpose of this book to expose techniques wider knowledge of which might frustrate investigation of crimes or regulation infringements. Nor is it the purpose of this book to consider how the information acquired by the techniques legislated, through inductive analysis, subsequently could be used not only evidentially but also to create new meaning—as 'intelligence', in the language of law enforcement. Such issues are much discussed elsewhere and would detract from our focus if included here. (The intelligence agencies have been invested with the same powers to further their own—usually non-evidential—purposes.)

Although RIPA2000 has been described as a very puzzling statute (*R v W, Attorney-General's Reference (No. 5 of 2002)* [2003] EWCA Crim 1632 at para. 98), and the IPA2016 may yet come to be so viewed, there is nevertheless a certain elegance and simplicity to their legal architecture (admittedly, a conclusion perhaps not immediately apparent to the casual observer and arrived at only after more than a decade of study and writing five editions of this book; a conclusion which might not be shared widely). As far as possible the statutory provisions are environment- and technology-neutral. Simply put, certain investigative conducts are regulated by statute when legally protected human rights are engaged irrespective, for instance, of whether the investigation is taking place in the 'real' physical world or in the 'virtual' online digital world. RIPA2000 and IPA2016 regulate the conduct of investigators, not the use of specific tools or technology.

Expert commentary on covert investigation law and policy ranges from the broadly supportive to arguments that suggest the law not only fails to give sufficient effect to human rights principles, but even undermines long-established protections in procedural law governing more conventional methods of investigation (D Ormerod, 'ECHR and the exclusion of evidence: trial remedies for Article 8 breaches?' [2003] *Crim LR* 61, 62). Since the second edition of this volume came out, Simon McKay has published a significant addition to the available legal commentary with his forensic and insightful analysis of the construction of covert investigation law in the UK (*Covert Policing: Law and Practice*, Oxford University Press, Oxford, 2011). Amongst other discussions, McKay unpicks the structure of RIPA and argues that the legislation—which 'only regulates activities that are used in support of substantive investigations'—needs to be studied in a three-part framework that encompasses conceptual, substantive, and practical/operational aspects (McKay, Chapter 1, particularly p 14). McKay's audience is as much the parliamentarian and the policy-maker as it is the legal practitioner. Law enforcement practitioners will discover between the covers comprehensive and provocative discussion that goes beyond the scope possible to achieve in the *Blackstone's Practical Policing* series.

Since the third edition was written, significant episodes of mismanagement of covert investigations have come to public attention. Consequently the legitimacy of covert investigation, characterized simultaneously by both moral justification and lawfulness, has been called into question, and this has triggered clarion calls for reform. It is not enough that the use of covert investigation methods must be lawful (in order to satisfy human rights standards): the methods employed must be morally justifiable in the circumstances and the manner of their execution must itself be morally justified (in order to satisfy the demands for legitimacy). Moral justification can be regarded as the foundation of ethical conduct. The ethics of investigation are multi-layered and multi-faceted. What will characterize the ethics of any given investigation will be the management of it.

Our approach to the fourth edition was to update the law chapters, but also to elaborate those chapters which addressed management issues. In updating the content to reflect recent new legislation, we have maintained the two-part approach first adopted for the fourth edition: the first part sets the context for the management of covert investigation, and the second part presents a summary introduction to the law.

It is worthwhile here setting out the background to Part One. The number of philosophers studying to any significant degree the morality and the ethics of investigation (and of covert investigation in particular) is surprisingly small, considering that this is such a significant area of public policy and such an important aspect of the government–citizen relationship. Relatively little in the way of academic attention has been focused on the ethical boundaries of covert investigation. The subject matter is neither easy nor straightforward, given that all that is lawful is not necessarily morally justified, and all that might be morally justified is not necessarily lawful.

Published since the third edition of this book, the College of Policing Code of Ethics (the content of which is essentially a code of professional standards conduct rather than an ethical philosophy of policing per se) addresses just twenty words of general guidance to covert investigators in the four short paragraphs devoted to the topic. The contribution can be seen to exemplify the confusion that can arise in this field from conflation. Investigators are called upon to be ethical in their use of covert investigation (Code of Ethics, p 5, para 1.16)—being ethical in this context meaning adhering to the police Code of Ethics: 'officers who authorize or perform covert policing roles must keep in mind at all times the principles and standards set out in the Code of Ethics' (para 1.7).

This exhortation is presented within the chapter of the Code devoted to honesty and integrity, without any apparent recognition of the inherent irony. Since all covert investigation necessarily involves deception, and since the use of deception is prima facie dishonest (whatever the justification), the effect of the police Code of Ethics as currently drafted is to define police use of covert investigation as an automatic breach of the police Code of Ethics. This is almost certainly not what the Code authors intended, and a confusion of presentation that is understandable, given that adequately and accurately summarizing such a complex area in a document as short as the police Code of Ethics would be beyond the most parsimonious and accomplished wordsmith. But it highlights the vulnerabilities of sound-bite philosophy and the fact that setting professional standards expectations about complying with the law will not necessarily address fundamental moral questions nor explicate ethical conundrums.

A small number of philosophers in this field, led by John Kleinig and Seumas Miller, have produced books and academic papers on various aspects of ethical policing and investigation. There is much more to be explored, especially in relation to covert investigation. Although this volume is not the place to do justice to that debate, the first chapter presents a basic introduction to some of the fundamental considerations that may help to determine when recourse to covert investigation will be morally justifiable. As much as anything, the chapter—we do not claim it to be definitive—is an initial contribution to the wider and deeper debate that must be held on the moral justification for covert investigation: a debate that is essential for the legitimacy of covert investigation because legitimacy comprises both lawfulness and moral justification. RIPA addresses only the lawfulness element within this equation. It is the use to which the tools of the law are put that determines whether the standards of moral management have been met.

So the first chapter of Part One sets the context for the moral management of covert investigation and points the way towards some of the wider and more detailed literature in this arena. The starting point is that investigation primarily serves the purpose of the criminal justice system (or regulatory and administrative system, as may be the case) as a social good. Investigation is not an end in and of itself, nor does it primarily serve the purpose of the investigating agency—an argument that may be inconsistent with the ways in which some police investigators perceive their role. (Perceptions can mislead self as well as others.)

Having presented the context for initial consideration of when the use of covert investigation might be morally justifiable, the book moves on to consider the statutory principles that currently underpin the availability and purpose of covert investigation as a tool. An explanation of the authorization and governance framework as it currently exists is set out in Chapter 3, together with considerations for authorizing officers. Discussion then turns to practical management issues, beginning with ways of understanding the operating environment within which it is proposed to deploy covert investigation techniques both from a strategic perspective and from an operational perspective. It is contended that the operating environment for covert investigation is far broader than many investigators, their supervisors, and senior managers appreciate, and that proper understanding of the operating environment will lead to more measured and less controversial use of covert investigation. Part One closes with a chapter on general management issues concerning recourse to covert investigation.

In Part Two, the statutory elements of covert investigation are considered in turn. Investigators are required to use the least intrusive means of investigation that will achieve their objective; accordingly Part Two starts with directed surveillance, the least intrusive of the surveillance environments. Intrusive surveillance, together with its frequent partner in the portfolio, property interference, is considered next, before discussion turns to the different ways in which covert investigation engages with computers. Surveillance of communications and the data generated thereby is considered next. Although posited within the context of directed surveillance in the statutory framework, the use of CHISs engages some of the most significant moral issues arising from relationship manipulation and privacy intrusion within the sphere of covert investigation. That arena is considered next, before a technical discussion of overseas deployment is presented. The book closes with reflections on what good practice covert investigation looks like.

Chapters are structured around questions that have been frequently debated by colleagues. Because each chapter is intended to be a self-sufficient reference guide, readers of the entire volume will notice that repetition of some points has been preferred to cross-referencing within this volume—an approach consistent with the preference of the publishers. Various features (definition boxes, bullet-point lists, key points) have been included in the chapters to render the information more readily accessible and digestible. Based on available sources, the information is up to date as of January 2018. This arena continues to develop both through case law and statute, and more than ten years on since coming into force, RIPA continues to ignite different and sometimes contradictory interpretations. Gradually the body of case law, which must be considered the definitive interpretation of the statute alongside the statute itself, is growing, but this incremental accumulation is slow. The reality is that many issues which might be challenged have not yet been scrutinized by the courts.

Covert investigation methods often provide incontrovertible evidence because of the level of intrusion by investigators into the private lives of citizens. Such intrusion is only permitted within strict statutory and procedural frameworks and, for a defendant faced with incontrovertible evidence, the only defence strategy left available in the adversarial trial system is to attack the investigation procedure and seek exclusion of the incontrovertible evidence on the basis that it was unfairly obtained and prejudicial to the defendant.

It is hoped that this revised and updated fifth edition will continue to promote investigator and senior manager awareness in order to minimize the risk of unwitting abuse of these powers and to minimize the misuse of procedure leading to technical acquittals of defendants against whom the evidence is strong enough to convict. The latter will fail society by not protecting citizens from crime and the former will fail society by not protecting citizens from abuse of authority. This consequence has led Parliament to the current reconsideration of what powers should be invested in investigators.

As always, publisher as well practitioner needs have characterized this fifth edition. To minimize production costs and to make room for new material, it has been necessary to omit some material that featured in previous editions. The first two editions contained in appendices sizeable relevant extracts of both RIPA and the Police Act 1997 (PA97), updated by the authors because at that time there were no consolidated texts of the Acts as amended. With the establishment of the government website <http://www.legislation.gov.uk>, there now exists a ready means for readers to access the latest available version of each law as amended. The website gives each law both as originally enacted and as subsequently amended. Where there are outstanding amendments still to be updated on the website, this is indicated. Thus there is no longer a need to include consolidated extracts in this volume.

Likewise the relevant Codes of Practice are now readily available online at <https://www.gov.uk/government/collections/ripa-codes>, having been revised and updated in the relatively recent past. So this book no longer features the Codes reproduced as appendices.

The revised and new Codes of Practice incorporate example scenarios. Accordingly we have omitted from this edition many of the example scenarios included in previous editions. Those that remain in the main text have been reviewed and revised to take into account comments made by the Chief Surveillance Commissioner about the inclusion of scenarios in the Codes of Practice. The intention of this volume has always been to provide investigators, authorizing officers, and others with an interest in covert investigation with a structure for consideration of the issues arising. Statute and case law remain the definitive guides to what is and is not permitted. No book or code can anticipate all the permutations that will confront investigators on a daily basis, but by offering frameworks for practitioner consideration based on our own observations and the documented observations of others, this volume aims to assist investigators in finding their own way through the maze of covert investigation.

Maintaining the affordability of the fifth edition of this book in the context of continued rising production costs has necessitated the omission of the legislative and case tables that were previously included. The chapter on mobile phones that was included in earlier editions has been omitted to make way for necessary discussion of the new legislation.

The former Association of Chief Police Officers (ACPO), in association with the then National Centre for Policing Excellence, published *Practice Advice on Core Investigative Doctrine* in 2005 (whilst the first edition of this book was being produced)—the first time that the police service has defined investigative doctrine. These professional mantles have been assumed by the College of Policing, but the principles outlined on page 103 of the 2005 doctrine, regarding covert policing, remain pertinent and are equally applicable to non-police investigators undertaking covert investigation. They bear quotation here, providing the doctrinal context within which this book should be read and to which this book seeks to make a contribution.

Principles underpinning a covert investigation strategy which investigators should consider

- Have a good working knowledge of intelligence processes and the National Intelligence Model.
- Become fully cognizant of all current, pertinent intelligence material prior to the instigation of an operation.
- Anticipate the need for covert policing and make early and timely bids for such resources (failure to make an early request may undermine the investigation and valuable material may be lost).
- Ensure that the covert policing strategy is proportionate to the overall objectives of the investigation.
- Know how to obtain advice and guidance for covert options.
- Have a thorough understanding of RIPA 2000 and the relevant aspects of the Police Act 1997. (*To which knowledge of the IPA 2016 should now be added.*)
- Understand public interest immunity (PII) procedures and legislation, and the Criminal Procedure and Investigations Act.
- Ensure that operations are run on a 'need-to-know basis' and that operational security is maintained at all times.
- Consult the Crown Prosecution Service at the earliest opportunity (in more complex cases this may be prior to the commencement of the operation).
- Establish a review mechanism if necessary. In serious or complex investigations which involve a high degree of risk, a senior officer must authorize and/ or review all operations.

Further information and reading

Covert tactics must be appropriately authorized and any deployments must be shown to be proportionate, lawful, accountable, necessary and ethical.

College of Policing Code of Ethics, p 5, para 1.6

The covert investigation legislative landscape

Police Act 1997	Regulation of Investigatory Powers Act 2000	Investigatory Powers Act 2016
Interference with property and entry onto land (Part III)	Directed surveillance Intrusive surveillance Covert human intelligence sources (Part II) Accessing encrypted digital data (Part III)	Interception of communications (Part 2) Communications data (Part 3) Electronic equipment interference (Part 5) Bulk interception warrants; bulk acquisition warrants; bulk equipment interference warrants (intelligence agencies only) (Part 6) Bulk personal dataset warrants (intelligence agencies only) (Part 7) Oversight arrangements (Part 8)
Covert surveillance and covert human intelligence source code of practice	Covert surveillance and covert human intelligence source codes of practice Code of practice for investigation of protected electronic information	Interception of communications: code of practice Code of practice for the acquisition, disclosure and retention of communications data Equipment interference: code of practice Intelligence services' retention and use of bulk personal datasets: code of practice Bulk acquisition of communications data: code of practice National security notices: code of practice

Underpinning the primary legislation and codes of practice is an extensive corpus of secondary legislation in the form of Statutory Instruments and Orders, too numerous to include here.

PART ONE

Managing Covert Investigation

Moral Foundations for Covert Investigation

> Knowledge acquisition that is critical to intelligence-led policing is almost never a morally neutral project.
>
> (John Kleinig, 'The ethical perils of knowledge acquisition', *Criminal Justice Ethics* 28(2) (2009), 201–222, at 218)

Just because investigators can, does not mean that investigators should.

In the search for a moral foundation to ensure the ethical use of covert investigation methods, if one was looking for a maxim to summarize sound management of covert investigation, then this surely is it. Having both statutory authority and resource capability does not equate to moral justification nor should it predetermine investigation management choices. As the criminal justice ethicist Professor John Kleinig has observed, the moral limits of an action (for example, the justifiable use of deception) may be crossed before the legal limit (in his example, entrapment) is reached (*The Ethics of Policing*, Cambridge University Press, Cambridge, 1996, 135).

Covert investigation operates in an arena of permanent tension between *preserving respect for individual human dignity* and *maximizing utility so long as any good generated outweighs any harm caused* (a philosophy and approach often called utilitarianism). The tension exists precisely because, although the law is written in black and white, how and when and even why legal tools should be used is far from clear cut. The prevailing circumstances of any given episode create a greyscale veil through which use of the black-and-white letter of the law must be interpreted.

Human dignity as a concept differs from that of human rights. Whilst not specifically protected in UK law, human dignity is distinguished in international law and some non-UK jurisdictions (the 1949 German constitution for instance). Human dignity, an inherent characteristic of personhood, founds claims to human rights (Kleinig and Evans 2013, 559). Statutory human rights engaged by covert investigation have qualified protection in UK law—there are occasions when the infringement of these rights by public authorities will be lawful (see Chapter 2)—but even when it is legally justifiable to infringe an individual's statutory rights, it can be argued that it is still necessary when choosing to employ and when conducting covert investigation to do so in a manner that preserves respect for human dignity, particularly the dignity of those who are subject to collateral intrusion. Herein lies the engagement of the profession of covert investigation with ethics.

Further information and reading

For discussion of human dignity in this context see, for example:

- John Kleinig and Nicholas Evans, 'Human flourishing, human dignity, and human rights', *Law and Philosophy* 32 (2013), 539–564.
- Tatjana Hörnle, 'Criminalizing behaviour to protect human dignity', *Criminal Law and Philosophy* 6 (2012), 307–325.

- Thomas Finegan, 'Conceptual foundations of the Universal Declaration of Human Rights: human rights, human dignity and personhood', *Australian Journal of Legal Philosophy* 37 (2013), 182–218.
- Aharon Barak, *Human Dignity: The Constitutional Value and the Constitutional Right* (Cambridge University Press, Cambridge, 2015).

Those who regard themselves as crusaders against crime might be expected to view the purpose of the law as primarily being for the benefit of crime-fighting (protecting the citizen from the unacceptable conduct of other citizens), to which end such advocates might argue there should be few or no limits (a crime-control philosophy). An alternative perspective might view the law as a necessary constraint on the use of power by those to whom it is entrusted (protecting the citizen from the unacceptable conduct of the state and its agents: a due process philosophy). Orbiting in the same solar system is a third perspective: the notion that state agents derive their authority over citizens as much from the legitimacy of their individual official actions as from statute that establishes their legal role and purpose; that lawfulness and legitimacy must necessarily coexist for any given investigative action to be the right thing to do in the circumstances.

Legitimacy is thus characterized by ethical use as well as legal compliance.

Perceived legitimacy fosters public consent, reducing the need for dependence upon police compulsion (Legrand and Bronitt illustrate this in connection with public order policing: 2015, 10). What constitutes ethical use does not appear to have been explicitly defined—although the public recognizes unethical practice when it is exposed: for example, the infiltration conduct of the now-disbanded Metropolitan Police Special Demonstration Squad, which has been documented by both Her Majesty's Inspectorate of Constabulary (HMIC) and by investigative journalists (HMIC, 2012; 2013; Evans and Lewis, 2013); consider also the surveillance actions of some local authorities in trying to regulate and investigate non-criminal misbehaviour (see *Jenny Paton and others v Poole Borough Council* (2010) IPT/09/01/C). Each of these examples in their own way triggered public offence and outrage.

In a speech given to the Current Legal Issues Seminar held at the Supreme Court, Brisbane, on 6 August 2015, Professor Simon Bronitt noted the:

> tendency for acute ethical issues (what may be termed the 'awful but lawful' issue) to be reduced to mere technical questions of legal compliance, suppressing wider moral, ethical and human rights dimensions raised by use of those techniques.

There is work yet to be done to complement covert investigation legal frameworks and codes of practice with guidance for investigators, applicants, and authorizing officers on the moral issues engaged at every step of the covert investigation planning and decision-making process and on the ethical execution of covert methods: covert investigation is not an arena amenable to techno-cratic justice or its associated decision-making. (We are grateful to Professor Bronitt for sharing his text with us and allowing its citation: he in turn drew upon a phrase coined by Nikos Passas in the context of corporate offending in 'Lawful but awful: legal corporate crimes', *The Journal of Socio-Economics* 34(6) (2005), 771–786.)

This first chapter is intended to be an introduction to the sort of dialogue and its associated lexicon that will be necessary to use when debating and developing practitioner guidance on the ethics of covert investigation. Any future developed guidance will be derived from a professional and philo-sophical narrative that explains the 'what for', the 'when', and the 'why' of covert investigation. Meanwhile, this chapter serves to assist investigators and authorizing officers in structuring their considerations and measuring their actions.

1.1 **In the Community Interest?**

The working-draft narrative adopted here starts with an understanding of the context for investigation and its role in the governance of society.

Institutions fundamental to a democratic society are a *legislature* elected by the citizens and *a criminal justice system* that operates independently from both legislature and government executive. In a liberal democratic society thus equipped, ideally individuals should be free to enjoy their autonomy in search of a satisfied and fulfilled life (howsoever each individual defines this) to the extent that fulfilment of such ambition does not unjustifiably harm the moral interests of another. In pursuit of individual satisfaction, individual au-tonomy should be free from unjustifiable let or hindrance from government or other citizens. In this regard the liberal democratic criminal justice system (including all its constituent elements) exists for one purpose: dispassionately to resolve disturbances to peaceful public order that arise from conduct that infringes the moral interests of another to the extent that it warrants crimin-alization. Although such actions may create individual instances of victimiza-tion of community members, crimes are nonetheless primarily offences against the community's public order: objectively, individual victimization from this perspective is coincidental. (Although, subjectively, it is unlikely to feel coinci-dental to a victim.)

As a process, the criminal justice system can be sub-divided functionally into constituent parts. *Information-gathering* (undertaken by investigators) informs *fact-finding* (by either magistrates or jurors, depending on the tribunal, leading to a determination of legal guilt or not guilty beyond reasonable doubt), which in the event of conviction in turn informs *sanction decision-making* (sentencing by magistrates or judges, depending on the tribunal), which sanctions are then *implemented* (by fines offices, probation, or prison staff).

From this perspective, the role of the information-gatherers and the sub-process of the information-gathering are seen to be the foundations of a just and reliable criminal justice system (which may be defined as a system which scrutinizes all proven and relevant evidence to achieve accurate decision-making in applying the law), which itself is a key component of democratic society. The proper functioning and integrity of the criminal justice system is determined and characterized in the first instance by the integrity of the information-gathering process and the integrity and professionalism of the agents giving effect to that process. Distortion or diversion of the information-gathering process compromises the proper functioning of the criminal justice system, an outcome that is detrimental to the community interest in having a just and reliable criminal justice process that resolves the disorder which disrupts a safe and peaceful society.

1.2 **Moral Purpose and Covert Investigation**

That which has utilitarian logic from a government or investigator perspective does not necessarily accord with the moral integrity—and therefore legitimacy—of the criminal justice system. Political or practitioner rhetoric that speaks of police 'fighting crime' injects a particular perspective and thus partiality into what properly should be dispassionate and impartial information-gathering within the context of the proper operation of the criminal justice system. (Integrity in information-gathering helps legitimize both the crime-control and due-process models of criminal justice.) Performance management that articulates success in terms of outputs (convictions secured, for example) rather than in terms of outcomes (unbiased decisions reasonably and logically arrived at based on all relevant information dispassionately and impartially obtained) is an architecture of accountability that misconceives what properly should be held to account if the community interest in a fair and just criminal justice system is to be served. It is an architecture that could be seen to create a perverse incentive that directs the focus of investigators towards a politically chosen output measurement rather than towards the outcome of a common good.

Since no investigator (in the UK trial process) performs the role of determining legal guilt or innocence, it follows that investigators can only influence those whose specific role it is to make such determinations through the investigators' selection of information to put before the fact-finders and decision-makers. Although distanced by design from the function of such determination, investigators nevertheless share moral responsibility in the making of the final determination and the consequences arising therefrom because the discoveries and disclosures of the investigators inform the fact-finding and decision-making sub-processes. If management measurement is not aligned with system moral purpose, then the investigator is confronted with the unfair demand of serving two masters whose interests may not coincide and may come into conflict.

The manifestation of New Public Management (Savage, 2007, Chapter 3), which focuses on performance rather than purpose, on outputs rather than outcomes, when applied to the criminal justice system and its agents, has the effect of compromising both the collective good of the criminal justice system and the integrity of its agents (such as the investigators of crime allegations). Management by metrics, as opposed to management for moral purpose, in this instance (unwittingly, no doubt) creates a perverse incentive to discover and disclose only that which will result in conviction: collateral kudos for the agency being bought with the vulnerability of creating the potential for miscarriages of justice. (Proper and appropriate expenditure of public monies is also a collective good but, likewise, the outcome of sound budgeting is not necessarily demonstrated by output measurement.)

The risk of miscarriage of justice also arises when investigators are motivated by misconstrued moral purpose—for example, a belief that their role is to fight for the victim rather than act dispassionately for systemic purpose, or a belief that acts that would constitute so-called noble-cause corruption are justified in the so-called fight against crime.

1.3 Covert Investigation and a Moral Theory of Policing

The criminal justice system exists not to convict criminals or to avenge victims, but to discover and consider the relevant and proven facts of all criminal allegations each according to their merits and *to apply the rule of law fairly* in response to those facts in order to achieve and preserve a just society (for a more in-depth discussion of these issues, see Kennedy, 2005, Chapter 1).

Any given individual's subjective notion of justice will not necessarily coincide with an objective view of what constitutes a just society. Consequently, the criminal justice system, and its constituent elements (which include investigators of crime), exist properly to serve the collective good of the community. All individuals are held to have both individual and communal interest in a sound criminal justice system, alongside any particular individual moral interests to which they are also entitled or to which they lay claim.

Investigators are agents (component elements) of the criminal justice system that exists to protect fundamental moral rights. Criminal justice ethicist Seumas Miller puts it this way: 'the protection of fundamental moral rights—specifically justifiably enforceable (aggregate) moral rights—is a collective good to which the members of the community have a joint right' (Miller, 2010, 264). The police are, perhaps, the most publicly visible of these elements. Paradoxically, many of the tools of policing are themselves *prima facie* infringements of individual moral right and human dignity: the denial of liberty and autonomy through arrest; the denial of peaceful possession of property through search and seizure; and the infringement of privacy through both overt investigation and covert surveillance. Miller and Blackler propose a moral theory of policing in which 'harmful and normally immoral methods are on occasion necessary in order to realize the fundamental end of policing, namely the protection of justifiably enforceable moral rights' (Miller and Blackler, 2005, 26). Perhaps it has not often been thought of in this way, but that is what the Regulation of Investigatory Powers Act 2000 (RIPA2000)—and now also the Investigatory Powers Act 2016 (IPA2016)—ultimately seeks to achieve: a framework in which otherwise morally offensive conduct may on occasion (when simultaneously lawful, legitimate, necessary, and proportionate) be utilized by public authorities to protect justifiably enforceable collective moral rights in which each individual citizen has personal and collective interest.

The protection of justifiably enforceable moral rights offers a perspective subtly—yet significantly—different from the siren call of fighting crime or the value-for-money exhortation to meet performance accountability targets. Political constructs—the rhetoric of fighting crime; the mantra of performance management; the emotional appeal of victim interest representation—are intrinsically subjective and therefore partial perspectives promoted and proselytized in a context of conflict resolution that more properly needs and warrants impartial, independent, objective investigation to serve a collective good (this being the accurate operation of the criminal justice system). Moral rights, intrinsic to each person (citizen and non-citizen), founded both upon their individuality and the fact that they are community members (irrespective of citizenship status), and guarantors of individual dignity, can provide a more objective benchmark against which to evaluate (proposed) actions that, all things being equal, would otherwise violate or infringe such moral interests. (The definition of moral rights is a debate outside the remit of this book: for the sake of argument here, and as a foundation for the following consideration of the law and practice of covert investigation, let the point stand that accountability against moral interest, rather than management metrics relating to cost and outputs, may better serve the community interest in the collective good of a fair and just criminal justice system.)

1.4 Addressing the Imbalance of Power in Criminal Justice

When an individual person is accused of crime, the state has the option to bring significant resources to bear against that person in proving the crime, and upon conviction in enforcing sanction. It is an asymmetrical balance of power—the might of the state and its agencies against the relative powerlessness of the individual—that is intended to be redressed by well-established principles: the presumption of innocence; the privilege against self-incrimination (which includes the right to silence); and a burden of proof beyond reasonable doubt placed upon the prosecution. The adversarial trial model employed in the UK privileges the principle of challenging one's accusers and their supporting witnesses to prove their allegations. This is overt justice in open court—public authorities and witnesses put to the test to ensure the factually guilty are found legally guilty and that the factually innocent are not erroneously found legally guilty.

In this context, and from the perspective of the investigator, covert investigation presents numerous advantages. In addition to the powers of arrest and search/seizure, covert investigation methods often provide the means for third-party lay witnesses to be replaced in the information-gathering and testimony processes by professional police surveillance witnesses and the recorded, technocratic evidence of surveillance devices. The evidence gathered through covert investigation often reveals the suspect condemning him- or herself through their own actions. Such evidence, properly presented, may be incontrovertible. (For an agency whose efficiency is measured by the number of convictions, covert investigation methodology thus holds obvious attractions, although UK jury laws prohibit evaluation of the probative weight attached by jurors to evidence gathered covertly, compared to overtly gathered evidence, and covert investigation may or may not be cost-effective depending on which resources are needed to obtain any given piece of information.) Covert investigation is a powerful weapon in the investigation armoury which further biases the asymmetrical power relationship.

But investigator advantage and convenience is not a justification strong enough necessarily to outweigh dignity-based claims to rights. Surveillance is not just an investigative tactical option: it is a *prima facie* infringement of moral autonomy. Intuitively, it seems likely that none of us would wish to be subject to 24/7 police surveillance, even if this hypothetically was the most 'efficient' means of preventing and/or detecting crime. Even—perhaps especially—when we have nothing to hide, each of us needs private space in which, simply, to be ourselves, rather than to be a subject of surveillance.

1.5 **Moral Management in Context**

This is the context for the moral management of covert investigation. If the state intends to bring its powerful resources to bear in surveilling individuals, then the grounds for doing so must not only be justifiable but must also outweigh any countervailing moral interest claim on the part of anyone who is surveilled and outweigh any normal expectations on the part of the community. The ends will not necessarily justify the means, because at stake are the shared values that make it worthwhile for an individual to engage in society (for a more detailed critique of the means–end rationale in this context, see Kleinig, 2009). When individuals are denied dignity and privacy, when they are disengaged from the community or disenfranchised by the actions of the state, when they have no investment in society, then individuals have little incentive to comply with social norms. Society then is at increased risk of self-interested disorder. These sentiments apply equally to investigators as to the investigated. If investigators use morally harmful, intrusive covert methods simply because they can, regardless of defined moral and legal boundaries, the community's consensual support for the criminal justice system and its agents, upon which the successful operation of the system relies, will be withdrawn. Misuse of covert investigation powers is its own form of self-interested public disorder.

Covert investigation offers investigators the opportunity to gather information about an individual in circumstances in which the individual is either not aware that information is being gathered, or otherwise believes that information is not being gathered. Confronted by often incontrovertible evidence, few other tactics present themselves to the defendant other than to seek exclusion of such evidence or to instil doubt into the minds of fact-finders by raising questions of propriety about the integrity of the investigation and the investigators. The onus on the investigator is to ensure that use of covert investigation is not only lawfully justified but also morally justified. If the former test is not met, exclusion of evidence will be sought. The latter may be tested in a number of ways, including scrutiny through rigorous investigator cross-examination at trial, and/or public inquiry into perceived investigator misconduct. The investigator's legal obligations are expressed in RIPA2000 and IPA2016 founded upon the principles articulated in the Human Rights Act; the moral obligation on investigators to perform their duties professionally and properly is perhaps less well defined but overarches the legal obligations.

1.6 **Morally Justified?**

So when will recourse to covert investigation methods be morally justifiable, if at all? (Note: we distinguish justifiable recourse to such methods, which characterizes morally sound law, from the actual execution of such methods, which must be ethical in and of itself.) Only, we argue, when all the criteria discussed below are present together.

Firstly, *the proposed use of covert methods must be consistent with the general moral theory of policing* presented above.

Secondly, *there must exist reasonable suspicion that the individual about whom information is to be gathered has committed or is going to commit a crime.* To be clear: there must first exist a demonstrable and reasonable suspicion of criminality (or serious criminality, depending upon which investigation methods are being considered). The fact that covert investigation subsequently discloses exculpatory rather than incriminating information does not invalidate that element of moral justification provided by this criterion if the original suspicion was reasonable in the circumstances. Indeed, the discovery of exculpatory information is consistent with the principle that investigators should impartially gather all relevant information—but that would be a collateral benefit of any given covert investigation. In and of itself, seeking exculpatory information intuitively does not seem to justify the moral harm of covert intrusion, although it can be argued that there is a public interest in ensuring innocent persons are not put on trial.

Difficult to justify also, within the scope of this second proposed criterion, is the intentional covert surveillance of individuals who are *not* suspected of being involved in crime, but whose associations with the suspect may assist investigators in locating the suspect: the whereabouts of the suspect are unknown but it is thought by investigators that, by covertly monitoring the movements of an otherwise innocent individual believed to be an associate of the suspect, the innocent individual will unwittingly lead the investigators to the subject. This utilitarian approach seems to be allowed for within the Covert Surveillance and Property Interference Code of Practice (hereafter CSPI Code) (para 3.11). The surveillance of innocent people who are being used as a means to an end directly engages that person's moral interests in ways rather different from those in which a suspected criminal's moral interests are engaged. This seems to be true even if the innocent associate is aware of the suspect's criminal conduct: it is certainly true where the innocent associate knows nothing of, and has no reason to suspect, the suspect's alleged involvement in criminality.

The innocent associate is an individual who has a moral right not to be covertly used as a tool by the authorities. Such investigator conduct is an infringement of an individual's autonomy and dignity, as is the deception exercised by investigators against the innocent associate. The innocent associate is not suspected of crime and all things being equal should not attract any attention of the authorities, let alone the intrusion and indignity of covert surveillance. Such investigator conduct is an infringement of privacy and autonomy, compounded by the fact that the authorities will record information obtained about the innocent person's life. The innocent associate, in circumstances of covert coercion, unwittingly betrays a family member or friend. Such investigator conduct is an infringement of the trust upon which the innocent associate's relationship is built: the relationship is forever tainted. All of this holds true whether the innocent associate and suspect subsequently become aware of the investigator conduct or not (see Harfield, 2012 for more detailed and exampled discussion of these issues).

Where an individual is engaged in crime, their moral claims stand to be countervailed by the weightier claims of those whose moral interests would be unjustifiably harmed by the criminal conduct. The innocent associate not involved in crime can be seen to fall within this latter category by virtue of being a community member, but in the present circumstances the innocent associate has specific moral claims that are not so obviously overcome as the moral claims of the suspected criminal. The claim of the innocent associate not to have their moral interests infringed by the authorities is greater precisely because the innocent associate is not involved in crime: the infringement of their moral interests by investigators is thus a more serious harm requiring a higher degree of justification. Ultimately, the information gained by the investigators in these circumstances may be used in fulfilment of the purpose of the criminal justice system, and those who knowingly engage in crime cannot expect to be immune from investigation. But where an innocent associate is used without their knowledge to gather information about a third party, in circumstances in which the moral claims of the innocent associate are seriously and significantly infringed in doing so, intuitively—if such covert surveillance can be justified at all—it seems that at the very least the tests of proportionality and necessity must be applied to a greater standard than that to which they are applied when covert investigation methods are deployed directly against an individual actively engaged in crime (equivalent, perhaps, to the difference in degree between an investigator's 'reasonable suspicion' and a fact-finder's 'beyond reasonable doubt').

Similar issues arise if it is proposed to conduct covert surveillance on an individual identified as a potential informer (Covert Human Intelligence Sources Code of Practice, hereafter CHIS Code, para 3.23; the ethical issues inherent in using informers are discussed in more detail in Harfield, 2012). Pre-recruitment surveillance can inform investigators about the suitability of the identified potential informer for recruitment and future tasking as a covert human intelligence source. In addition to the ethical issues already considered in relation to the innocent associate, one other factor warrants consideration in this context. The information being gathered by investigators will be used firstly to determine whether or not the potential informer should be approached by a recruiting team, and secondly (if recruited) to manage the working relationship with the CHIS. The argument is not strong in supporting moral justification for such surveillance, but the use to which the information gathered would be put might be argued to be ultimately to the benefit of the potential informer because it will inform the investigator's duty of care towards the informer, if recruited. Parallel with these moral considerations are the statutory considerations: 'covert surveillance in such circumstances may or may not be necessary on one of the statutory grounds' (CHIS Code, para 3.23).

Thirdly, *the crime must be of sufficient seriousness to warrant recourse to otherwise immoral methods* (this *moral* consideration is not to be confused with the *statutory* requirement for proportionality that will be considered in more detail in Chapter 2). The moral rights of the community (of which individual victims/potential victims form part) to be protected from serious crime or to have such a crime investigated and prosecuted as fully as possible must, in the circumstances, outweigh a suspected individual's moral rights to privacy. (See Seumas Miller, John Blackler, and Andrew Alexandra, *Police Ethics* (Waterside Press, Hook, 2006), 258–262 for a discussion of privacy in this context.) Just as a right to privacy is not absolute, neither are all crimes sufficiently serious to warrant use of covert investigation methods. (Whilst too large an issue to be discussed here, seriousness in this context is understood to be a reflection of the harm caused or likely to be caused. Harm against the community interest in a peaceful society is created both by criminal actions and by any misconduct on the part of criminal investigators.)

Fourthly, *there should be no other, less morally harmful means of securing the required information.* Deployment of covert investigation should, in relation to the specific piece of information sought, be the last resort (and even then might not be justified in the circumstances). The intrusion of privacy and infringement of autonomy inherent in covert investigation will not be justified either morally or in law if the information sought already exists in a form accessible to the investigators (for example, the records of another agency).

Fifthly, *the specific piece of information sought by means of covert investigation must itself be significant to the investigation*: significant, in these circumstances, being understood to mean that the investigation could not proceed or be properly completed without the specific piece of information that covert investigation could provide. Information that is merely interesting rather than of significant use, desirable rather than essential and necessary, may not be sufficient in itself to meet this moral criterion.

Even then, notwithstanding that these minimum criteria are met, the circumstances of any given investigation may impose additional moral considerations on any proposed use of covert methods. All things being equal, these criteria would seem to be the basic minimum required to be met for the use of covert investigation to be justified.

Further information and reading

Rationalization is neither rationality nor justification. It is, however, an ever-present temptation for inexperienced or careless decision-makers and a consequence of fallacy. These are some examples of inappropriate and misguided rationalization being articulated:

- If it's legal and permissible, it's proper.
- If it's necessary, it's ethical.
- It's for a good cause.
- It won't hurt anyone.
- Everyone is doing it this way.
- It's okay if I don't gain personally.
- I'm fighting fire with fire.

These fallacious lines of thought corrupt (in the sense of subvert or pervert) logic and objectivity when making arguments (for example, an argument in support of a surveillance authorization application). They are examples of how *not* to approach decision-making in the ethical use and moral management of covert investigation.

These examples are drawn from Michael Josephson, *Making Ethical Decisions* (Josephson Institute of Ethics, Los Angeles, 2002), 27–29 (see <http://josephsoninstitute.org/MED/> (accessed 22 July 2015)).

1.7 **Conclusion**

Improper use of covert investigation methods by state agents—which constitutes a misuse or an abuse of their empowerment to use such methods—will never be justifiable either in law or ethics.

Investigator legitimacy is reinforced when use of investigation powers is simultaneously lawful and morally sound. For recourse to covert investigation to be morally sound, ultimately it must properly and fairly serve the purpose of the criminal justice system as a common good (not any more immediate personal or professional purpose of the investigators). To serve the purpose of the criminal justice system, covert information-gathering must be lawful and executed in circumstances where the moral interests of the individuals subject to investigation and collateral intrusion are justifiably—and only to the extent necessary—outweighed by the countervailing moral interests of others.

Four current pieces of legislation, in essence and to the extent possible, translate into statute the protection of community interest in the common good of a fair and just criminal justice system, and the protection of individual enforceable moral claims from unjustifiable state interference against individual autonomy through covert investigation. The Acts in question are the Human Rights Act 1998 (HRA), the Regulation of Investigatory Powers Act 2000 (together with its related secondary legislation and Codes of Practice), the Investigatory Powers Act 2016 (together with its related secondary legislation and Codes of Practice), and Part III Police Act 1997 (PA97). A growing corpus of case law has now refined interpretation of the 1997 and 2000 statutes, and future case law will refine interpretation of the 2016 statute. Such law establishes when and how covert investigation may lawfully be used—may, not should—but that, in and of itself, does not make general recourse to or specific use of such methods automatically ethical.

RIPA2000 and IPA2016 are laws that empower public authorities on occasion to override the law that otherwise constrains public authority power. Even if only sub-consciously, having access to such trump cards must influence and prejudice investigator attitudes to covert investigation. Moral considerations, focused on preserving respect for human dignity, rebalance the equation tipped by RIPA2000 and IPA2016 in favour of the investigator. RIPA2000 and IPA2016 require investigators only to act lawfully: it is respect of human dignity that requires investigators to act ethically. The two approaches are not mutually exclusive (and in the arena of policing public disorder, for example, have been identified as complementing each other so as to achieve a desired outcome at minimal social and moral cost: see Legrand and Bronitt, 2015, 11–12).

For the use of covert investigation to be ethical in any given instance, it requires more than merely the circumstances (lawfulness, accountability) to be ethical: the moral worth of any given covert investigation, when viewed from the perspective of the common good that is the purpose of the criminal justice system and to which the information-gathering is contributing, will be characterized by the management of the investigation and the decisions made during its course by the investigators and authorizing officers. Such decisions will cement or corrode investigator legitimacy.

Case study

When people are asked to define a moral dilemma (on the basis of anecdotal experience), nine out of ten will actually probably describe a moral choice—the choice between doing the right thing and doing the wrong thing, when doing the wrong thing perhaps would be less uncomfortable than doing the right thing for the person having to choose. A moral dilemma exists when all the options are morally (and almost always also materially) harmful: the lose-lose situation when there are no right answers because all the outcomes are bad.

Investigators face multiple moral choices daily, but true moral dilemmas are confronted less frequently (although certain investigations are more likely to give rise to such dilemmas than others). Such dilemmas can arise when managing a covert investigation issue. In one real-life instance the dilemma was created not out of the legislation but out of organizational policies intended to give effect to the intent of the legislation. In this instance, complying with the law was the easy part: managing the conflicting policy directions was the hard part, for which none of the resolution permutations that presented themselves offered a way out free from significant moral harm. Nor was there anything intrinsically wrong with any of the organizational policies engaged. Each was logically sound in purpose and rationally designed. But a perfect storm of circumstances had converged which no policy-maker might reasonably have foreseen (or even if they had, they might equally reasonably have dismissed as highly unlikely to happen). No matter which course of action was decided upon, one or more policies would have to be breached. That in itself arguably would constitute its own moral harm (and nowadays a breach of the College of Policing Code of Ethics), but existing independently of the policy breach harms were the significant moral and material harms that the policies ultimately were intended to help prevent. The circumstances meant that different possible courses of action would have led to different bad outcomes, but whatever decision was made, the outcome would be bad.

At that point there is no other form of guidance but an individual's own moral compass.

When a (lose-lose) decision has to be made that involves taking what appears to the decision-maker to be the least harmful option (and others may rank the harm inherent in each option differently), such decisions and the rationale underpinning them should be meticulously and contemporaneously documented because they will be scrutinized forensically later by others who might never have been in such a situation. Such decisions are unlikely to be cost-free for the decision-maker, even if the cost is only angst and sleepless nights. Investigators and managers unwilling to put themselves in this precarious position might be advised to take a career path that avoids having to engage in or manage covert investigation.

Further information and reading

The moral theory of policing is presented in Seumas Miller and John Blackler's book *Ethical Issues in Policing* (Ashgate, Aldershot, 2005), Chapter 1. Seumas Miller returned to this theme in his book, *The Moral Foundations of Social Institutions* (Cambridge University Press, Cambridge, 2010) Chapter 9.

John Kleinig's seminal work is *The Ethics of Policing* (Cambridge University Press, Cambridge, 1996): in relation to covert investigation issues see, particularly, Chapters 7 and 8. See also his paper 'The ethical perils of knowledge acquisition', *Criminal Justice Ethics* 28(2) (2009), 201–22.

Morally problematic issues in the management and utilization of informers are considered in the context of Miller and Blackler's moral theory of policing by Clive Harfield in 'Police informers and professional ethics', *Criminal Justice Ethics* 31(2) (2012), 73–95.

On the purpose of the criminal justice system, see Helena Kennedy, *Just Law: The Changing Face of Justice—and Why It Matters to Us All* (Vintage, London, 2005).

On the implications of public perceptions of fairness in the criminal justice system, see Denise Meyerson, 'Why should justice be seen to be done?' *Criminal Justice Ethics* 34(1) (2015), 64–86.

On New Public Management and police reform, see Stephen Savage, *Police Reform: Forces for Change* (Oxford University Press, Oxford, 2007), Chapter 3.

On the actions of the Metropolitan Police Special Demonstration Squad and implications arising, see:

1) For official inquiries:
    HMIC, *A Review of National Police Units Which Provide Intelligence on Criminality Associated with Protest* (HMIC, London, 2012).
    HMIC, *A Review of Progress Made Against the Recommendations in HMIC's 2012 Report on the National Police Units Which Provide Intelligence on Criminality Associated with Protest* (HMIC, London, 2013).
    HMIC, *An Inspection of Undercover Policing in England and Wales* (HMIC, London, 2014).
2) For a journalistic documentary narrative:
    Rob Evans and Paul Lewis, *Undercover: The True Story of Britain's Secret Police* (Faber & Faber, London, 2013).

The College of Policing Code of Ethics stipulates that 'covert tactics must be appropriately authorised and any deployments must be shown to be proportionate, lawful, accountable, necessary and ethical' (p 5). The College's ethics webpage is accessible at <http://www.college.police.uk/What-we-do/Ethics/Pages/Code-of-Ethics.aspx> (accessed 16 July 2015) and the Code itself is accessible at <http://www.college.police.uk/What-we-do/Ethics/Documents/Code_of_Ethics.pdf> (English) and <http://www.college.police.uk/What-we-do/Ethics/Documents/Code_of_Ethics_Welsh.pdf> (Welsh).

See Tim Legrand and Simon Bronitt, 'Policing the G20 protests: "Too much order with too little law" revisited', *Queensland Review*, 22(1) (2015), 3–14, for a discussion of how policing focused on protecting human rights negated the need to rely upon some of the most draconian laws ever enacted in a purportedly liberal democratic society.

See H Packer, 'Two models of the criminal process', *The University of Pennsylvania Law Review* 113(1) (1964), 1–68, for presentation of the crime-control and due-process models of criminal justice.

Statutory Principles in Covert Investigation

The purpose of investigation is to discover fairly and record accurately information that will subsequently be used as the basis for significant decision-making and, in the case of criminal justice decisions, also to determine culpability. (Investigation is not an end in and of itself.) The decisions made may have severe adverse consequences for those subject to them (imprisonment of those convicted, for example), and it is important for establishing and sustaining public confidence in the administrative, regulatory, and criminal justice systems that such decisions are, and are seen to be, arrived at fairly. Wide and varied research has consistently shown that people will generally accept adverse decisions made against them if they feel the process leading to those decisions has been undertaken fairly (such research is summarized and discussed by Denise Meyerson in 'Why should justice be seen to be done?', *Criminal Justice Ethics* 34(1) (2015), 64–86).

The UK legislative framework regulating the use of covert investigation is intended to ensure that the use of such methods does not give rise to unfairness in either the administrative regulation or the criminal justice processes. What constitutes unfairness and unjustifiable conduct on the part of authorities in these contexts is derived from the Human Rights Act 1998 (HRA). Covert investigation law has been drafted so as to give effect to investigator and agency statutory obligations imposed by the HRA.

2.1 Which Statutory Human Rights Are Principally Engaged by Covert Investigation?

The key principles in this context are the right to fair trial protected by Article 6 of the European Convention on Human Rights and Fundamental Freedoms 1950 (ECHR) and the right to respect for private and family life protected by Article 8 ECHR. Section 6 HRA makes it unlawful for UK public authorities (including those who act on their behalf, s 6(3)(b)) 'to act in a way which is incompatible with a Convention right'.

The right to fair trial is concerned with procedural fairness and is engaged from the moment an investigation commences. Not only must the trial process itself be fair, but the pre-trial processes by which evidence is discovered for use at trial must be fair, because if such processes are not fair, then it follows that the trial which relies upon the information so gained cannot be fair (see generally Ashworth, 2002, 35–36).

The right to respect for private and family life is defined in Article 8(1) ECHR:

> Everyone has the right to respect for his private and family life, his home and his correspondence.

This is reinforced by Article 1 of the First Protocol to the ECHR set down in Paris, 20 November 1952:

Every natural and legal person is entitled to the peaceful enjoyment of his possessions.

'It would be a strange reflection on our law if a man who had admitted his participation in the illegal importation of a large quantity of heroin should have his conviction set aside on the grounds that his privacy has been invaded', observed Lord Nolan (*R v Khan* [1997] AC 558); see also *Attorney-General's Reference (No. 3 of 1999)* [2001] 2 AC 91, which asserted that the interests of crime victims and the public should be taken into account.

And indeed that is not the intention of the ECHR, because the right to respect for private life is qualified by Article 8(2). In certain circumstances public authorities may infringe the Article 8(1) right:

There shall be no interference by a public authority with the exercise of this right except such as is in accordance with the law and is necessary in a democratic society in the interests of national security, public safety or the economic well-being of the country, for the prevention of disorder or crime, for the protection of health and morals, or for the protection of the rights and freedoms of others.

Article 1, Protocol 1, ECHR is similarly qualified:

No one shall be deprived of his possessions except in the public interest and subject to the conditions provided for by law and by the general principles of international law.

Further information and reading

Protocol 1 provides 'public interest' as grounds justifying deprivation of property. There is no similar justification for intrusion into private life in Article 8. A Ashworth, *Human Rights, Serious Crime and Criminal Procedure* (Sweet & Maxwell, London, 2002), particularly Chapters 2 and 3, provides a comprehensive discussion of 'public interest' in the context of covert investigation.

Thus investigators planning covert operations or managers supervising or authorizing such activity know from the outset that such investigation is likely to breach Article 8(1), given domestic effect in UK law by s 6 HRA, and that they can only proceed in certain prescribed circumstances which have come to be considered by the European Court of Human Rights at Strasbourg (hereafter ECtHR) in a framework of sequential tests:

(1) Does the investigative act fall within the scope of Article 8? (2.2.1)
(2) If yes, has the Article 8 right been interfered with by a public authority? (2.2.2)
(3) If it has, was this interference in accordance with the law? (2.2.3)
(4) If it was lawful, was the interference pursuant to a legitimate aim as identified in Article 8(2)? (2.2.4)
(5) Even if it was both lawful and pursuant to a legitimate aim, was it still necessary, and no more than necessary (ie proportionate), in a democratic society? (2.2.5)

> Investigators must comply with the standards set by these tests and defendants will seek to disrupt a prosecution by arguing that, whilst tests 1 and 2 have been met, one or more of tests 3, 4, and 5 have not.

2.2 What Do the Article 8 Tests Mean?

Where covert surveillance undertaken for the relevant statutory purpose is likely to produce *private information about any person*—whether or not that person is the subject of the investigation—then authorization will be necessary and both applicants, but more especially authorizing officers, have to consider in detail how the proposed conduct engages with Article 8 ECHR. What do the Article 8 ECHR tests mean for investigators and authorizing officers?

2.2.1 Does the investigative act fall within the scope of Article 8?

If the proposed investigative activity *is intended* or *is likely* to gather information about the private life of an individual (whether or not that individual is the subject of the investigation), then such activity will fall within the scope of Article 8. If the plan is physically to watch an individual in order to observe that individual's movements or associations, or to listen to his or her conversations, or to photograph or video what he or she does, or to deploy a third party to interact with the subject in such a way as to acquire information, or to monitor his or her movements by technical tracking devices, then whether the desired product is to be used for evidential or intelligence purposes, rights protected by Article 8(1) will be infringed. This includes the rights of any third parties present in the surveillance arena, regardless of whether such third parties are associated with the investigation subject or not.

Which gives rise to both legal and ethical issues when it is intended to conduct observations of a public space in order to identify individual present in that space. *Perry v UK* (2004) 39 EHRR 3, a case that actually centred on incorrect application of the Police and Criminal Evidence Act 1984 (PACE) Code D, has implications for surveillance of public spaces because of the very broad interpretation that the ECtHR applied to the likelihood that private information might be obtained: 'the respect for private life under Article 8 of the Convention brings with it decades of developing jurisprudence' (see N Taylor, 'Policing, privacy and proportionality', *EHRLR* (2003), Special Issue, 86).

The manner of the observation, the way in which a record is made of what is being observed, and the use to which information gathered and recorded by observation is used are all of relevance here. Where such observations undertaken by investigators are unlikely, of themselves, to produce any private information because the observations will merely trigger an immediate response to spontaneous events, then no prior authorization seems necessary because Article 8 has not been engaged (such circumstances are hypothesized in the examples given in para 2.24 of the CSPI Code).

But if such general observations undertaken by investigators are simultaneously recorded, using digital cameras for example, which would have the evidential advantage of corroborating the eye-witness accounts of the observers, then if the recordings were to remain available for further analysis, and if the possibility existed that information on the recordings could be cross-checked with other information already held by the investigation agency or planned to be gathered by the investigation agency at some future date, private information about all persons in the surveillance arena has been gathered. In such circumstances it may be necessary to have authorization in place before the observations commence because the accumulation of recorded imagery, particularly repeated over time, will inevitably gather private information. For example, for passers-by who happen regularly to pass through the surveillance arena during the period of each day that the observations are planned to take place, to be present in a public place is not to surrender the right to privacy nor, arguably, does it reduce one's expectation of privacy. The fact of being present in a public space does not in and of itself justify a third party making a record of that presence.

Inevitably when in a public place an individual will be casually observed by other individuals also present. Casual observation does not infringe privacy. But if a note or some other form of record is made of an individual's presence in a given place at a given time, then it is no longer a case of casual observation: information has been gathered which, taken together with any other relevant information, may amount to private information, thus engaging Article 8 rights.

Similar considerations would seem to apply when public authorities access social media sites. In his final report before ceding surveillance governance to the Investigatory Powers Commissioner, the Chief Surveillance Commissioner observed (OSC [Office of Surveillance Commissioners] *Annual Report 2016–17*, para 15.2) that:

> ... one major consequence of the OSC inspections has been the emergence, during the course of discussions, of investigations being made by public authorities through use of social media and the Internet. For example, it may help to show whether counterfeit goods are being offered for sale on a Facebook page, or reveal that someone who claims to be living alone as a single parent has a social media page which provides a different story, or perhaps, particularly sensitive, enable a check to be made whether concerns about the welfare of a child or vulnerable adult may be justified. When individuals choose to go public or advertise themselves, they cannot normally complain that those who look at their social media sites are disregarding their rights to privacy. However if the study of an individual site becomes persistent, issues under the legislation may arise.

If the purpose of accessing social media is to observe and record information over a period of time, then consideration should be given to whether or not any authorization is required, the decision in each instance depending upon the nature of the circumstances. Initial individual social media access may not warrant authorization, but persistent monitoring may.

Further reading and information

The issues arising when individuals going about their lawful business in public places are imaged, and the recorded images are subsequently used for some purpose of which those imaged are not aware, are considered in Clive Harfield, 'Body-worn POV technology: moral harm', *IEEE Technology and Society Magazine* 13(2) (2014), 64–72.

2.2.2 If yes, has the Article 8 right been interfered with by a public authority?

The HRA 1998 applies to public authorities. 'It is unlawful for a public authority to act in a way which is incompatible with a Convention right', prescribes s 6. A public authority is defined in the HRA as a public body including 'a court or tribunal' (s 6(3)(a)) and 'any person certain of whose functions are functions of a public nature' (s 6(3)(b)), which includes not only public authorities but private contractors carrying out a public function on behalf of the authority.

Public authorities empowered to undertake directed surveillance under ss 28 and 29 RIPA2000 are identified in Schedule 1 to that Act (see Chapter 6), whilst those authorities permitted to undertake intrusive surveillance are identified in s 32(6) RIPA2000 (see Chapter 7). Authorities empowered in law to interfere with property are identified in s 93 PA97 (see Chapter 8). The latest publicly available published versions of both Schedule 1 and s 32 can be accessed online via <http://www.legislation.gov.uk/ukpga/2000/23/contents> (accessed January 2018).

2.2.3 If a public authority has so interfered with Article 8(1) rights, was this interference in accordance with the law?

The ECHR makes reference to 'in accordance with the law', 'prescribed by law', and 'lawful'. Starmer identifies three criteria as a test to ensure compliance with the principle of legality thus established (K Starmer, 1999, 166):

(1) domestic law must identify the legal basis for any restriction on an ECHR right;

(2) persons likely to be affected by such a restriction must be able to access the relevant domestic law; and

(3) the relevant domestic law must be clear and comprehensible so that anyone should be reasonably able to identify or foresee whether or not their behaviour is breaking or might break the law.

The principle of legality is considered to be satisfied by the following categories of law:

- statute
- delegated legislation such as Codes of Practice
- common (or case) law
- European Community law.

The extent to which these categories are truly accessible to the layperson is debatable. The potential difficulty in identifying the latest consolidated text of any given statute as amended has already been referred to. Codes of Practice, held to satisfy the principle of legality (*Barthold v Germany* (1985) 7 EHRR 383), are certainly intended to make the law more comprehensible to the non-lawyer. The layperson is unlikely to be sufficiently familiar with stated cases in common law for them to be regarded as properly accessible, but through professional legal representation a layperson may be considered to have sufficient access to common law decisions. The common law was held to meet the principle of legality in *Sunday Times v UK (No. 1)* (1979–80) 2 EHRR 245, reinforced by the decision in *Huvig v France* (1990) 12 EHRR 528 that 'law' could be understood in a substantive sense rather than just in a statutory sense.

As was demonstrated in *Malone v UK* (1984) 7 EHRR 14, following *Silver v UK* (1983) 5 EHRR 347, internal or official guidelines are not sufficient to constitute being in accordance with law, even where published, particularly where the criteria for interpretation of such guidelines remains unpublished.

The PA97, RIPA2000, and IPA2016 make provision for certain covert investigation tactics. Public authorities complying with such provisions will therefore be doing so in accordance with statute law supported by codes of practice. Note, however, that 'it does not follow … that because an act of covert surveillance is lawful it can never result in a contravention of the Convention rights' (*Re McE* [2009] UKHL 15, at para 71). Other tests have to be met.

2.2.4 If it was lawful, was the interference pursuant to a legitimate aim as identified in Article 8(2)?

If the actions of the public authority pass the legality test, they must then be considered within the context of the legitimacy test. The legitimate reasons for interfering with an Article 8(1) ECHR right are prescribed in Article 8(2).

For public officials engaged in law enforcement the legitimate reason provided by Article 8(2) is:

- the prevention of disorder or crime.

For state agents undertaking other forms of regulatory function or public protection, other legitimate reasons apply:

- the interests of national security
- the interests of public safety
- the interests of the economic well-being of the country
- the protection of health or morals
- the protection of the rights and freedoms of others.

There is no scope for adding to this list of reasons and they should be interpreted strictly within the ordinary meaning of the language. Article 18 ECHR prescribes that none of the restrictions permitted should be applied for any reason other than for the reasons prescribed (Starmer, 1999, 177).

2.2.5 Even if it was both lawful and pursuant to a legitimate aim, was it still necessary and proportionate in a democratic society?

The final test is that of necessity in a democratic society. This test incorporates the concept of proportionality which is concerned with balancing the often conflicting interests of the individual and the wider community. Thus Sedley LJ in *B v Secretary of State for the Home Department* [2000] 2 CMLR 1086:

> a measure which interferes with a human right must not only be authorised by law but must correspond to a pressing social need and go no further than is strictly necessary in a pluralistic society to achieve its permitted purpose; or, more shortly, must be appropriate and necessary to its legitimate aim.

More recently, in *Wood v Commissioner of Police for the Metropolis* [2009] EWCA Civ 414 at 82, reliance was exclusively put upon *S and Marper v United Kingdom* (Application Nos. 30562/04 and 30566/04) at 101:

> An interference will be considered 'necessary in a democratic society' for a legitimate aim if it answers a 'pressing social need' and, in particular, if it is proportionate to the legitimate aim pursued and if the reasons adduced by the national authorities to justify it are 'relevant and sufficient'.

An action can be authorized as 'necessary' because it meets one of the grounds outlined in s 28(3) RIPA2000, but that should not be confused with the 'necessity' test established by the ECHR and subsequent case law. A proposed action can be RIPA2000-compliant but not ECHR-compliant.

Further information and reading

See K Starmer, *European Human Rights Law* (Legal Action Group, London, 1999), 170. See also B Fitzpatrick, 'Covert human intelligence sources as offenders: the scope of immunity from the criminal law', *Covert Policing Review* (2005), 15–32, at 20.

(The authors are grateful to Kingsley Hyland, CPS, for drawing their attention to Sedley LJ's dictum quoted above.)

Section 28 RIPA2000 imposes a specific obligation upon authorizing officers to consider proportionality in a two-fold test in relation to directed surveillance. Firstly, authorizing officers must ensure that the surveillance is necessary for the purpose of preventing or detecting crime or that it is necessary for preventing disorder. Secondly, they must believe that the proposed investigation method is proportionate to what is sought to be achieved by it, although the term 'proportionate' is not defined in either statute or the ECHR. A similar obligation is imposed in relation to s 29 RIPA2000 and the authorizing of covert human intelligence source (CHIS) deployments. Consideration of whether conduct to be authorized is proportionate to what is sought to be achieved is required as part of the general duties in relation to privacy enacted in IPA2016 (s 2(4)(c)), as elaborated in relation to specific duties (for example, s 23(1)(b)).

The phrasing of the proportionality test in s 93 PA97 is slightly different but essentially amounts to providing the same protection for suspects and third parties. For property interference to be authorized, the officer must believe that it is necessary because it is likely to be of substantial value in the prevention or detection of serious crime (a higher threshold than for directed surveillance) and that the desired objective cannot be reasonably achieved by other means.

The RIPA Covert Surveillance and Property Interference Revised Code of Practice (CPSI Code) at paras 3.4 and 3.5 elucidates the principle of proportionality slightly differently, stating:

> If the activities are deemed necessary on one or more of the statutory grounds, the person granting the authorization or warrant must also believe that they are proportionate to what is sought to be achieved by carrying them out. This involves balancing the seriousness of the intrusion into the privacy of the subject of the operation (or any other person who may be affected) against the need for the activity in investigative and operational terms.

> The authorization will not be proportionate if it is excessive in the overall circumstances of the case. Each action authorized should bring an expected benefit to the investigation or operation and should not be disproportionate or arbitrary. *The fact that a suspected offence may be serious will not alone render intrusive actions proportionate.*

> (Emphasis added)

In the Investigation of Protected Electronic Information Code of Practice (IPEI Code) the proportionality test is expressed slightly differently again. Stipulating that the imposition of the requirement to disclose the protected electronic information 'should be proportionate to what is sought to be achieved by obtaining the disclosure', the Code goes on to say (para 3.39):

> This involves balancing the extent of the intrusiveness of the interference with an individual's right to respect for their private life against the benefit to the investigation or operation being undertaken by a relevant public authority in the public interest.

The difference in the way the balancing consideration is expressed superficially seems a matter of mere semantics, but actually is significant and could divert consideration: investigators and authorizing officers may be tempted to interpret 'need for the activity' broadly. It is amenable to such a reading. But 'benefit to the investigation' reminds them that the focus for consideration of proportionality is a narrow one. The seriousness of the offence being investigated does not, in and of itself, render any given investigative action proportionate.

The CSPI Code (para 3.6) advises that the following elements of proportionality should therefore be considered:

- balancing the size and scope of the proposed activity against the gravity and extent of the perceived crime or offence—bearing in mind that 'the fact that a suspected offence may be serious will not alone render intrusive actions proportionate' (CPSI Code, para 3.5);
- explaining how and why the methods to be adopted will cause the least possible intrusion on the subject and others;
- considering whether the activity is an appropriate use of the legislation and a reasonable way, having considered all reasonable alternatives, of obtaining the necessary result;
- evidencing, as far as reasonably practicable, what other methods have been considered and why they were not implemented.

The language of this extract has clear implications, particularly for authorizing officers: it will not be sufficient to itemize these bullet points in an authorization template form with a tick box to be marked as demonstration of such considerations having taken place. Such considerations will need to be fully documented, with reasoned decisions recorded.

Further information and reading

The Equipment Interference Code of Practice issued pursuant to s 7 IPA2016 offers its own interpretation of proportionality considerations for those persons empowered to issue warrants under this Act (para 4.18):

- The extent of the proposed interference with privacy against what is sought to be achieved.
- How and why the methods to be adopted will cause the least possible interference on its subject and others.
- Whether the activity is an appropriate use of the legislation and a reasonable way, having considered all reasonable alternatives, of obtaining the necessary result.
- What other methods, as appropriate, were either not implemented or have been employed but are assessed as insufficient to fulfil operational objectives without the use of the proposed investigatory power.

- Whether there are any implications of the conduct authorized by the warrant for the privacy and security of other users of equipment and systems, including the internet, and an explanation of why (if relevant) it is nevertheless proportionate to proceed with the operation;
- Where a bulk equipment interference warrant is available (intelligence agencies only), the safeguards set out in Chapter 3 of Part 6 of the IPA2016.

The effect of s 125 IPA2016 on the cancellation of equipment interference warrants is to impose on the chief officer issuing the warrant under Part 5 IPA2016 a duty to maintain a continuous review of proportionality issues in each instance a warrant is issued, from the moment the warrant is issued until the warrant is cancelled or otherwise ceases to have effect.

These multiple interpretations of 'proportionality' set out in the various Codes of Practice for different covert investigation methodologies seem to have much in common, but it will be the responsibility of each authorizing officer to ensure that, when proportionality is addressed in any given authorization or warrant that the correct formula from the relevant Code is adopted.

Investigators and authorizing officers, resisting the urge to find an objective that justifies a technique, must be clear from the outset what evidence or intelligence it is that is sought and how it relates to the investigation as a whole. When reviewing existing authorities and considering applications for renewal, investigators and authorizing officers must consider whether the proportionality has changed and if so, how. It may be that as a result of the evidence or intelligence gained, the continued use of surveillance (in order to obtain new specific pieces of information or evidence) is proportionate. But it may equally be possible that surveillance has in fact produced the specific evidence or intelligence that was the original objective of the authorized action and that further surveillance merely to secure more of the same is disproportionate.

Consideration of proportionality for authorizing officers is a balancing act, but one in which it is easy to confuse what properly should be balanced. Taylor succinctly draws the crucial distinction: 'a balancing exercise takes place that requires a consideration of whether the interference with the right is greater than is necessary to achieve the aim ... this is not an exercise in balancing the right against the interference, but instead *balances the nature and extent of the interference against the reasons for interfering*' (emphasis added, 2006, 26). McKay elaborates in practical terms: 'an assessment of the proportionality of the resources deployed in an operation cannot be properly undertaken without knowing the nature of the offences being investigated, the evidence required to prove them and the likely dividend to society in preventing and detecting the offence or likely outcomes' (2006, 49).

Although the nature of the offence may offer partial justification for the deployment of certain methods (a test purchase operation being a case in point), it is not the *seriousness* of the offence or the *extent of the harm* derived from the offence that must be balanced but *the use of coercive and intrusive methods* against the value of the evidential product derived therefrom (Ormerod, 2006, 77–78).

With case law having precedence over policy, even policy set out in Codes of Practice issued pursuant to primary legislation, it is worth rehearsing guidance from the European Court of Human Rights on the interpretation of proportionality:

KEY POINTS ON PROPORTIONALITY

(1) Have relevant and sufficient reasons based on reliable information been put forward for conducting the proposed covert investigation in that particular way? *Jersild v Denmark* (1995) 19 EHRR 1.

(2) Could the same evidence or intelligence be gained by a less intrusive method? *Campbell v UK* (1993) 15 EHRR 137.

(3) Are the decision-making process by which the application is made and the authorization given demonstrably fair? *W v UK* (1988) 10 EHRR 29; *McMichael v UK* (1995) 20 EHRR 205; *Buckley v UK* (1997) 23 EHRR 101.

(4) What safeguards have been put in place to prevent abuse of the technique? *Klass v Germany* (1979–80) 2 EHRR 214. See para 59 in which it is argued safeguards represent the compromise between defending democratic society and individual rights.

(5) Does the proposed infringement in fact destroy the 'very essence' of the ECHR right engaged?

(Based on Starmer, 1999, 171, 175–176)

If there is no information or evidence to support the deployment of investigation methods that will infringe Article 8(1), then an unjustifiable infringement will take place.

Further information and reading

- S McKay, 'Approaching the Regulation of Investigatory Powers Act 2000', *Covert Policing Review* (2006), 46–53.
- S McKay, 'Privacy, proportionality and other human rights principles', *Covert Policing: Law and Practice* (Oxford University Press, Oxford, 2011), Chapter 2.
- D Ormerod, 'Recent developments on entrapment', *Covert Policing Review* (2006), 65–86.
- N Taylor, 'Covert policing and proportionality', *Covert Policing Review* (2006), 22–33.

The Codes of Practice accompanying RIPA2000 and the PA97 are available online at <https://www.gov.uk/government/collections/ripa-codes> (accessed January 2018).

As yet untested in the courts is the issue of cumulative 'disproportionality'. A single covert investigation action may not, in and of itself, be disproportionate. But a series of sequential authorizations within the context of a single investigation arguably may lead to an overall response that, cumulatively, is disproportionate. This is another issue that authorizing officers may wish to keep in mind when considering reviews, renewals, and supplementary applications. The latest editions of the RIPA2000 Codes of Practice recognize the consequences of accumulation as a potentially problematic area in relation to the definition of 'private information': 'the totality of information gleaned may constitute private information even if individual records do not' (CSPI Code, para 2.6).

2.2.6 Collateral intrusion and proportionality

Authorizing officers are particularly advised (CSPI Code, para 3.8) to take account of the possibility of obtaining private information about persons (other than the subject of the authority) coincidentally present in a surveillance arena (so-called 'collateral intrusion'):

> The same proportionality tests apply to the likelihood of collateral intrusion as to intrusion into the privacy of the intended subject of the surveillance
>
> (CSPI Code, para 3.9)

This stipulation increases the onus of consideration upon authorizing officers.

2.3 What Are the Consequences of Investigator Malpractice?

There are five possible adverse consequences for investigators who have not acted properly during a covert investigation:

- a stay of proceedings (where investigators are considered to have unfairly entrapped an offender or enticed an offence that would not otherwise have been committed);
- exclusion of evidence from trial;
- becoming the subject of a complaint (and possibly associated civil litigation) either under the jurisdiction of the Investigatory Powers Tribunal, the Independent Police Complaints Commission, or individual agency procedures; or
- being subject to adverse comment from the Investigatory Powers Commissioner; and
- (for police officers) being subject to disciplinary action for breaching the police Code of Ethics.

IPA2016 provides that unauthorized interception specifically is unlawful. Breaches of RIPA2000 Parts 2 and 3 result in surveillance that will be unauthorized and so non-compliant but which will not, of itself, be unlawful. Nevertheless, acting in a way which is incompatible with a Convention right is unlawful under s 6 HRA.

Section 78 PACE provides for the exclusion from trial of unfair evidence as follows:

> A court may refuse to allow evidence on which the prosecution proposes to rely to be given if it appears to the court that, having regard to all the circumstances, including the circumstances in which the evidence was obtained, the admission of the evidence would have such an adverse effect on the fairness of the proceedings that the court ought not to admit it.

PACE does not impose an absolute duty upon courts to exclude unfairly obtained evidence. The power to do so is discretionary. Section 78 PACE ensures that a court is competent to consider whether or not, *in the interest of ensuring fair trial*, evidence obtained by unlawful covert investigation should be excluded. If the court decides that it would be unfair to admit evidence that had been unlawfully obtained, for instance through improperly authorized or unauthorized surveillance, then such evidence must be excluded. Since PACE came into force 'there have been many such cases under section 78' (M Zander, *The Police and Criminal Evidence Act 1984* (3rd edn, Sweet & Maxwell, London, 1996), 171).

Neither Europe nor the UK has followed New Zealand's example in automatically excluding any evidence that has been secured in breach of the New Zealand Bill of Rights Act (Starmer, 1999, 298–299). When considering whether to not admit evidence that has been unfairly obtained, both UK and Strasbourg courts have taken a broad view when having regard to all the circumstances and apply a standard test: *what would be the effect on the fairness of the trial if evidence that had been obtained unlawfully is admitted?*

The ECtHR has held that rules of evidence regarding admissibility are primarily the preserve of domestic courts, Strasbourg's role being to determine the fairness of a trial as a whole (*Schenk v Switzerland* (1991) 13 EHRR 242). It would appear that the requirements of a fair trial do not necessarily demand the exclusion of evidence unlawfully obtained. But as *Schenk v Switzerland* illustrates, careful consideration will be given to the probative weight of the evidence, and the opportunities available to the defence to challenge the evidence and any other relevant factors in a given case before unlawfully obtained evidence will be admitted by the court. In both *Khan v UK* (2000) 31 EHRR 1016 and *PG v UK* [2002] Crim LR 308, the ECtHR unanimously found breaches of Article 8, yet no unfairness arising from the evidence adduced therefrom. 'Technical breaches especially of qualified rights might not impact on fairness' (David Ormerod, 'ECHR and the exclusion of evidence: trial remedies for Article 8 breaches', [2003] *Criminal Law Review* 61–80, 61, 66). Unattractive though the unlawful or non-compliant activities of investigators might be, the courts have held that there are circumstances in which evidence improperly obtained should nevertheless be put before the jury. The Court of Appeal has held that exclusionary rules cannot be employed merely to express disapproval of the manner in which investigators have secured relevant evidence (*R v Chalkley and Jeffries* [1998] 2 All ER 155). Critics have argued that 'the courts routinely admit covert surveillance evidence owing to its reliability, despite acknowledged breaches of Article 8' (Ormerod, 66 and 67; see also Kingsley Hyland's commentary appended to the case report of *R v Khan (Imran)* [2013] EWCA Crim 2230 in Crim LR 204, 7, 520–524). 'A problem with this approach is that it does nothing to encourage or exhort police officers to uphold the law and to conduct ethical investigations' (Sybil Sharpe, 'Covert surveillance and the use of informants' in Mike McConville and Geoffrey Wilson (eds), *The Handbook of The Criminal Justice Process* (Oxford University Press, Oxford, 2002), 59–74, at 70). The same could be said in relation to other investigators.

The unlawful or non-compliant conduct of investigators, whether deliberate or unwitting, can never be condoned. The fact that courts have not always excluded evidence unlawfully or improperly obtained as a result of covert investigation does not excuse investigators from always complying with procedural law. Admission of the evidence notwithstanding, such judgments are serious indictments of the investigators concerned for acting unlawfully or improperly, thereby compromising their integrity, that of the organization for which they work, and the integrity of the criminal justice and public regulatory systems as a whole.

The independent Investigatory Powers Tribunal (IPT) is an independent court with unique powers established pursuant to s 65 RIPA2000 which investigates and as necessary adjudicates complaints by individuals that they have been subject to unlawful interference and or human rights violations by public authorities using RIPA2000 and IPA2016 powers. The tribunal determines its findings according to the same principles that are applied in judicial review, ss 67(2) and 67(3)(c) RIPA2000. The tribunal shall then investigate the authority under which the individual concerned acted, pursuant to s 67(3)(b) RIPA2000. No frivolous or vexatious complaint will be entertained. Complaints will not normally be investigated if they are made more than a year after the date of the alleged incident. The tribunal has the power to award compensation or make such other order as they see fit and their decisions are final, not being subject to appeal. By virtue of s 68(6) and (7), anyone working for an organization empowered with covert investigation powers under RIPA2000 or IPA2016 shall provide the tribunal with such documents or other information as is required.

For complaints arising out of conduct relating to covert investigation which does not fall within the specific remit outlined, the normal complaints procedures relating to the investigator's organization apply.

Complainants also have recourse to civil suit against investigators who are alleged to have breached Article 8 rights, pursuant to ss 7 and 8 HRA.

Further information and reading

The Investigatory Powers Tribunal publishes its judgments on its website: <http://www.ipt-uk.com> (accessed 21 December 2017).

The IPA2016 create the Investigatory Powers Commissioner (IPC) and other judicial commissioners (s 227), who, together with the Investigatory Powers Commissioner's Office (IPCO), have assumed responsibility for the functions previously performed by the Surveillance Commissioners, the Intelligence Service Commissioner, and the Interception of Communications Commissioner, all of which roles have been abolished (s 240). The IPC is invested with a 'broad remit to keep under review the use of investigatory powers' (IPA2016 Explanatory Notes, para 638). The use of the more intrusive covert methods will be subject to prior approval by the IPC, whilst the use of other surveillance powers will be subject to inspection and audit. Non-compliance and poor professional practice are likely to be the subject of adverse IPC comment in much the same way that such issues attracted concerns voiced by the Chief Surveillance Commissioner.

Further information and reading

The IPCO website provides further information and will publish the Annual Reports of the ICPO, <https://www.ipco.org.uk> (accessed 21 December 2017).

In July 2014 the College of Policing published its Code of Ethics pursuant to s 39A Police Act 1996 as amended by s 124 Anti-Social Behaviour, Crime and Policing Act 2014. The first standard set in the Code of Ethics is that of honesty and integrity and, in relation to covert policing, this chapter of the Code requires that 'covert tactics must be appropriately authorized and any deployments must be shown to be proportionate, lawful, accountable, necessary and ethical' (para 1.6 of Standard 1). Thus the standards set in the Code of Ethics incorporate and elaborate the standards set by the Article 8 tests. Whilst a breach of the Code of Ethics by a police investigator will not automatically attract sanction in and of itself, 'behaviour that does not uphold the policing principles or which falls short of the expected standards of professional behaviour set out in this Code of Ethics will be dealt with [*inter alia*] according to the severity and impact of any actual, suspected or alleged breach' (para 5.1.5 of the Supplementary Notes). Failure to comply with the requirements of RIPA2000 and IPA2016 (or any other procedural law) is conduct that will harm public confidence in the integrity of the criminal justice system and its component elements such as the police. Loss of public confidence is a significant harm, given the reliance placed within the criminal justice system upon the cooperation of the public. (The uses to which local authorities were putting directed surveillance is an instance of misuse that damaged public confidence and led to changes in the law constraining more tightly local authority use of directed surveillance. The actions of certain members of the now disbanded Special Demonstration Squad are equally likely to have damaged public confidence in the police service.)

Causing a significant harm logically seems to equate with a severe breach of the Code of Ethics. Moreover, failure on the part of a state agent, such as an investigator or a manager of investigations, to comply with the requirements of their statutory empowerment is, in and of itself, a moral harm and therefore intrinsically unethical.

In this context, judicial discretion to admit evidence unlawfully obtained does not provide mitigation. Indeed, the fact that judicial discretion has had to be brought to bear is prima facie evidence that a police investigator has acted unlawfully and therefore, by the definition set out in the Code of Ethics, unethically. It follows, having established high public expectations, that if the College of Policing Code of Ethics is to have meaning and influence, and if it is to enjoy credibility with the public (and not itself be a cause of loss of public confidence), all police investigators and authorizing officers who are found to have acted unlawfully under RIPA2000, IPA2016, or PA97 must expect to be held accountable under the Code of Ethics and accordingly sanctioned. Time will tell whether this is the interpretation adopted by the police service.

2.4 **Scotland**

The jurisdiction focus of this book is England and Wales. RIPA2000 also applies to Northern Ireland. The use of covert investigation in the separate criminal jurisdiction of Scotland is provided for by the Regulation of Investigatory Powers (Scotland) Act 2000 (RIP(S)A). Where all proposed covert investigation conduct is likely to take place in Scotland then authorizations should be sought and granted pursuant to RIP(S)A, to which a separate code of practice applies. There are limited exceptions and these are explained in para 1.18 of the Covert Surveillance and Property Interference Revised Code of Practice issued pursuant to s 71 RIPA2000.

2.5 **Conclusion**

This chapter has set out primary statutory principles and tests that have to be met for covert investigation methods provided for by RIPA2000, IPA2016, and PA97 to be undertaken lawfully. There exists a second aspect to lawful covert investigation that reinforces the adherence to and compliance with these statutory principles: the authorization of covert investigation. It is to that subject that we now turn.

3

Authorization and Governance

Covert investigation that is subject to RIPA2000, IPA2016, and PA97 must be authorized before the use of covert methods commences (unless the prevailing circumstances fall within the exceptional and tightly defined parameters of emergency authorization). The role of the authorizing officer is the most important role within the overall management and governance of lawful covert investigation: it is the authorizing officer (be that an investigation agency senior manager, a public servant, judicial officer, or a government minister) who considers and documents the statutory determinations of proportionality and necessity, and who satisfies him- or herself that the appropriate risk management strategies have been identified and implemented, before any given use of a covert investigation tactics is embarked upon. The governance architecture is multi-faceted, with agency self-authorization (subject to external prior approval in certain cases); oversight in the form of the Investigatory Powers Commissioner; and an independent Investigatory Powers Tribunal adjudicating allegations of misuse. Further detail will be the subject of the law chapters following this general discussion of the covert investigation management. Here the general and generic issues concerning authorization as a mechanism are considered.

3.1 **The Context for Authorization**

Within the context of due process protection and the adherence to procedural fairness, *preserving the integrity of the criminal justice system (or, as appropriate, an administrative or regulatory determination system)* is the key issue arising from the use of covert investigation. Investigators, because they are acting outside the public arena and so are beyond overt scrutiny, must be capable of being held to account for their actions by other means. As much as the citizen wishes to be protected from being harmed by crime, agents within the criminal justice system must not misuse their powers and authority in providing that protection: to do so would be to cause harm not only to the subject of the investigation (who would thus be subject to unfair treatment) but also to the wider community interest in having a morally sound criminal justice system. The secrecy of covert investigation limits the ways in which investigators can be managed and held to account in this arena. Equally important in protecting the integrity of the criminal justice system is protecting investigators from malicious allegations that they have acted improperly.

Four principles can be said to underpin the governance and regulation of covert investigation undertaken to detect and prosecute crime or regulatory infringements:

- evidence to sustain a prosecution (or other enforcement action) or intelligence to facilitate investigation management must be obtained in a manner that preserves the integrity of the criminal justice or administrative systems and their actors;

- statutory rights of the person(s) being investigated must not be infringed except where there is statutory provision to do so;
- the rights and privacy of other citizens not suspected of criminal involvement or regulatory misconduct must be protected and collateral harm as a consequence of covert investigation should be minimized through effective investigation management; and
- the professional integrity of investigators must be demonstrated or, if necessary, its absence exposed.

These principles for the management of investigations in which it is proposed to deploy covert methodology are derived from the Article 8 statutory and case law tests discussed in Chapter 2:

(1) Does the investigative act fall within the scope of Article 8? (2.2.1)
(2) If yes, has the Article 8 right been interfered with by a public authority? (2.2.2)
(3) If it has, was this interference in accordance with the law? (2.2.3)
(4) If it was lawful, was the interference pursuant to a legitimate aim as identified in Article 8(2)? (2.2.4)
(5) Even if it was both lawful and pursuant to a legitimate aim, was it still necessary, and no more than necessary (ie proportionate), in a democratic society? (2.2.5)

Further information and reading

The four management principles and the context in which they apply are considered further in C Harfield, 'The governance of covert investigation', *Melbourne University Law Review*, 34(3) (2010), 773–804, which compares contrasting governance frameworks for covert investigation in England and Wales and New South Wales (Australia).

In 'Law, morality and the authorization of covert police surveillance', *Australian Journal of Human Rights* 20(2) (2014), 133–164, C Harfield presents theoretical consideration of how ethical authorization can, and in some instances perhaps cannot, be achieved within the current governance architecture.

3.2 What Benefits and Disadvantages Arise from the UK Regulatory Regime?

The role played by continental European prosecutors (usually a branch of the judiciary or else trained as judges) and investigating magistrates (where such a role exists) means that continental European investigators nearly always have some form of judicial supervision, particularly for methods likely to engage ECHR rights. The perceived advantage of judicial oversight is that it is considered to be a guarantor of the integrity of the criminal justice system and a means of ensuring that investigators do not act unfairly or unlawfully. Many have argued for judicial oversight of covert investigation within the UK, which would put covert investigation on a par with overt coercive investigation methods, such as the execution of production orders and search warrants which require judicial authority and which, so it is argued, is necessary in order to comply with ECHR. Self-regulation by investigators is, as a mechanism, vulnerable either to deliberate abuse or to ignorant (even if well-intentioned) misuse and inadequate training.

These latter concerns prompted Parliament to constrain the privilege of self-authorization by local authorities and to introduce a requirement on local authorities to seek judicial approval before planned use of authorized direct surveillance can commence (s 23A RIPA2000, as amended by s 38 Protection of Freedoms Act 2012). Parliament also restricted the circumstances in which local authorities could use directed surveillance. These legislative changes came about in direct response to public concerns about how local authorities were employing the powers with which they had been invested (see, eg, 'Local authorities launched 10,000 snooping operations last year', *Daily Telegraph*, 22 July 2008, <http://www.telegraph.co.uk/news/uknews/2446314/Local-authorities-launched-10000-snooping-operations-last-year.html>, accessed 21 July 2015: a very similar story appeared in the *Daily Telegraph* a few months later on 1 November 2008).

The IPA2016 consolidates previous governance regimes (the Chief Surveillance Commissioner; the Interception of Communications Commissioner; and the Intelligence Service Commissioner) into a single entity: the Investigatory Powers Commissioner's Office (IPCO) (<https://www.ipco.org.uk>, accessed 04 January 2018). Oversight is managed through annual inspections, notification of authorities, and, in certain types of investigation, prior approval for proposed actions.

This approach has its critics. Whilst declaring a preference for judicial supervision, the ECtHR nevertheless found parliamentary oversight and independent scrutiny of investigator self-regulation, particularly if undertaken by persons with judicial experience, to be an acceptable alternative to direct judicial supervision and therefore such a regime is compliant with Article 8(2). This principle, applied by the ECtHR in *Klass v Germany* (1979–80) 2 EHRR 214, 235, was enacted in the now repealed Interception of Communications Act 1985 (IOCA), and was found sufficient by the court in *Esbester v UK* (1994) 18 EHRR CD 72 (see also *Christie v UK* (1993) 78-A DR 119; *R v Lawrence* [2002] Crim LR 584; and Ferguson and Wadham (2003), 103), hence the IOCA scheme was reproduced with only minor adjustments in the PA97 and RIPA2000. Elsewhere, differently structured internal authorization regimes have been found to be inconsistent with the rule of law (*Kopp v Switzerland* (1999) 27 EHRR 91).

Further information and reading

- A Ashworth, *Human Rights, Serious Crime and Criminal Procedure* (Sweet & Maxwell, London, 2002) Chapter 2, for a discussion of the debate and various authorities.
- G Ferguson and J Wadham, 'Privacy and surveillance: a review of the Regulation of the Investigatory Powers Act 2000' [sic] *EHRLR* (2003) Special Issue 101, for a further general introductory discussion of the issues.
- S McKay, *Covert Policing: Law and Practice* (Oxford University Press, Oxford, 2011), Chapter 1, for a general introduction to covert policing law and the proposal of a specific analytical framework with which to examine the mechanics of RIPA2000.
- M Seneviratne, 'Policing the police in the United Kingdom', *Policing and Society* 14(4) (2004), 329–347, for discussion about the pitfalls of self-regulation and how these can be overcome.

The regulatory regime, where it is not judicial, should be independent from the investigating authorities and must be seen to be guarding against the abuse of powers by investigators. This has translated itself into what many investigators regard as a bureaucratic nightmare of form-filling. Because of this widely held perception, it is worth rehearsing the benefits of the written authority process to the investigator.

The process of seeking written authority:

- helps investigators structure their operations appropriately;
- enables authorizing officers to demonstrate how they have considered the issues of privacy, legitimacy, necessity, and proportionality;
- records the decision-making process throughout an investigation;
- is a substitute for alternative methods of due process control.

It is a means by which not only the justifications for infringing ECHR qualified rights are recorded in a transparent form, but also by which the investigator can be protected from subsequent allegations of abuse of authority and malpractice.

Self-regulation subject to scrutiny arguably is a more flexible authority regime, from the operational perspective, than one requiring investigators to go to court on a regular basis, perhaps as often as several times a day, to seek a judicial warrant for the investigative activity to be employed, which for many would provide a greater guarantee of rights protection. The current authority regime seeks to balance the need for operational flexibility and responsiveness against the obligation to protect citizens' rights. It gives investigators a flexibility they would certainly miss if it was withdrawn, and being asked to account for their actions in writing could be seen as a small price to pay for such an operational and investigation management advantage.

But there are practical problems that should be acknowledged by investigators, authorizing officers, their senior executives, and external commentators. To use a police example: authorizing officers in the National Crime Agency (NCA) deal with covert investigation daily, are very experienced in considering the human rights issues, and have become very familiar with the provisions of the PA97 and RIPA2000, and will likely become equally proficient with the IPA2016 arrangements. Their opposite numbers in territorial local policing, by and large, do not have the same daily operational familiarity with covert investigation and not infrequently have additional authorizing duties under PACE as well as a wider range of managerial and community issues to deal with, all of which place competing demands on their time in addition to their RIPA2000/IPA2016 obligations. It is not unknown for a superintendent to find him- or herself in a position in which the demands of the authorizing officer role protecting human rights and ensuring the integrity of an investigation appear to conflict with the demands of their performance management role in meeting monthly targets: 'force strategic priorities and cost-effectiveness, of themselves, provide insufficient basis for authorization' (OSC *Annual Report 2009–10*, para 5.8; see also OSC, *Annual Report 2008–09*, para 5.26). Authorizing officers in other public-sector organizations similarly have other duties competing with their RIPA2000 obligations for attention and time, and the lack of adequate training and daily experience of authorizing surveillance amongst non-police authorizing officers has been commented upon in the OSC, *Annual Reports 2005–06* and *2006–07*, although the Chief Commissioner also noted that lack of experience as a consequence of lack of use of covert investigation powers is also a consequence of complying with the principle that covert investigation is a matter of last resort (OSC, *Annual Report 2008–09*, para 5.4, with comment on the dividend from investment in training at para 5.27 (see also the OSC *Annual Report 2016–17*, para 4.3).

All of this appears to reinforce the jurist argument that supervision of covert investigation should be confined to the courts. But there are a number of wider issues that militate against such a move. Leaving aside the overarching issue of how much surveillance is desirable in any given society, the amount currently being undertaken in the UK, based on the annual reports of the OSC, could fundamentally alter the relationship of the judiciary to the trial process. For instance, issuing a search warrant for a specific item or items of known evidence in order to render it accessible at trial tends to be a single event; however, a covert investigation operation is an entire sequence of related events intended to identify evidence, and so judicial oversight would involve a greater degree of engagement with investigation management. To some this might be desirable, but it would reduce the independence of the judiciary from the pre-trial process. The question arises whether such investigation function falls outside proper judicial function (if the judiciary is to remain fully independent from the executive), although this issue lies beyond the primary purpose of this book.

The second wider consideration concerns promotion of the rights culture and integrity of the criminal justice system. Why confine to the judiciary pre-trial consideration (as well as final determination at trial) of how the rights of an individual suspect should be balanced against the rights of the wider community and the powers of the state acting on behalf of the wider community? Investigators who daily might take actions that engage the ECHR rights of an individual should themselves be engaged in identifying how those rights ought to be protected and how any necessary breaches of qualified rights can be minimized. Rather than abdicating such decision-making to others, self-regulation (subject to external scrutiny) affords the opportunity to increase the professionalism of investigators and helps to instil in state agents the very values that the ECHR seeks to protect. It forces investigators and authorizing officers to confront the ECHR daily. The concepts, which would otherwise remain remote arguments at *voir dire*, become ingrained in the daily thinking of investigation practitioners and managers. Within such an approach the trial process, adjudicated by the judiciary, remains the final guarantee of individual rights, independent from the investigation process.

Confronting such issues imposes upon those empowered to resort to covert investigation the obligation to be well-versed in the appropriate legislation and the interpretation placed on the statutes by the courts. Thus the starting point for any investigator or authorizing officer is the primary and secondary legislation (the statute and any supporting statutory instruments), supplemented by case law. The latest available versions of UK statutes will be found online at <http://www.legislation.gov.uk/>, a database searchable by title and year. The website indicates where amendments have been enacted. Statutory instruments are to be found online at <http://www.legislation.gov.uk/uksi> (both sites accessed 18 June 2018).

Further information and reading

Relevant legislation and case law can also be accessed via the following subscription websites: <http://www.westlaw.co.uk> or <http://www.lexisnexis.co.uk>; or via the following free (at the time of writing) website: <http://www.bailii.org>.

3.3 Key Actors in the Self-authorization of Covert Investigation

In the self-authorization regime there are two key actors: the *applicant* and the *authorizing officer*. As a matter of organizational process, individual agencies may insert a gatekeeping role between these two with the remit to quality-assure applications before they are considered by the authorizing officer, but in terms of delivering statutory obligations, it is the applicant and the authorizing officer upon whom responsibilities fall in the self-authorization process.

It is important not to confuse the roles of *applicant* and *authorizing officer*. The roles are distinct but can become blurred, particularly if the application process is automated and computerized for the purposes of process management and creating supporting documentation as the application proceeds. It is the applicant and authorizing officer who stand to be cross-examined in court about the application and the authority (although it is the gatekeeper who is most likely to face the annual IPCO inspection team).

Given their particular responsibilities, authorizing officers will wish to be wary of accepting applications on face value without careful scrutiny. An applicant may well have considered issues of legitimacy, necessity, and proportionality in the body of the application, but authorizing officers have a legal duty to consider such matters for themselves and will undoubtedly bring additional perspective to such consideration. An authorizing officer who merely rubber-stamps the application will not have discharged his or her legal obligation under the Act.

At the risk of over-simplification but for the purposes of introductory illustration, the key roles are distinguished in Table 3.1, which identifies (for the purpose of elucidating the distinction) four sequential management stages of the overall application/authorization/review process (to which external prior approval may be added in certain cases).

Table 3.1 The roles of applicant and authorizing officer distinguished

Applicant role	Authorizing officer role
First stage—application	**Second stage—initial authorization**
Identify intelligence/evidence gap required to be filled.	Do not rubber-stamp the application: actively consider what is being requested. Be prepared to authorize less than is being sought. Test all assumptions relied upon in the application. Read all the intelligence reports relied upon.
Document and demonstrate the gap and why the desired information is relevant and important to the ongoing investigation.	
Seek advice about and consider all possible solutions.	The application may look similar to others, but how is it different and what individual considerations will this difference demand in considering and, if approved, phrasing the authorization?
If covert surveillance is sought, seek feasibility study from appropriate technical staff.	Have less intrusive methods been attempted to obtain the desired information/evidence? (What were they?)
Undertake comprehensive risk assessment of proposed action. Complete and submit application for consideration by authorizing officer (AO). Where collaborative arrangements exist between police forces or other agencies, identify to which	If not, why not?
	Is the proposed action lawful?
	Is the proposed action necessary?

Table 3.1 (continued)

Applicant role	Authorizing officer role
AO application should be made as per the collaboration protocol.	Is the proposed action proportionate? (Part of this consideration requires full understanding of the technical capabilities of any proposed equipment: can the equipment achieve more than is actually necessary or proportionate? If so, why is not less sophisticated equipment being used? If that is not possible, how will the overly sophisticated equipment be used so as not to secure more product than is proportionate?)
	Where equipment is to be deployed, will its subsequent retrieval require authorization?
	Determine the schedule for reviewing the authority.
Third stage—monitoring execution (ongoing review)	**Fourth stage—review/renewal/cancellation**
Ensure that the action undertaken is that which is being authorized, which will not necessarily be that which was sought in application.	Rigorously, robustly, and regularly review ongoing authorities to ensure that they remain valid, necessary, and proportionate.
During conduct of the surveillance, gather information to inform updated risk assessment in the event that review is necessary and renewal desired.	Do not necessarily wait until the end of the authorized period to conduct a review if changed circumstances demand earlier review.
If a previously unidentified individual is iden-tified during the course of surveillance, seek immediate review and, if necessary, emendation or extension of the authorization from the AO, or, if necessary, a new authorization.	Immediately cancel authorizations on completion of surveillance or when any of the legitimacy, necessity, or proportionality tests are no longer met, whichever is the sooner.
Review will generally be required wherever circumstances change.	
Fully document all the above—be prepared to be cross-examined in court	

3.4 **Who Is an Authorizing Officer?**

Within the different agencies and organizations empowered with recourse to covert investigation, the roles identified as having responsibility for authorizing the use of such methods are defined in various statutory instruments. Mirroring the demarcation between basic directed surveillance and the more morally problematic intrusive surveillance, different ranks of manager and

45

senior manager are identified in relation to the authorization of directed and intrusive surveillance.

In relation to directed surveillance (see Chapter 6), authorizing officers within agencies empowered to self-authorize directed surveillance are listed in the Schedule to the Regulation of Investigatory Powers (Directed Surveillance and Covert Human Intelligence Sources) Order 2010 (No. 521). Authorizing officers in respect of interfering with property (see Chapter 8), communication interception (see Chapter 11), and accessing communications data (see Chapter 10) are identified in Part III PA97, and Parts 2, 3, and 5 IPA2016.

Authorizations in deployments that are likely to acquire confidential information or where a juvenile CHIS is involved are undertaken by more senior managers in the relevant agencies and the authorizing officers in these circumstances are listed in Annexe A to the CSPI Code and Annexe A to the CHIS Code.

Further information and reading

As at 4 January 2018, the only version of the 2010/521 Order and accompanying Schedule available online at <http://www.legislation.gov.uk/uksi> was the version of the Order as originally made, which takes no account of changes in organizations or other amendments since 2010.

3.5 When Is External Authorization or Approval Needed?

In certain categories of surveillance, agency self-authorization is subject to external approval before the planned covert activity can commence.

Local authorities authorizing directed surveillance within the scope of their powers to do so must seek from a relevant judicial authority (as defined in s 32A(7) RIPA2000) an order approving the grant of the authorization (s 32A(2) RIPA2000). The planned directed surveillance cannot commence until the grant order has been made.

Those agencies empowered to undertake intrusive surveillance or to deploy a relevant source may not commence the planned activity until the authorizing officer has received prior written approval from the Investigatory Powers Commissioner (see Chapters 7 and 12).

An external prior approval or granting order ensures that the practitioner intentions of the investigating agency have been subject to independent review prior to implementation: it serves as a check to ensure that the statutory tests of proportionality and necessity have been met. Magistrates can refuse to make a grant order if not satisfied that the relevant grounds under s 28(2) or s 29 RIPA2000 have been met and exist at the time the grant is considered. The IPC can withhold prior approval or quash an authorization made under the urgency provisions if the Commissioner is not satisfied that the requirements of s 32(2) (a) and (b) RIPA2000 have been met.

3.6 **Is Authorization Necessary?**

There has been much police practitioner concern about the perceived bureaucracy inherent in authorizing covert investigation. This issue featured prominently in the Home Office/Association of Chief Police Officers (ACPO) review of RIPA2000 which reported in 2005. (The review has not been published, but a redacted copy has been lodged in the House of Commons Library for the benefit of Parliamentarians, *Hansard* HC, 20 June 2007, col 1967W; see also Home Affairs Committee, *A Surveillance Society?* Fifth Report of Session 2007–08, HC58i & HC58ii (TSO, London, 2008), starting at para 311.) Home Office opinion, supported at the time by the OSC and by the then HM Chief Inspector of Constabulary Sir Ronnie Flanagan in his 2008 *Review of Policing: Final Report* (para 5.55), was that police forces, through their desire to be thorough in their accountability, had over-complicated their own procedures and that significant duplication was involved in the police authorizing processes that had evolved. This can, perhaps, be explained in part by the police service and other public authorities coming to terms with very new and radically different legislation which even such authorities as the Law Lords have found difficult to interpret.

The use of covert investigation does not automatically require authorization. RIPA2000 is not a law that manages covert actions; it is a law that renders lawful and compliant covert actions in circumstances where Article 8 ECHR rights are engaged. 'Where *directed* surveillance would not be likely to result in the obtaining of any private information about a person, no interference with Article 8 rights occurs and an authorization under the 2000 Act is therefore not appropriate' (Covert Surveillance and Property Interference: Revised Code of Practice, para 1.14: investigators and authorizing officers will need to be aware that what constitutes private information has been broadly interpreted by various courts (see Chapter 2 at 2.2.1.)).

Nor is a RIPA2000 authorization required in circumstances in which the investigating agency has 'another clear legal basis for conducting covert surveillance likely to result in the obtaining of private information about a person' (CSPI Code, para 1.15; see also S McKay, *Covert Policing: Law and Practice* (Oxford University Press, Oxford, 2011, 6–9)).

The nature of intrusive surveillance and property interference is such that those agencies empowered to engage in such conduct (far fewer than the number empowered to utilize directed surveillance) will always require authorization under the relevant Acts.

In a significant contribution to covert investigation case law, the Investigatory Powers Tribunal (IPT) in *C v Secretary of State for the Home Department* (IPT/03/32/H, 14 November 2006) draws a distinction between the *core functions* of an investigating, governing, or regulatory agency and the *ordinary functions* commensurate with managing a large organization. Thus it was held that whilst it was necessary for police forces to authorize surveillance conducted in the prevention and detection of crime (a core function of policing), it was not necessary to authorize under RIPA2000 surveillance that was being conducted in relation to a former employee's disputed medical pension claim against a police force (human resource management being an ordinary function of a large organization).

If surveillance is for the purpose of preventing and detecting crime (the only purpose for which most organizations listed in Schedule 1, RIPA2000, as amended, can authorize surveillance), and the proposed activity engages the qualified rights protected under Article 8 ECHR, then the activity must be authorized under RIPA2000 and the PA97, as required.

3.7 What Issues Have Arisen from Independent Inspections of Covert Investigation?

The governance role assigned to the Office of Surveillance Commissioners initially under Part III PA97 and then extended by Part IV RIPA2000 has been re-assigned to the Investigatory Powers Commissioner and the Investigatory Powers Commissioner's Office under Part 8 IPA2016. OSC annual reports nevertheless remain a basis for authoritative guidance until over-ruled by any subsequent equally authoritative reinterpretation.

Further information and reading

OSC *Annual Reports* published since 2002–03 are available to download from the archived website of the Office of Surveillance Commissioners which is now accessible via the National Archives at <http://discovery.nationalarchives.gov.uk/details/r/C16807> (accessed 17 July 2018). The final OSC Annual Report (2017) is accessible via the 'Publications' page of the PCO website (accessed 4 January 2018).

The OSC annual reports contain an insight into how well or otherwise public authorities are handling their statutory obligations in respect of these covert investigation methods and are a source of guidance to investigators and authorizing officers alike. In the early reports the Chief Surveillance Commissioner highlighted instances of good and poor practice identified during inspections. Latterly this practice has been dispensed with in favour of more general observations, partly as a response to a general improvement in covert investigation standards amongst police forces. Yet there remain perennial issues, and with the recent significant increase in directed surveillance undertaken by non-police organizations, issues encountered early on by the police service are now being encountered by other agencies.

In 2001 the Chief Surveillance Commissioner felt it necessary to highlight the 'poor wording' in the applications for property interference submitted by police chief officers. 'There have been examples where Chief Officers have authorized the removal of property to attach surveillance equipment to it but have failed to authorize the entry on to property necessary to do so or even the return of a vehicle after the device has been fitted' (OSC *Annual Report 2000–2001*, para 15.9). 'Insufficiently specific applications and authorizations' were still an issue in 2004 (OSC *Annual Report 2003–2004*, 11). In the reporting year 2006–07, 67 unauthorized surveillance operations were reported to the OSC, most occurring because of inadequate explanation and lack of understanding between authorizing officers and staff as to what activity precisely had been authorized (OSC *Annual Report 2006–2007*, para 5.3). In 2010–11, 129 'irregularities' were reported to the Chief Commissioner (OSC *Annual Report 2010–2011*, para 3.2).

The need for comprehensive precision in both applications and authorizations cannot be overemphasized. Actions that have not been specifically authorized will not be lawful.

Deficiencies identified by the OSC have included:

- failure to authorize or authorization of the wrong type;
- the conduct of surveillance beyond that which was actually authorized, and conversely, the authorization of multiple tactics many of which, in the event, were never used;
- poorly presented and inadequately considered arguments about the proportionality of the authorized activity;
- inadequate intelligence cases made in support of an application;
- inadequate risk assessments, particularly in relation to CHIS authorizations;
- excessively detailed intelligence cases made in support of an application;
- confusion about the statutory definitions of directed and intrusive surveillance;
- confusion about the definition of a CHIS (the OSC has strongly criticized the emerging trend of deploying 'tasked witnesses' (OSC *Annual Report 2006–2007*, para 8.9), a term of uncertain and non-statutory origin which, in the experience of the OSC, may embrace 'impropriety'; if, as the OSC supposes, there are insufficient trained handlers and controllers, and senior investigating officers are not sufficiently trained in the deployment of CHISs, the creation of new labels will not render the tasked activity lawful);
- errors in detail such as car registration numbers and incorrect addresses leading to surveillance of subjects or property other than those actually identified in the authorization;
- lateness in notification, renewal, and cancellation;
- commencement of operations requiring a Commissioner's prior approval before such had been granted;
- failure to explain urgency in oral authorizations;
- authorizations given by staff without power to do so;

- authorizing more than was sought on an application (there may, of course, be very good reasons for authorizing officers authorizing less than an applicant had applied for once proportionality and necessity had been considered);
- delegation of reviews by authorizing officers to their deputies;
- continuing failure on the part of authorizing officers 'properly to demonstrate that less intrusive methods have been considered and why they have been discounted in favour of the tactic selected' (OSC *Annual Report 2008–09*, para 5.8);
- codes of practice not readily available to practitioners;
- persistent use of template phrases, formulaic constructions, and 'cut and paste' in both applications and authorizations (which indicate failure on the part of authorizing officers to execute their statutory duty to consider each case on its merits) (see, for example, OSC *Annual Report 2013–14*, para 5.15).

Overall, the OSC frequently identified the lack of adequate training and refresher training in RIPA2000 and covert investigation management as a theme common to all the public authorities empowered to undertake covert investigation. In 2007–08 an apparent improvement in the training of authorizing officers was evident on inspection (OSC *Annual Report 2007–08*, para 8.3), but a lack of specialist training concerning the authorization and deployment of CHIS was recorded (para 9.5). Criticism was to the fore once more in the OSC *Annual Report 2008–09*, in which the Chief Commissioner lamented the fact that 'too many ACPO officers and senior executives have yet to receive formal training in this legislation' (para 5.22). The Chief Commissioner felt it necessary to observe (para 5.27):

> Public authorities which invest in training usually achieve a higher standard of compliance. The quality of training is variable.

Subsequently the Chief Commissioner observed that the failure of authorizing officers to describe 'the particulars of each case in a manner that is bespoke to the particular investigation' (ie the reliance of both applicants and authorizing officers on the use of formulaic phrases) is 'probably the consequence of poor training' (OSC *Annual Report 2009–10*, para 5.1). With the inclusion of magistrates in the authorization regime since the amendments to RIPA2000 brought about by the Protection of Freedoms Act 2012, OSC concerns about poor training have now been voiced about the apparent 'disparate levels of knowledge within the magistrates' court' (OSC *Annual Report 2013–14*, para 5.25). In his final report, the Chief Surveillance Commissioner drew attention to the need for continued training of local authority officials even though RIPA2000 powers might be infrequently used (OSC *Annual Report 2016–17*, para 4.3), and for the extension of law enforcement agency training to include proper and lawful deployment of surveillance tactics in the virtual world (OSC *Annual Report 2016–17*, para 13.2).

Such deficiencies heighten the risks of improperly authorized or unauthorized investigations taking place. Such investigations will, by definition, be noncompliant, thus undermining the integrity of the criminal justice and other public regulatory systems.

On the frequent complaint about the bureaucracy of self-regulation under RIPA2000 and PA97, the OSC originally offered this palliative: 'conscientious completion of the application form will incline the judge, if the authorization is called into question, to uphold it, if he can' (OSC *Annual Report 2003–2004*, 8); a maxim supported indirectly by the decision in *R v Kennedy and others* (unreported, 2001), in which proceedings were stayed due to inadequate police records and documentation, and by the upholding of the conviction in *R v Paulssen* [2003] EWCA Crim 3109. Despite *minor* infringements of RIPA2000 leading to a technical failure of authorization continuity, the judge in *Paulssen* held that police had acted in good faith even if the authorization process had been incorrectly applied. More recently, however, the Chief Surveillance Commissioner took a rather different stance, observing that much of the perceived bureaucratic burden surrounding RIPA2000 and the PA97 'does not result from the legislation or the Codes. It is largely the making of law enforcement agencies who often repeat the same statements in different sections of the forms' (OSC *Annual Report 2006–2007*, para 12.1): 'unnecessary repetition and verbosity produce self-inflicted bureaucracy' (OSC *Annual Report 2006–2007*, para 8.6). Such bureaucracy is symptomatic of poor training (OSC *Annual Report 2007–08*, para 8.7).

Unnecessary repetition and verbosity, together with reliance upon formulaic constructions, is regarded as evidencing a lack of clear and concise preparation in application and in authorization consideration. The use of tick boxes and template phrasing gives rise to the suspicion that authorizing officers, for instance, have failed in their statutory duty to consider proportionality properly. Criticism of the use of templates and formulaic language has been a perennial theme in OSC *Annual Reports* (for example, *2008–09*, para 5.1; *2009–10*, para 5.13; *2010–11*, para 5.7).

A key vulnerability in the employment of stock phrases or the use of imprecise language and broad constructions is that specific conduct will not be found to have been authorized even if both applicant and authorizing officer think that it is covered by the deliberately vague and generalized nature of an authorization that seeks to be all-encompassing. There are no short cuts in the application and authorization process. Precision does not have to be bureaucratic. Investigations can often develop dynamically in unexpected directions: in such circumstances review and, if necessary, the seeking and granting of new authorizations will be the appropriate approach to ensure that the surveillance product is not subsequently vulnerable to being ruled inadmissible as evidence.

It is fundamental to a proper authorization process that covert activity has been specifically authorized. It is incompatible with this principle that

51

authorizations be so loosely framed as to permit activity not anticipated at the time of authorization.

(OSC *Annual Report 2009–10*, para 5.13)

Linked to this is the issue of organization guidance and the use of hypothetical scenarios. Scenarios can be equally useful or vulnerable to misinterpretation if regarded as a 'one-size-fits-all' solution. There is also the temptation to word an authorization so that it fits an apparently relevant scenario rather than the circumstances of the actual matter at hand. 'Examples given in handbooks tend to be inflexibility applied leading to a wrong conclusion which consideration of the specific facts of the case would have avoided' (OSC *Annual Report 2008– 09*, para 3.15). The Chief Commissioner expressed concern at plans to include scenarios in the draft revised codes of practice (OSC *Annual Report 2008–09*, para 3.15), and subsequently criticized their actual inclusion in the published versions (OSC *Annual Report 2009–10*, para 5.3).

The Chief Commissioner made plain that OSC 'inspections are and will continue to be based on the most authoritative and current judicial interpretation of the legislation' (OSC *Annual Report 2009–10*, para 3.6), and that such interpretation will be accorded precedence over any organization guidance or ministerial policy statement that is at odds with the OSC view (para 3.7; see also OSC *Annual Report 2008–09*, para 5.1). It reasonably may be anticipated that this will be true of IPCO inspections in the future. To ensure compliance with RIPA2000, IPA2016, PA97, and the Article 8 tests, authorizing officers and the organizations for which they work will wish to have access to the best training available and, just as importantly, the time available free from other operational demands to undertake the authorizing and review functions properly pursuant to the statutory obligations imposed upon them.

If, in a period of severe public-sector economic stringency, the necessary resources and training are not made available to resolve the multiple issues raised by OSC inspections, then the stark political consequence is that recourse to covert investigation as a tactic (without which some serious criminality cannot adequately be investigated) will have to be abandoned (see OSC *Annual Report 2013–2014*, para 5.19) until such time as more resources become available or different political decisions are made about resource allocation.

4

Understanding the Operating Environment

Covert investigation cannot safely or securely be undertaken unless those managing such methods understand the operating environment in which the methods are to be deployed. (Safety and security are interests in which investigators, those acting on their behalf, those being investigated, and third parties each have a moral claim.) Understanding the operating environment requires a holistic recognition of the vulnerability and harm landscape in order appropriately to manage systemic and individual interventions that may be needed along the *continuum of corruption*, which ranges from lack of sufficient competence amongst staff at one end to serious (and often criminal) abuse of public power and position for personal gain at the other.

The acquisition, security, use, and dissemination of information obtained by, and concerning the use of, covert investigation methods, together with the state of investigator knowledge in relation to any given investigation, create an arena vulnerable to compromise and a market for corruption in which lack of sufficient competence can have significant adverse consequences. Corruption vulnerability awareness is the foundation of resistance and resilience against corruption. Information about investigation targets, tactics, and techniques is of high value to those being investigated. Its acquisition, through unwitting, careless, or deliberate disclosure by investigators, facilitates evasion of surveillance by those being investigated and so frustrates the proper purpose of the criminal justice and regulatory systems for which ends investigation is being undertaken.

4.1 **Strategic Perspectives**

The vulnerability and harm landscape can be envisioned from a variety of perspectives in order to achieve holistic understanding. At the strategic level, areas of vulnerability that must be managed by an organization can be marshalled into four categories:

- organizational *purpose*;
- organizational *process*;
- organizational *product*; and
- *people* working (directly for, on behalf of, or in partnership with) the organization.

Specific vulnerabilities—elements within each category that potentially could be compromised if not adequately and securely managed—can be mapped across the categories to define a strategic perspective at the organization-wide level. This is the perspective that executive leadership needs to understand in order to appreciate how best to structure the organization and appropriately trained staff for the safe and secure deployment of covert investigation methodology. (The Senior Responsible Officer, a mandatory role by virtue of the Communications Data Code, para 3.31 and a recommended role in the CSPI

Code, para 3.28, could assume organizational responsibility for maintaining this strategic perspective.) Once specific vulnerabilities have been identified, responses can be devised and implemented.

Table 4.1 illustrates this in practice with a case study example concerning the management of covert investigation using informers, possibly the most problematic area of covert investigation for an organization to manage. We suggest that this model framework can be applied equally across other aspects of covert investigation management.

The *Purpose-Process-Product-People* (P4) analytical framework proposed here is an overarching, strategic approach to problem identification in the arena of covert

Table 4.1 The 4 Ps Vulnerability Management Framework

Areas of vulnerability	**Purpose** of organization (including contributory purposes of organizational sub-units)	**Processes** contributing to organization purpose	**Product** (within organizational context)	**People** (as contributors to organizational purpose)
Vulnerability	*Law enforcement agency within criminal justice system* 1. Obtain reliable intelligence 2. Without compromising organization 3. Influence of asset recovery strategy?	1. Identifying/ recruiting informer 2. Identifying/ recruiting handler (including self-selection) 3. Meeting informer in remote location (so as not to risk exposing informer links to investigating agency) 4. Briefing informer 5. Debriefing informer 6. Analysing information 7. Disseminating intelligence	1. Informer identity 2. Handler identity 3. Information provided by informer (reliability thereof) 4. Information provided by informer (valued asset to be protected) 5. Access to raw information 6. Access to analysed intelligence 7. Use made of that knowledge product	1. Informer 2. Handler 3. Source management 4. Departmental command 5. Law enforcement staff outside the source-handling environment but with access to product *[?associate vulnerability— family/ friends/ colleagues of handler]*

(continued)

Table 4.1 (continued)

Areas of vulnerability	**Purpose** of organization (including contributory purposes of organizational sub-units)	**Processes** contributing to organization purpose	**Product** (within organizational context)	**People** (as contributors to organizational purpose)
Response to vulnerability	Organizational structure: minimize staff exposure to informers by having specialist units rather than general access Recruitment and training strategy for handlers Recruitment and risk management strategies for informers Accountable processes for tasking, deployment, and dissemination to ensure alignment with organizational purpose and to ensure informer serves organizational purpose and not vice versa Articulated principles in relation to use of informers and derived product to foster professionalism Independent oversight	Appropriate identification of intelligence need Tasking according to intelligence gap Authorization of deployment Record of decision-making and rationale Two handlers at every meet: electronic corroboration if feasible Proper record of meeting Accountable rewards Proper pre-dissemination analysis and sanitization Appropriate dissemination flows	Protected identities (informers and handlers) Corroboration of product Location security Building/office security IT security Review of potential evidential use of product No dissemination of/acting on product likely to expose source	Continuous risk assessment of informer (including through covert surveillance if necessary) No dissemination of/acting on product likely to expose source Use of specialist source-handling staff, remotely located Regular vetting and training of handlers—including corruption vulnerability training Regular vetting and training of handler managers—including corruption vulnerability training Continuous risk assessment of source management Training of senior investigating officers Risk-assessed dissemination

investigation management as an initial step in problem solving. Its counterpart is the equivalent understanding of to whom or to what harm may be caused if the specific areas of vulnerability are not managed appropriately and successfully. From an ethical perspective, it can be argued that no matter how attractive the desired end product, the risks posed in achieving it may not justify the means (see J Kleinig, *Ethics and Criminal Justice: An Introduction* (Cambridge University Press, Cambridge, 2008), 104). Again, the categorization is four dimensional.

Unmanaged vulnerabilities can give rise to harm being caused to:

- *the organization utilizing covert investigation* (for example, reputational damage and litigation costs arising from misuse of such methods by inadequately trained staff);
- *the staff* of the organization utilizing covert investigation (for example, hazardous deployments and moral harms such as separation from family through prolonged surveillance or infiltration);
- *the subject(s) of the investigation* (for whom, for example, conviction will result both in moral harm such as societal condemnation, and in material harms— such as court-imposed sanction or denial of future employment); and last, but by no means least,
- *the legitimate interests of third parties*—which range from the interests of the community as a whole in having an effective criminal justice system characterized by integrity, to individuals such as associates (non-criminal or criminal) of the investigation subject, or non-associated members of the public, who will be subject to collateral intrusion by virtue of being present in the surveillance arena during surveillance.

Where harm is likely to be caused and cannot be prevented, avoided, or mitigated (for example, an accused cannot and should not avoid the harm of sanction imposed upon conviction), then the causing of harm, even if it is just a minor trespass coincidental to an authorized covert intervention, must be justifiable in the circumstances. As with areas of vulnerability at the level of strategic organizational management, likely harms can similarly be mapped. These can be mapped at the strategic level also for the organization, its staff, and third-party interests, but it is at the operational level that most investigators will engage with this issue, in the form of operational risk management.

4.2 **Operational Perspectives**

The key message is NOT that covert investigation is too risky to undertake but rather that with proper management of identified vulnerabilities and mitigation of preventable harms, covert investigations can be successfully concluded, with every operation contributing to accumulated operational and organizational learning. The risks of intervention have always to be balanced against the risks of non-intervention.

Managing operational vulnerability is a complex and developing subject and it is one that investigators and their managers conducting and supervising covert investigations have to consider when planning, authorizing, executing, and reviewing such operations. The Chief Surveillance Commissioner drew attention to the importance of sound risk assessment and professionalism in risk management in his final report to the Prime Minister (see for example, OSC *Annual Report 2016–17*, paras 13.5; 13.6; 14.1; 14.2). In his summary of areas for improvement, the Chief Surveillance Commissioner identified that vulnerability (and therefore risk) arises when undue influence is brought to bear by senior investigating officers on those with daily management and authorization responsibilities for covert investigation operations (para 14.3(i)).

There may be no right answer and any given decision may have to be based on a professional judgment taking into account any number of factors (eg what is known, what is unknown, and what can reasonably be surmised). It is helpful to have a framework within which to make such considerations, and with which to identify appropriate risk control measures and so determine a risk management strategy. This chapter presents some models to use as such a framework.

Risk in relation to specific deployments of covert investigation can be viewed from three perspectives. Firstly, risk analysis constitutes one of the analytical tools and techniques within the National Intelligence Model (NIM): if an issue is assessed through the NIM business management process as warranting attention at, and subsequent action is derived from, a tasking and coordinating meeting, then the determination of an appropriate intervention constitutes the first step in the proportionality rationale. Spontaneous serious incidents aside, should covert investigation methods be used in operations not initiated under the NIM process?

Secondly, there is the issue of identifying vulnerability associated with tactical options in the planning stage of an operation and then managing the risks throughout the operation before reviewing operational risk management at the conclusion of individual interventions and completed investigations. In an era in which partnership is promoted assiduously, the various perceptions of risk and priorities complicate risk management in multi-agency investigations. In partnership and collaborative working, analysis of vulnerabilities either has to be undertaken jointly from the outset, or else should be a two-stage process in which organizations individually assess risks and then collaborate in finding the most appropriate intervention or management strategy once the matter requiring intervention is raised in a multi-agency forum. (Partnership-working, in and of itself, generates its own intrinsic vulnerabilities.)

Covert investigation operations generating either intelligence or evidence then create a third arena of vulnerability in relation to the storing, utilization, and dissemination of the covert investigation product.

4.3 **What Positive Obligations Are Imposed on Investigators?**

The failure to consider vulnerabilities and apply an appropriate risk manage-ment strategy constitutes at best poor working practice, at worst negligence. In certain circumstances such omission goes beyond mere negligence. Court interpretations of Article 2 ECHR place upon public authorities the positive obligation to protect life. *Osman v UK* [1999] 1 FLR 193 illustrates this point (see also K Starmer, *European Human Rights Law* (Legal Action Group, London, 1999) 89–90, 199–200 for general discussion). A positive obligation was held to exist where 'the authorities knew or ought to have known at the time of the existence of a real and immediate risk to the life of an identified individual or individuals from the criminal acts of a third party and that they failed to take measures within the scope of their powers which, judged reasonably, might have been expected to avoid that risk' (*Osman v UK* [1999] 1 FLR 193, note 19 at para 116).

This general principle can be held to apply elsewhere even where positive obligations under the ECHR do not apply: investigators and investigation man-agers should take reasonable measures to manage foreseeable risks. Application forms for covert investigation authority, both in paper form and in the various software versions commercially available, usually include pages or boxes that have to be completed to demonstrate that the applicant has identified the risks involved with the application and determined an appropriate risk management strategy. The risks anticipated and how they are managed might have a bearing on the necessity and proportionality arguments supporting the application. Experience has shown that risk assessments for covert investigation applications are not infrequently omitted altogether on initial submission. Those that are submitted are often inadequate. And even where a risk assessment is included on first submission, for subsequent reviews and renewals the assessment is almost never revised and is very often dispensed with a perfunctory 'no change'.

Surveillance conducted for covert investigation may not produce the intel-ligence anticipated, nor the evidence sought, but the one guaranteed product of covert surveillance will be vital information with which to review the risk assessment.

At initial application, risk assessments will be estimations. Investigators will identify what they think the risks of the operation might be and how these anticipated risks should be managed. Managers and authorizing officers will review such assessments from their own perspectives, considering any add-itional risks posed by the operation to the organization as a whole. Once a period of surveillance has been conducted, information about risks will have been updated by default in one or more of three ways: new risks may have been identified; previously anticipated risks may now be discounted; or pre-viously anticipated risks will have been confirmed. It is important that this information is captured and included in subsequent risk assessments on submission of investigation authority reviews and renewal applications.

Where initial surveillance has demonstrated that there are no additional risks to take into consideration, and none that can now be dismissed, and where there has been no compromise of staff or equipment, then this should be incorporated in the risk assessment attached to the review consideration or renewal application. It is not simply a case of stating 'no change'. What was previously an initial estimation is now supported by empirical and observational information. An initial estimation has become an informed evaluation. At the very least, such a revised risk assessment might say: 'Following x hours/days of surveillance, no new risks associated with this operation have been identified. None of the previously identified risks can be discounted. There is no intelligence to indicate that staff or surveillance techniques deployed in this operation have been compromised. Therefore the current risk management plan remains valid.'

Risk management or reduction is as dynamic a process as is the manifestation of the risks themselves. It must be held under constant review. In some operations it will be so dynamic that the commanding officer will have undertaken several revised risk assessments during the course of any given phase of the operation, possibly within a very short space of time and with little or no opportunity to record the rationale at the time, in which case documenting the variation as soon as practicable after the event must suffice.

Further information and reading

The revised CSPI and CHIS codes of practice specifically draw attention (para 3.8 in both codes) to the fact that *authorizing officers* should take into account the risk of obtaining private information about persons who are not subject to the surveillance or property interference activity (collateral intrusion). The codes of practice are admissible as evidence in criminal or civil proceedings and code provisions must be taken into account by any court or tribunal if considered relevant to the matter before them.

(CSPI Code, para 1.6; CHIS Code, para 1.5)

4.4 The Benefits of Thorough Risk Assessment

The added value of sound risk assessment to covert investigation is to be found at a number of levels. Some operations involve physical danger to staff. All covert investigations run the risk of investigators acting unlawfully in the absence of effective management or in cases where enthusiasm exceeds knowledge and competence, both of which vulnerabilities could result in trials not proceeding or being discontinued because of improper or unlawful investigator conduct. Depending on particular community sensitivities, a clumsily managed operation might result in public disorder.

Particularly where an operation engages Article 8 rights, risk assessment helps validate the thinking of applicant and authorizing officer alike, producing the following benefits:

- professional, credible risk management/reduction processes;
- reviews of working assumptions, taking into account changing risk circumstances;
- a process for real-time decision-making amenable to subsequent review (either in an operational debrief or a subsequent public enquiry);
- reduction in the number of perverse decisions;
- reduction in corporate/personal liability.

The demonstrable dangers in covert investigation include the death of surveillance staff; the compromised safety of CHISs; compromised investigations, tactics, techniques, and technology; corruption within investigation teams; organizational and individual reputational damage; and loss of public confidence in agencies investigating criminality. The risk of all these adverse outcomes can be mitigated and minimized through appropriate risk management.

4.5 **Identifying Risks and How to Manage Them: The Model Approach**

Structuring thinking around established conceptual models aids precise consideration of risk issues. Section 4.6 of this chapter briefly introduces three risk assessment models currently in use amongst different law enforcement organizations. (Anecdotally, the authors have also been told that there are forces which do not apply any structured approach to risk assessment of covert operations: lack of a systematic approach to risk management is itself a vulnerability giving rise to its own risks.)

It is helpful to apply *risk assessment* models to all the different facets of risk, otherwise regarded as the different 'at risk' groups: risk to the organization; risk to staff and other resources engaged in the operation (including for this purpose technical equipment, remotely deployed CHISs, and members of the public who allow their premises to be used as observation points); risk to the subject of the operation; and risk to third parties such as members of the public unconnected with the investigation but likely to be present in the surveillance arena.

It is suggested here that use of a risk assessment model is a useful tool to aid risk identification and section 4.6 briefly introduces three different models identified to the authors as currently being used in different UK law enforcement agencies.

Once risks have been identified, a determination has to be made on how to manage them. For this there are the RARA and TTTT *risk management* models (see 4.7), which can be used in conjunction with the vulnerability assessment.

The culmination of this consideration should be a structured risk management plan or risk reduction strategy for those risks, amongst the many identified, which are likely to cause the most harm. The use of models aids thinking for both applicants and authorizing officers and should thus facilitate a more succinct written assessment, ensuring that it does not become a bureaucratic nightmare that actually adds nothing of value to the investigation or its management.

Overarching the risk management plan or reduction strategy must be the assessment of how the identified risk control measures themselves might engage the ECHR rights of staff, investigation subject, and general public.

Although the investigator and manager have primary responsibility for risk assessment and management, on occasion they will need to draw upon expert advice when encountering specialist fields and techniques. For instance, experts from computer crime units will be best placed to advise on what sort of electronic footprints will be created when computers are used to conduct e-surveillance. Non-experts will not necessarily appreciate the full range of risks to be managed in specialist arenas.

4.6 **Models of Risk Identification**

Created by former Deputy Assistant Commissioner, John Grieve, whilst serving with the Metropolitan Police Service, is a model that helps an investigator and the manager to begin to identify risks associated with any given operation, often referred to as the '3 Ps L E M' model because of its acronym (PPPLEM). From this original idea, which informed the designs of early computerized authorization management systems, other models have subsequently been elaborated as different perspectives on risk have been identified. The PPPLEM model (the acronym translates as shown in Table 4.2), applied to the four risk groups, will help identify the risks inherent in any given operation. A matrix is a useful aid to complete the assessment, with the 'at risk' groups placed on the vertical axis and the PPPLEM elements placed along the horizontal axis (Table 4.3).

It may well be the case that not all the elements of the model apply to all the 'at risk' groups. Indeed, if there was something significant to say in each of the matrix boxes, the proposed operation should probably be considered too risky!

The advantage of using this model lies not only in helping structured consideration: it demonstrates and records the thought processes of investigators and managers alike and in this way saves the trouble involved in composing lengthy prose to make the same point. More detailed discussion can thus be

Table 4.2 The PPPLEM model for risk assessment

P—Police and community risks	Alternatively, public and organizational risks. In general terms: what are the risks to the organization within the community of engaging in this operation? Is there any general risk to/from the community at large? Adverse publicity? Public disorder possible? What are the risks to the organization from the investigation subject/staff/public at large? What are the risks to the community from the organization engaging in this operation? What are the risks to the community from the investigation subject? What are the risks to the community from the organization staff? What are the risks of not doing anything?
P—Physical risks	What are the physical risks to staff/subject/third parties? Organization premises or premises borrowed for the purpose?
P—Psychological risks	What are the psychological risks to staff/subject/third parties?
L—Legal risks	What are the legal risks to the organization? Its staff? The subject? Third parties?
E—Economic risks	What are the economic risks to the organization? Its staff? The subject? Third parties? The community? Cost of operation? Possible litigation claims?
M—Moral risks	What are the moral risks to the organization? Its staff? The subject? Third parties? Can the operation be justified morally as well as legally? Is there a danger that the very essence of the ECHR will be breached as well as the Article 8 rights in question? What are the risks of not doing anything?

Table 4.3 PPPLEM matrix

PPPLEM matrix	Police/ community	Physical	Psychological	Legal	Economic	Moral
Organization						
Staff						
Subject						
Third parties						

Table 4.4 The PLAICE model for risk assessment

P	Physical risks
L	Legal risks
A	Risks to organizational assets
I	Information and information technology risks
C	Risk of compromise to staff, tactics, and techniques
E	Environmental risks

saved for those risks identified through the vulnerability and RARA models as requiring particular management (see 4.7).

The PLAICE model of risk assessment, advocated by Roger Billingsley, formerly of the Metropolitan Police Service, is summarized in Table 4.4. Once again, specific risks within each of the above categories are to be identified and documented, together with the proposed control measures. The importance of documenting and continually reviewing risks and reasoning is emphasized, particularly in relation to defending the service and staff against subsequent litigation. For the purpose of using this model, Billingsley suggests that 'information technology' should include sensitive data gathered using technology and the systems used to process, analyse, and document such data. The environment, readers are reminded, should include possibly hostile environments overseas when deploying staff abroad on covert investigations.

Further information and reading

See R Billingsley, 'Risk management: is there a model for covert policing?' *Covert Policing Review* (2006), 98–109.

Developed as a response to managing the impact of austerity funding cuts on operational policing and to foster a common lexicon and methodology for risk modelling in law enforcement, the Management of Risk in Law Enforcement (MoRiLe) programme has produced both strategic and tactical risk models which have been authorized as Approved Professional Practice, alongside the National Intelligence Model and the National Decision Model. A scoring guide has been produced that is multi-faceted (identifying victims, the community, the environment, and geographical scope as key impact areas).

Further information and reading

The MoRiLe scoring guide is too large to reproduce here. Further information can be obtained from Chris Dowen (Programme Lead) via <https://polmorile. wordpress.com/2015/11/29/management-of-risk-in-law-enforcement-morile/> (accessed 20 December 2017).

The MoRiLe model seems best suited to helping to determine whether costly covert investigation resources should be deployed, and to assessing the possible consequences of such deployment that may need to be managed post-execution. On the information provided to the authors, it does not appear to be a direct substitute for either the PPPLEM or PLAICE models and it can be envisaged that, in conjunction with the National Decision Model, a combination of applications may be used at different planning and execution stages of any given investigation utilizing covert investigation methodologies.

The issue here is not which model is used but that some model of structured consideration and reasoning should be used to identify risks and appropriate control measures. The PPPLEM, PLAICE, and MoRiLe models are not mutually exclusive—and each relies on good intelligence for any meaningful consideration of risk to be undertaken.

4.7 **Vulnerability and Risk Strategy Models: RARA and TTTT**

Vulnerability, *probability versus impact*, can be measured as two scales of 1 to 10, one for each of probability and impact. Alternatively it can more simply be expressed in terms of 'high', 'medium', or 'low' set in a matrix, with one axis representing probability and the other impact (Table 4.5). Both approaches assist in determining mitigation priorities.

Greatest vulnerability, and therefore risk, will be inherent where the probability and impact are both high or where one is high and the other medium. These are the risks that require management or a reduction strategy (see Table 4.5).

Risks that are both low in impact and low in probability need not concern the investigator, investigation manager, or authorizing officer too greatly.

Once the vulnerability factor has been identified, risk management and reduction prioritization can be undertaken. For this the RARA model can be applied.

Table 4.5 Impact/probability matrix

High impact	*Contingency required plan*	ACTION REQUIRED	ACTION REQUIRED
Medium impact		ACTION REQUIRED	ACTION REQUIRED
Low impact			
Impact/Probability matrix	Low probability	Medium probability	High probability

There are four strategies that can be adopted in relation to any given risk: **remove** it, **avoid** it, **reduce** it, **accept** it—hence RARA. This is a sliding scale of strategies. Preferably, operations should be planned so as to remove all risks. This ideal world is rarely achievable, however. Changing tactics to achieve the same objective may afford a means of avoiding a risk. If the risk cannot be removed or avoided, then there may be measures that can be put in place to reduce the risk. There will be a number of risks that investigators will wish simply to accept. This might be because the risks have a low vulnerability factor: low probability/low impact.

As with the PPPLEM model, Billingsley offers an alternative to RARA—the TTTT model: **terminate, treat, transfer**, or **tolerate**. In essence, albeit with the second and third elements reversed, the TTTT model is intended to achieve exactly the same outcome in the same way as the RARA model.

Potential control measures aimed at reducing the likelihood or adverse consequences of any given risk may themselves have risks attached. It may not be possible, for instance, to deploy a full surveillance team to provide protective cover for the deployment of an undercover operative because the surveillance team itself would show out in the deployment arena. In such a case, alternative means of providing protection and rescue for such operatives must be devised, or else the desired evidence or intelligence must be acquired by other means—a way of avoiding identified risks.

As with the PPPLEM and PLAICE models, the application of the RARA or the TTTT model in determining a risk management strategy and appropriate control measures illustrates and records the thought processes of the decision-takers based on available information at the time, and herein lies its value to investigators, managers, and authorizing officers.

4.8 Conclusion

Successful risk assessment depends upon having information that is as accurate as possible and as up to date as possible. Such information is to be found, in part, as a by-product of surveillance. If such information has not been recorded and assessments consequently reviewed, then individuals and organizations are vulnerable not only to the risks inherent in the investigation, but to the risk of—and consequences from—being negligent.

There is always scope for the unforeseen to occur. Use of these models to aid risk management will not alter that truism. These models cannot accurately predict the future. They will help identify those risks that can reasonably be foreseen. They will help prioritize a risk management strategy according to whether any given risk can be removed, avoided, reduced, or accepted. The models must be utilized in conjunction with the latest available information and intelligence. In the event of something unforeseen occurring that leads to particularly adverse consequences, the documented use of these models may well determine whether the investigators and the organizations concerned can be shown to have done everything that was rea-sonable in the circumstances or whether they are vulnerable to a civil claim based on negligence.

Besides the models for structured consideration of risk discussed earlier, force crime managers have three strategic approaches to managing risk: through training; through process; and through physical security. Staff engaged in covert investigation must be appropriately trained and skilled. CHISs, for instance, should be managed through dedicated source units with handlers and controllers appropriately qualified to national standards. Foot and vehicle surveillance require different skills and different levels of training. Those intending to use specialist technical equipment must understand its operation, capability, and limitations.

Risk management through procedure does not seek to stifle innovation and creativity, but it does seek to protect staff through adherence to established processes and statutory provision, such as surveillance authorization, that provide structure and frameworks tested through experience. Incorporated in this should be consideration of the necessity to conduct security-vetting of key staff involved in covert investigation. Security-vetting of key roles reduces the vulnerability of organizations and of their staff to compromise and cultivation by hostile elements keen to acquire access to information held by organizations or to compromise on-going investigations. In connection with this, in 2001 ACPO adopted the Government Protective Marking Scheme.

Further information and reading

There are four levels of protective marking: 'TOP SECRET', 'SECRET', 'CONFIDENTIAL', and 'RESTRICTED'. Documents falling outside all of these areas of sensitivity are 'UNCLASSIFIED'.

Top Secret

Compromise would:

- Threaten directly the internal stability of the UK or friendly countries
- Lead directly to widespread loss of life
- Cause exceptionally grave damage to the effectiveness or security of UK or allied forces or to the continuing effectiveness of extremely valuable security or intelligence operations
- Cause exceptionally grave damage to relations with friendly governments
- Cause severe long-term damage to the UK economy.

Secret

Compromise would:

- Raise international tension
- Seriously damage relations with friendly governments
- Threaten life directly or seriously prejudice public order or individual security or liberty

---

- Cause serious damage to operational effectiveness or security of UK or allied forces or the continuing effectiveness of highly valuable security or intelligence operations
- Cause substantial material damage to national finances or economic and commercial interests.

Confidential

Compromise would:

- Materially damage diplomatic relations, that is, cause formal protest or sanctions
- Prejudice individual security or liberty
- Cause damage to operational effectiveness or security of UK or allied forces or the effectiveness of valuable security or intelligence operations
- Work substantially against national finances or economic and commercial interests
- Substantially undermine the financial viability of major organizations
- Impede the investigation or facilitate the commission of serious crime
- Seriously impeded the development or operation of major government policies
- Shut down or otherwise substantially disrupt significant national operations.

Restricted

Compromise would:

- Adversely affect diplomatic relations
- Cause substantial distress to individuals
- Make it more difficult to maintain the operational effectiveness or security of UK or allied forces
- Cause financial loss or loss of earning potential to, or facilitate improper gain or advantage for, individuals or companies
- Prejudice the investigation or facilitate the commission of crime
- Breach proper undertakings to maintain the confidence of information provided by third parties
- Impede the effective development or operation of government policies
- Breach statutory restrictions on disclosure of information.

See also Clive Harfield and Karen Harfield, *Intelligence: Investigation, Community, and Partnership* (Oxford University Press, Oxford, 2008) 155–158, on maintaining a professional intelligence environment, the principles of which apply also to managing covert investigation and the product thereof.

Alongside procedural security, physical security is an additional means of risk management. Unauthorized disclosure takes place either when hostile elements access directly intelligence and sensitive evidence acquired through covert investigation (from which tactics and techniques may be deduced and so compromised) or when such elements through corruption or blackmail secure complicity from a member of the intelligence or covert investigation staff in passing on the acquired product. Assuming that the measures above have been implemented, the risk of the latter scenario, whilst not eradicated, is reduced. Removing the opportunities for self-initiated unauthorized access is a means to reduce the former risk.

Physical security means quality locks on doors (for instance, a combination of monitored personal key card and digital lock access would be an example of good security); a clear desk policy; regular password-changing on computers; security filing cabinets in locked offices for classified hard-copy documents; and locked offices for those computer terminals networked to sensitive databases. It also means regular review by the organization's security officer.

Every deployment of covert investigation risks the exposure and compromise both of techniques and methods and the identity of individuals performing the various CHIS roles. It is too easy for the documentation of risk assessment and management strategies to be perceived, erroneously, as bureaucratic box-ticking. Documentation is necessary in order to ensure colleagues and partners are aware of the issues and the strategies for dealing with them. But that is just a supporting function for the main principle: ongoing, perpetual, dynamic risk assessment underpins the successful deployment of covert investigation. Without it, the chances of a successful operation (ie acquisition of the desired objective, lawfully, without compromising methods, techniques, or personal safety; the adducing of evidence secure from procedural challenge at trial) are significantly reduced.

Managing Covert Investigation

5.1 **Introduction**

At the risk of inducing apoplexy in die-hard detectives, the key to successful covert investigation management is to think like managers, not investigation practitioners. The reflective reader will recognize from the previous chapters and those which follow that managing covert investigation is more than just ensuring the quality and accuracy of authorization applications: it involves skilled investigation management together with complex resource management in an environment in which there are frequently many competing priorities for scarce skills and capacity. Securing a covert investigation authority may be easier than securing the resources needed to execute the covert investigation activity. Investigators planning the use of covert techniques will need to plan for circumstances in which the resources are not available: and if an alternative means of obtaining the intelligence/evidence is available, that immediately raises questions about the proportionality of the proposed action. Alternatively, there may be occasions on which covert investigation methods offer a less resource-intensive means of acquiring information that could also be obtained by non-intrusive means: the issue for managers in these circumstances is whether authorization can be given lawfully in circumstances where desired information could be obtained in a way that engages Article 8 rights at lesser cost than a method that would produce the same information for greater expense but without engaging Article 8 rights. At trial, judges will be concerned with compliance with the law rather than management theory. McKay observes:

> It is likely that in the future, legal challenges will be mounted based on the central question of whether covert policing resources were justified at all having regard to the circumstances of the case as well as scrutinizing the human rights issues increasingly assiduously.
>
> (S McKay, *Covert Policing*, Oxford University Press, Oxford, 2011, para 2.01)

In the event that resources are available, the proportionality test is met, and an authorization is granted, management of the covert investigation does not stop when the specific activity is completed and the authorization cancelled. There then exists the covert investigation product that has to be managed, and the organizational learning from each operation to be captured and, as appropriate, disseminated.

In functional terms governance of covert investigation can be viewed as a three-tier hierarchy:

- Statute and case law—mechanisms defining what investigators can and cannot do with the case law remedy providing a form of indirect governance through adverse consequences, such as the (discretionary) exclusion of evidence, and establishing external scrutiny mechanisms.
- External inspection—auditable governance in which proper records demonstrate compliant/lawful and appropriate deployment.

- Internal management—procedures to prioritize appropriate operations in which covert investigation may be necessary to guard against overuse and unnecessary deployment.

(C Harfield, 'The governance of covert investigation', *Melbourne University Law Review*, 34(3) (2010) 801)

Professional management is thus the first layer of covert investigation governance and accountability: from the outset, empowered organizations have the opportunity to demonstrate that covert investigation has been used only when lawful, compliant, and appropriate, and not extravagantly.

KEY POINTS

- How does the proposed investigation/operation relate to NIM tasking and coordinating?
- What evidence/information is being sought? Is it essential or desirable?
- Is it already known (by another agency perhaps?) Can it be obtained by non-covert means?
- What are the resource implications of the proposed action?
- If used, what is the risk of covert investigation methods being exposed in the surveillance arena or at court?

Further information and reading

The revised CSPI Code recommends that within each organization undertaking covert investigation, a *senior responsible officer* (of at least the rank of an authorizing officer as identified in RIPA2000, IPA2016, and the PA97) should have executive responsibility for:

- the integrity of the process in place within the *public authority* to authorize directed and intrusive surveillance and interference with property or wireless telegraphy;
- compliance with Part II of the 2000 Act, Part III of the 1997 Act and with this code;
- engagement with the Commissioners and inspectors when they conduct their inspections; and
- where necessary, overseeing the implementation of any post-inspection action plans recommended or approved by a Commissioner (para 3.29).

It is suggested here that such a role could usefully have responsibility for ensuring not just the proper application for and granting of covert investigation authorities but the whole process of covert investigation management within an organization, which includes the preparatory tasks of prioritizing and selecting investigations to be supported by covert investigation and the post-investigation tasks of product and evidence management. Such an executive role provides strategic leadership of covert investigation as a function within the overall work of the organization. It is not suggested here that such a role should in any way erode or obscure the statutory responsibilities imposed on authorizing officers under the Act. In some jurisdictions, albeit operating a different governance paradigm for covert investigation, support mechanisms for senior investigators and authorizing officers have appeared to have absolved, or have created the vulnerability of absolving, such individuals of their statutory responsibilities (Harfield, 'The governance of covert investigation', 797). The recommended role of *senior responsible officer* is understood here to be one of overarching organization leadership in matters relating to covert investigation and not an operational role, notwithstanding that the recommendation is that the *senior responsible officer* has practical authorizing officer experience. The two roles are separate and should not be confused or conflated.

Nor should the senior responsible officer role recommended in the CSPI Code be confused with the senior responsible officer role mandatorily required pursuant to the Communications Data Code, para 3.31 (see Chapter 11.7 of this volume) or the senior responsible officer role mandatorily required pursuant to the CHIS Code, para 9.1 (see Chapter 13.5 of this volume). But there is no reason why the same individual should not undertake all three of these strategic roles and a case can be made for investing a single senior executive officer with these roles to achieve strategic cohesion in the overall management of covert investigation within any given organization.

5.2 Do You Really Need To?

The statutory requirement for necessity has already been considered (Chapter 2). There is, arguably, also a managerial necessity test. It is presumably only a matter of time (if the issue has not already been raised) before an operation that does not meet managerial necessity is challenged on the basis that the statutory necessity test is consequently undermined. The basic managerial test is simply expressed: how does the proposed investigation, or operation in support of an investigation, relate to organizational tasking and coordination?

Tasking and coordination procedures and policies will vary from organization to organization. Within the police service, the business processes within the framework of the National Intelligence Model (NIM) specifically provide for tasking and coordination and it is suggested here that any covert investigation within the police service will be undertaken pursuant to an appropriate tasking and coordination direction given either at Basic Command Unit (NIM Level 1) or at Force/Regional level (NIM Level 2), taking into consideration the principles of the National Decision Model and the Police Code of Ethics.

There are two generic circumstances that provide exceptions to this principle. The first is the distinction drawn between 'core' and 'ordinary' functions in the case of *C v Police & Secretary of State* IPT/03/32/H (14 November 2006). Where covert investigation is deployed in the management of staff for disciplinary and professional standards purposes, such action will not feature in fortnightly tasking and coordination meetings. The second circumstance is that of the spontaneous investigation, such as a crime in action (a kidnapping, for example), which will not reasonably have been foreseen in a planning meeting. The net practical effect would seem to be the confining of covert investigation to identified priority crimes and spontaneous serious crimes.

Definition: how are crimes prioritized?

Crimes can be prioritized for intervention in a number of ways:

- In response to a specific assessment of risk and threat.
- Through community consultation within the philosophical context of a police service and other agencies responsive to community needs.
- In order to meet (politically imposed) performance measures.

The weighting applied to these three approaches is a matter of judgement and influences the determination of necessity when considering applications for the use of covert investigation. Inevitably there will be variations between organizations, communities, and individuals in making such judgements and identifying priorities.

The deployment of covert investigation by other empowered organizations equally will be determined by the relevance of the proposed investigation to the core functions of the organization and whether or not the proposed investigation is compliant with the statutory purpose(s) for which the organization in question can undertake covert investigation.

The relationship between covert investigation powers and organization performance management is potentially fraught. In the absence of specific intelligence about ongoing criminality it is unlikely that covert investigation can be justified to meet performance targets such as types of offence investigated or types of operation undertaken. (For the Chief Surveillance Commissioner's concerns about performance target culture see, OSC *Annual Report 2008–09*, para 5.26 and OSC *Annual Report 2010–11*, para 5.6.)

Key issues confronting those managing the use of covert investigation in all agencies and organizations

- Is public opinion about any given public nuisance or crime issue (rarely founded upon hard data) a reliable legitimization for recourse to covert methodologies?

- What is perceived as serious, trivial, or perennial anti-social nuisance to be addressed will vary from community to community; from organization to organization.

- The importance of not confusing necessity in relation to preventing a harm to society with the proportionality of the method in relation to the specific product of the covert investigation.

- The importance of reviewing and monitoring use of covert investigation in order to ensure it is not being used inappropriately.

- In what circumstances, for which organizations, and by whom undertaken (eg elected or non-elected persons), consideration at a senior level about the politics of using covert investigation is appropriate? The 'necessity' test clearly could be a political issue and the political will of Parliament as expressed in statute should be the guiding principle; the proportionality test of methods used theoretically is apolitical but such determination could be vulnerable to political perception.

Further information and reading

For official consideration of the wider issues of surveillance see:
- Home Affairs Committee, *A Surveillance Society?* Fifth Report of Session 2007–08, HC58i & HC58ii (TSO, London, 2008);
- Home Affairs Committee, *A Surveillance Society? Information Commissioner's Response to the Committee's Fifth Report of Session 2007–08, HC1124* (TSO, London, 2008);
- House of Lords Select Committee on the Constitution, *Surveillance: Citizens and the State*, Second Report of Session 2008–09, HL 18-I and HL 18-II (TSO, London, 2009).

Where multi-agency partnership working is envisaged, partner organizations will wish to ensure that powers are applied for and utilized appropriately in order to avoid becoming vulnerable to challenges about whether one agency's powers have been used to achieve another agency's objectives when the latter would not normally have access to such powers: circumstances sometimes referred to as 'process-laundering'. In such circumstances it would seem prudent to ensure that tasking, coordination, objectives and responsibility for subsequent action based on covert investigation product were clearly identified at the outset in the planning documentation and joint-investigation policy book.

Covert investigation is intended to secure either specific intelligence to inform planned future intervention or evidence for use at trial or in regulatory enforcement. The intended final objective determines whether the information or evidence being sought is desirable or essential. Prosecutor or in-house legal advice may be helpful at this planning stage, particularly in more serious cases. There will be instances when no prosecution or definitive determination is possible without the covert investigation product. But there will be other instances when prosecution of a different (lesser) charge may be an option, which may not entail the need for covert investigation product to be acquired and adduced. It is not for investigators to second-guess sentencing or sanction in the event of a conviction or finding of regulatory breach, but if covert investigation product is going to make no difference to the possible sentence on conviction, then for investigation managers and covert capability resource managers such considerations may help prioritize the allocation of scarce skilled resources between investigations where covert product is essential and those where it is desirable.

Managers and investigators need to consider whether the information sought is already directly available and known to, or easily ascertainable, by other agencies, or whether it may be deduced or inferred from information already available elsewhere. Once again, at issue are partnerships and the impetus for better (lawful) information sharing between agencies and organizations: the beneficial obverse of the process-laundering vulnerability identified above. Authorizing officers, in discharging their duty to consider the proportionality of the proposed technique in relation to the information or evidence to be gained, will wish to be confident that the information is not already in the possession of a public authority in a position lawfully to share it. If another organization does have access to the information, then it should be obtained from that organization in the first instance subject to information-sharing protocols, unless making such a request to another organization poses a risk of harmful compromise: differences between organizations in vetting standards and other corruption prevention measures may be an issue here.

Both police and local authorities find themselves confronted with incident hot-spots (for example, thefts from unattended vehicles in public car parks or fly-tipping) in which the first issue of any investigation is to identify possible suspects (as opposed to trying to obtain identity details of a confirmed offender, such as a street drug dealer regularly operating in an area, whose identity is as yet unknown to investigators). If an operation is targeted at an area or location rather than a named or described suspect, what issues arise in considering whether an authorization for covert investigation (by definition this applies only to directed surveillance) is required? How can collateral intrusion be recognized and managed in circumstances where the parameters are imprecise? How can distinctions be made between capturing private and public information? If it is impossible to tell, is there an issue at all—or alternatively, is everything an issue because it is impossible to tell?

This is an issue in which case law would benefit those contemplating such operations: the jurisprudence on private information already discussed above provides some guidance. Courts have accepted that those actively engaged in criminality must expect to be investigated and therefore voluntarily assume the risk of interference with their right to have their private life respected (*Ludi v Switzerland* (1993) 15 EHRR 173). But collateral intrusion of third parties uninvolved in the suspected criminality will, in the case of a public car park or the remote country lane where fly-tipping takes place in addition to lawful passage, occur whether the offenders are known, or they are described but unnamed, or the purpose of the operation is to identify possible suspects. As ever, the precise circumstances of each operation will dictate the need for authorization. The fact that the purpose of an operation is to identify possible suspects rather than gather evidence or intelligence about named or described offenders, does not absolve applicants or authorizing officers from considering whether the proposed covert investigation engages human rights.

One discriminator that could inform such consideration is the nature of the intended intervention. Where general observations are kept with the intention of triggering an immediate reactive intervention to any crime witnessed by the observing investigators, then this might be considered to be within the general duties of an organization's statutory function, as opposed to a recourse to specific and exceptional powers. Where the observations are kept with the intention of securing information in order to inform subsequent intervention, then private information will probably be gathered about both individuals whose conduct reveals them to be suspects and third parties whose conduct engages no prohibition at all. The gathering of such private information (recalling the broad construction courts have applied to this concept) will probably require surveillance authorization. (See also CSPI Code, para 2.24 on general observation activities and OSC *Annual Report 2008–09*, para 5.26.)

5.3 What Are the Resource Implications?

If there is justification for covert investigation, then the operation to execute the covert method will need to be resourced properly and adequately. Covert investigation is often time-consuming and expensive (both in terms of actual and opportunity costs). Managers need to challenge themselves and investigators with the following questions:

- What is the required objective of the whole operation?
- What is the objective of the covert element (within the context of the whole operation)?
- How might it be achieved?
- Can it be afforded?
- Even it can be afforded, is the proposed action cost effective?
- What is the organization going to have to sacrifice, abandon, or postpone in terms of other work in order to resource and support a covert investigation? (What are the opportunity costs of a covert investigation?)

The first three questions provide the contextual framework within which the remaining three questions must be considered. Appropriate expenditure of public monies is an issue with its own moral significance.

Case study—the expense of technical support

An investigator wanted covert photographic surveillance of the rear of a house set in rural farmland. Avoiding the all-too-common professional discourtesy of telling the Technical Support Unit how to do their job by specifying the equipment they should use, the investigator instead, and quite properly, asked simply for the desired product: photographic evidence, suitable for use at court if necessary, of persons entering and leaving the premises via the rear door.

A feasibility study highlighted a significant consequence. There was a need to deploy the camera in an elevated position in order to obtain the desired product. There being no suitable natural features in which to disguise such a deployment, a manmade solution would have to be constructed. This solution on its own would have appeared out of place and so would attract undue attention. Therefore it would have to be disguised within the context of property improvement work, if the owners of the neighbouring property could be persuaded to accept such unsolicited enhancements. These were going to be very expensive photographs.

For managers, consideration of such circumstances must focus on whether the evidential value of the product obtained is proportionate to the cost of its acquisition. In this respect managers have their own proportionality considerations alongside those required by law of authorizing officers. That which is possible is not necessarily feasible.

There are four general resource areas for consideration:

- Skills capability and capacity—how many appropriately skilled staff are needed and available?
- Technical capability and capacity—feasibility study needed prior to authorization.
- CHIS requirement, if any—a specialism defined by interactive rather than remote surveillance.
- Sustainability of operation—once started can it be continued, and for how long?

These considerations, it is suggested, should be contemplated prior to detailed planning and authorization application. An established covert investigative method may exist, but can it be adequately and safely executed by available staff? Safety in this consideration is as much about not compromising the method as it is about ensuring the personal safety of staff. The case study above illustrates the value of undertaking technical feasibility studies at the early contemplation stage. The deployment of CHISs (be they informers, undercover officers, or test purchase officers) may require significant advance planning, especially if trained staff have to be borrowed from other organizations for the purpose. The sustainability of operation can, of course, be adversely affected by unforeseen events occurring after the commencement of the operation, either within the context of the operation itself or as a result of events elsewhere to which the organization has to respond by diverting effort from existing operations. There is little that can be done to avoid such spontaneous developments. But how might that which can be foreseen or reasonably anticipated (eg annual leave, requirements to attend court, planned events to which the organization has to respond) influence the sustainability of the action being contemplated? What will be the cut-off point if the desired product is not achieved in the anticipated timescale? (Repeated authorization renewals because the desired product has not yet been evidenced may accumulate to a quantum of intrusion that becomes disproportionate in the circumstances and so becomes unlawful; such circumstances might also call in question the intelligence on which the authorization was originally based.)

Protection of resources is also at issue. Consultation with the organizational security officer and with professional standards staff will identify opportunities to reduce the risk of compromising resources and investigations through proactive measures. This needs to be considered not only at the systemic level but also in relation to individual operations at the pre-planning stage. Planning following a compromise is too late.

These are the considerations that senior investigators and intending authorization applicants need to resolve prior to the detailed planning phase of a covert operation.

5.4 **Planning and Preparation**

It is increasingly common for investigators and applicants to be required to give a presentation to authorizing officers in order to enable the latter properly and fully to undertake their role. This is especially necessary for complex operations. With the expansion of the covert investigation legislative landscape, ever more work is required of authorizing officers in terms of their statutory responsibilities and it can be argued that if the individual concerned is not familiar with the investigation or the geographical area in which the operation is intended to take place, it will be difficult to make an informed judgement on many of the issues that will fall to be considered. A paper-based or electronic authorization system cannot provide answers to questions that may arise in the authorizing officer's mind while reflecting upon the legality, necessity, and proportionality of the proposed action: for example, what other tactics were considered? Why were they dismissed? How was the threat level arrived at?

A possible framework for approaching such presentations is suggested below. It may also serve to inform general operational planning, tasking and coordination meetings, and resource allocation meetings.

Checklist—Framework for authorization/planning presentations

- This operation is a priority because ...

- The objectives and outcomes of the operation are ...

- The objectives of the proposed covert investigation, within the context of the wider operation, are ...

- What sort of covert investigation is being contemplated? Will prior approval be necessary? Does it involve multi-phase action (ie reconnoitre, deployment, recovery; each of which will have to be specifically authorized) in order to achieve a single objective?

- It meets the legal framework compliance because ...

- The associated risks and threats are ... [refer to Chapter 4 for risk management]

- The impact on the community will be ...

- The impact on the organization (and/or partnership) will be ...

5.5 **Managing Deployment and Authorization**

Covert investigation activity is not an end in and of itself: it is a tactic that will be undertaken alongside other forms of investigation. The degree to which this takes place will vary from operation to operation. The relationship between the use of covert investigation and other investigation and intervention methods will need to be understood in order to achieve planned objectives and outcomes. In some cases covert investigation will be used in a simple role to corroborate intelligence and inform a search warrant application: depending on the physical evidence, witness testimony, and interview evidence that follows on from the execution of the search warrant, it may or may not be necessary to adduce the covert investigation product at trial. In more complex operations the interrelationship between different methods and constituent objectives will be more intricate. In other cases covert investigation will identify suspects against whom more conventional evidential opportunities can then be planned which may avoid the need to have to adduce the covertly obtained evidence at trial. Covert investigation may inform decisions about the point in the investigation plan that forensic evidence will be required; it might inform a parallel stream of financial investigation with a view to providing evidence at trial or information upon which to base asset freezing and recovery; it will always provide, collaterally, information about the nature of risks and threats involved in the investigation. Investigation and intelligence managers will be looking for new opportunities or lines of enquiry emerging from the intelligence picture developing as a result of the use of covert investigation.

Management of the investigation strategy runs in parallel with management of the investigation logistics. Basic command unit (BCU) covert investigations may require logistical support from level 2 resources, for which bids will have to be made to force managers. Such bids will have to be in conjunction with appropriate tasking and coordination direction and may be in competition with similar bids from other BCUs. Non-police agencies intending to undertake covert investigation may wish to buy in surveillance skills from other public sector organizations or from the private sector—the latter option does not avoid the need for RIPA2000 authorization because s 6 HRA is interpreted as including actions taken on behalf of a public authority by a third party.

Ongoing logistical management includes management of the authorization application, renewals, and cancellations. For those agencies empowered to undertake intrusive surveillance, prior approval must be received in writing from the Investigatory Powers Commissioner's Office (IPCO) before the covert activity can commence. Failure to comply fully with the prescribed schedules will render investigations vulnerable to being unauthorized and so subject, together with any evidence derived therefrom, to challenge in subsequent trial proceedings. One such challenge was made in *R v Paulssen* [2003] EWCA Crim 3109; however, the Court of Appeal upheld the conviction despite the failure of authorization continuity, which the Court viewed as only a minor technical infringement of RIPA2000. It is certainly not suggested here that investigators should rely on this case to avoid rigorous authorization management. Successful challenges at court may result in covert investigation product being excluded from evidence.

Larger organizations regularly engaging in covert investigation may wish to establish, if they do not already exist, central bureaux to assist in the management of the authority regime. Such bureaux can become centres of excellence and expertise which can greatly facilitate the appropriate and secure use of covert methods, manage the authorization process, ensure secure procedures for the handling and preservation of covert investigation product, and undertake operational reviews in order to capture organizational learning.

A consequential temptation of the central bureau concept is to have full-time or rota-based authorizing officers. The extent to which such individuals can meaningfully undertake the statutory considerations of legality, necessity, and proportionality, within the context of wider organization management issues, depends upon their familiarity with the investigation in question and the communities in which covert activity is to take place. The balance to be struck is between the authorizing officers being sufficiently independent of the investigation as to be able to be objective when considering and reviewing applications and their not being so independent that they are not sufficiently aware of the circumstances and so cannot arrive at an informed decision. (This is where presentations in support of an application can be of particular benefit.)

Further information and reading

The revised codes of practice detail specific requirements in relation to the keeping of records about covert investigation applications and authorizations.

The RIPA2000 Codes of Practice are available online at <https://www.gov.uk/government/collections/ripa-codes> (accessed 12 January 2018).

The IPA2016 Codes of Practice are available online at <https://www.gov.uk/government/consultations/investigatory-powers-act-2016-codes-of-practice> (accessed 12 January 2018).

5.6 Managing the Product: Dissemination, Disclosure, Debrief

Managing the product of covert investigation divides into three generic areas: dissemination of intelligence derived; the use of such product as evidence at trial; and organizational reflection on lessons learnt.

5.6.1 Dissemination of intelligence acquired

Covert investigation will generate intelligence tangential to the primary investigation objective. For example, as a result of surveillance, associations between criminals may be newly identified or those hypothesized corroborated; use of identified vehicles may be confirmed; links between criminals and businesses through which criminal profits might be laundered may be identified; all related to the primary investigation objective by virtue of being discovered in the authorized surveillance arena but not destined to be part of a prosecution case. Because it has both investigative tactical value and policy strategic value, such intelligence, building up a picture of criminal networks and markets, has to be documented and disseminated appropriately. This means not only to the correct colleagues, both within and outside the originating agency, but also in the correct fashion that takes measures necessary to ensure that covert techniques are not compromised.

Further information and reading

C Harfield and K Harfield, *Intelligence: Investigation, Community, and Partnership* (Oxford University Press, Oxford, 2008), particularly chapters 7–10.

It is equally possible, of course, that something is observed within the surveillance arena that has no direct or indirect relevance to the authorized investigation but which nevertheless warrants documentation and dissemination in timely and appropriate fashion.

Occasionally dilemmas will arise in which prompt dissemination of such intelligence, no matter how well sanitized, will disclose the existence of ongoing covert investigation simply because the information could not have been obtained in any other way. Investigation and intelligence managers and, if necessary, senior organization managers will have to confer in such circumstances and decide how best to proceed. It would be difficult to justify *not* acting on a piece of intelligence, particularly if harm could be prevented, just because of a reluctance to compromise an ongoing covert investigation through the dissemination of collateral intelligence: given the primary function of the police to preserve life and prevent crime, the latter duty will always be more important and so assume greater priority than the tactical desire not to disrupt an operation. This is similar to a dilemma frequently faced by CHIS controllers when a CHIS has acquired intelligence that could only have come from the CHIS and so acting on it (before the intelligence can be corroborated and its acquisition sanitized so as to disguise the involvement of a CHIS) would expose, compromise, and potentially endanger the CHIS.

Trying to balance intelligence value against investment costs (in terms of the investigation already underway and through support of which covert methods have produced the collateral intelligence) is not a straightforward equation. Nor is it a calculation that should overshadow statutory obligations in relation to legality, necessity, and proportionality.

5.6.2 Disclosure

Disclosure occurs in one of two ways: through revelation to the prosecutor pursuant to statutory obligations under the Criminal Procedure and Investigations Act 1996 (CPIA); or through unauthorized means such as careless information management or purposeful corruption.

The latter risk can be guarded against through the creation and maintenance of an appropriate professional and secure environment for the handling of sensitive intelligence or, as required, evidence acquired through covert investigation. Appropriate measures will include security vetting (a five-yearly process), interim review and management of vetting in between vetting processes, and proactive measures to prevent compromise and corruption.

Covert investigation methods will only remain effective to the extent that criminals remain ignorant of them, yet every trial represents an opportunity for those accused (and by extension the general public) to learn about the methods that brought them before the court. Revelation to the prosecutor, a statutory requirement enabling the prosecutor to fulfil his or her duty under s 3 CPIA, does not automatically mean disclosure to the defence. Circumstances exist under which sensitive information (such as covert investigation methods, the identity of a CHIS, or information that might facilitate future offences or aid future suspects to evade arrest) can be protected from exposure at court. The management of this issue is therefore of crucial importance and may warrant the appointment of a specialist covert investigation disclosure officer alongside the general disclosure officer on complex cases.

Potentially all information and material acquired through covert investigation, *and* the documentation relating to the authorization of covert investigation, is liable to disclosure at trial. Just because evidence or other material has been obtained by covert means does not mean that either the information or the methods used are automatically exempt from statutory disclosure. (The one exception to this is the product of intercepted communications, currently prohibited from use at trial by s 56 IPA2016—see Chapter 11 for further discussion of this and the relevance of 'Preston' briefings.) Investigators will need to liaise closely and fully with their prosecuting authorities in respect of information that they wish judges to withhold subject to a public interest (PII) order. Prosecutors have a continuing duty to review all material, both pre-trial and during the trial, to ascertain whether it undermines the prosecution case or assists the defence case. 'If no duty to disclose arises, then no issue of public interest immunity arises' (S McKay, 'Public interest immunity after *Edwards and Lewis v United Kingdom* and *R v C* and *R v H* and the role of special advocates', *Covert Policing Review* (2006), 110–124).

R v H and C [2004] 2 AC 134 provides the defining test that interprets the CPIA (as amended by the Criminal Justice Act 2003) and its associated Code of Practice.

....

Case law criteria: *R v H and C* [2004] 2 AC 134—public interest immunity (PII)

Full disclosure should be made of all material held by the Crown that weakens its own case or assists the defence. An exception from this rule may be justified if an important public interest has to be protected. If material does not undermine the Crown case or assist the defence, there is no requirement to disclose it or apply for PII. Sensitive/unused neutral material or sensitive/unused material damaging to the defence need not be disclosed and should not be brought to the attention of the court. PII should be sought only where absolutely necessary.

For further discussion, see S McKay, 'Public interest immunity after *Edwards and Lewis v United Kingdom* and *R v C* and *R v H* and the role of Special Advocates', *Covert Policing Review* (2006), 110–124, particularly 119–124.

....

Investigators seeking to protect information through PII have the option of having their application heard openly (defence present), privately (defence aware of the application but not present), or secretly (defence unaware of the application). The guiding regulations are to be found in the following:

- Magistrates' Courts (Criminal Procedure and Investigations Act 1996) (Disclosure) Rules 1997 (SI 1997/703);
- Crown Court (Criminal Procedure and Investigations Act 1996) (Disclosure) Rules 1997 (SI 1997/698);
- Criminal Procedure Rules 2005 (SI 2005/384).

There has been mixed case law on the issue of whether documentation from the authorization application process should be subject to disclosure. In *R v GS* [2005] EWCA Crim 887, the appellants sought disclosure of all documentation relating to the granting of OSC approval for intrusive surveillance, including the applications. Since only one of the defence counsel in the case expressed any concern about the lawfulness of the application procedure, the Court of Appeal regarded the remaining defence applications for disclosure as a 'fishing expedition' (at para 16 of the judgment).

Dismissing the appeal, the Court held (at para 32):

> it is not open to the criminal court to embark upon an examination of material underlying an approved authorization, to determine whether the correct statutory criteria have been correctly taken into account and so on, all of which go to the issue of lawfulness.

The Court went on to assert that production of the OSC signed approval forms, or alternatively the testimony of a Chief Officer supported by the approval forms, should be sufficient to establish lawfulness (para 35), and that evidence unlawfully obtained is not automatically rendered unfair and subject to exclusion under s 78 PACE. In *Jones* [2010] EWCA Crim 925 at 10, the Court noted that the original trial judge had read the authorization documentation and had determined that as nothing therein undermined the prosecution case, the documents did not fall to be disclosed.

In *R v Grant* [2005] EWCA Crim 1089, the Court took a significantly different view. The authorization processes in this case were subject to full scrutiny because of specific challenges made by the defence: notebook entries, deployment feasibility studies, and testimony from officers involved in making the applications and staff deploying technical equipment were all disclosed and admitted in submissions, to establish that there had been an intention on the part of investigators from the outset to use audio surveillance to capture privileged conversations between suspects and their legal advisors, and that such capture had not been an unforeseen collateral occurrence.

Further information and reading

For further detailed discussion of the cases considered above, see A Hopkins, 'Testing lawfulness: the authorization of interception of communications and covert surveillance under the regulation of Investigatory Powers Act 2000', *Covert Policing Review* (2005), 33–51, particularly 45–48.

The use of covert investigation by state agents against individual citizens is an illustration of the asymmetrical power relationship between state and citizen that the principles of due process at trial seek to rebalance in the interests of fairness. There may be justifiable arguments to protect methodology and identities through PII applications, but in the context of self-authorization or non-judicial prior approval, investigators cannot be surprised that transparency and accountability of decision-making will be subject to court scrutiny through disclosure.

5.6.3 **Debriefing**

Whilst it is true that every deployment of covert investigation risks compromising methods or personnel, it is equally true that each deployment offers opportunities for organizational learning. Such practice-based learning must be captured. Operational debriefing and investigation review are two structured ways of identifying useful lessons. Potentially there is an additional role here for a central bureau that facilitates the management of covert investigation within the organization. Such a bureau would thus become the centre of expertise within the organization. The police service already operates a structured murder investigation peer review system. It is worth considering whether regular internal or peer review of covert investigation deployment would help capture learning and identify areas for improvement—before such opportunities were identified through external audit and inspection by the OSC. Regular review also reinforces and demonstrates organizational responsibility and professional attitudes towards covert investigation. It can be used to demonstrate that covert investigation is not being used extravagantly.

In the police service the national capture of learning and good practice falls to the College of Policing. Good practice is promulgated through the various guidance manuals published by the College.

The IPCO inspection programme (which is not confined to the police service but includes all bodies empowered to undertake covert investigation) informs the annual report that the Investigatory Powers Commissioner must make to the Prime Minister and Scottish Ministers. Whilst the IPCO role is not primarily to capture and disseminate good practice, the annual reports (if not too dissimilar from the OSC annual reports now superseded) are likely to be a valuable source of information and insight into wider management issues concerning covert investigation.

In whatever form it takes, practice-based debriefing and organizational learning must inform both future strategic use of covert investigation and also the training of surveillance operatives and those who facilitate covert investigation. Failure to train staff adequately (which includes training delivery by 'well-meaning but inadequately-informed providers'), and failure to identify and adopt lessons to be learnt, both contribute to the diminution of the overall covert investigation skills base which the Chief Surveillance Commissioner has observed (OSC *Annual Report 2006–2007*, para 7.2; quote taken from para 10.5).

5.7 **Contracting Out, Joint Operations, and Collaborative Working**

Provisions exist for public authorities to engage in joint operations, collaborate with other public authorities in the purchase or services or undertaking of functions, or contract out some of their functions to private enterprise. Statutory provision for inter-agency and inter-force collaboration were consolidated and enhanced in the Police and Crime Act 2017 (see also ss 74, 78–80 IPA2016). The management rationale for these initiatives is to save money and share otherwise scarce skills and capabilities. In relation to covert investigation, such money-saving strategies give rise to additional considerations for senior responsible officers and for authorizing officers.

Any private enterprise undertaking public functions on behalf of a public authority will engage s 6 HRA 1998. When acting on behalf of a public authority, it will be unlawful for the private enterprise to act in a way which is incompatible with an ECHR right. Those subcontracted will be restricted in what they can do lawfully by what the contracting authority is empowered to do. Thus there will be occasions when private investigators in possession of the technical capability to undertake certain methods on behalf of private customers will not be able to employ such methods on behalf of public authorities because the latter are not empowered to use them. For example, the deployment of vehicle tracking devices constitutes property interference which, in the public authority arena, can only be utilized and authorized by a limited number of law enforcement and intelligence agencies under s 93(5) PA97 or s 5 Intelligence Services Act 1994. A local authority could not, therefore, ask a private investigator to undertake this method of surveillance, even though the private investigator might have the technical capability (see OSC *Annual Report 2010–11*, para 5.14).

Authorities investigating together in a joint operation may be in a position to pursue their own individual prosecutions or regulatory interventions arising from that operation. For example, arising from a joint operation, a police force might pursue criminal charges against some of the suspects identified whilst a local authority partner in the investigation might pursue regulatory matters within their own remit against other suspects identified. In such a joint operation it will be necessary to plan the investigation and prosecutions in such a way as to ensure that evidence obtained during covert surveillance is used appropriately and for a proper purpose. Where it is anticipated that evidence obtained using restricted covert surveillance powers might be relied upon for the prosecution of matters for which no covert power of investigation exists (simply because such evidence was secured during a collaborative or joint investigation), legal advice should be sought as to the likely admissibility of such evidence in the planned proceedings. It does not seem to have been the intention of Parliament, in making provision for joint operations and collaborative working, that collaboration should be used as a means to circumvent restrictions on the use of certain powers established in RIPA2000, IPA2016, and the PA97.

A third area of new complexity concerns the making of covert investigation applications for and the granting of authorities for such conduct within the context of collaborative working. The default position in both RIPA2000 and the PA97 is that applicants and authorizing officers must be members of the same organization. The exception to this principle exists when two or more *police forces* have entered into a collaborative working agreement pursuant to s 23 of the Police Act 1996 (for English and Welsh forces: s 12 of the Police (Scotland) Act 1967 for Scottish forces), *and* the collaboration agreement permits applicants and authorizing officers to be from different forces. Following the legislative changes enacted in the Police and Crime Act 2017 (ss 1 and 157), all 43 police forces and Police and Crime Commissioners have signed a National Collaboration Agreement that permits a Senior Authorizing Officer authorizing interference with property under s 93 PA97 to issue authorities 'not only in relation to their own force area but, where necessary and proportionate, in relation to other force areas' (OSC *Annual Report 2016–17*, para 5.1).

Where a collaborative working agreement is established for the purpose (*inter alia*) of facilitating covert investigation for the signatory parties, such agreements must document specific arrangements for the management of covert investigation between the partners. 'Mere agreement to share resources is insufficient' (OSC *Annual Report 2010–11*, para 5.12; see also CSPI Code, paras 3.15–3.22; covert investigations conducted under collaborative working arrangements, and the policies underpinning these activities, will be subject to coordinated inspection of all parties to the arrangements, OSC *Annual Report 2013–14*, paras 5.26–5.27).

The need to document the entire covert investigation process, from initial planning to subsequent evidential or intelligence product management, is an intrinsic part of covert investigation management and is imposed as a statutory duty on each public authority availing itself of covert investigation powers. Neither joint operations nor collaborative working agreements absolve individual partner agencies from maintaining their own records for each operation. However, the revised Code of Practice makes clear that duplication of authorizations amongst collaborating partners should be avoided (CSPI Code, paras 3.16–3.17).

Further information and reading

On joint operations and collaborative working see CSPI Code, paras 3.15–3.22; 6.9–6.10; 7.12–7.14; and CHIS Code, paras 5.9 and 6.13.

Contracting out, joint operations, and collaborative working may complicate the management of covert investigation and reinforce the need for public authorities to consider seriously the good practice recommendation in CSPI Code, para 3.28 that an executive-level senior responsible officer (with authorizing officer experience) be designated for the strategic management of covert investigation within the organization. These three strategic initiatives for making best use of scarce resources each give rise to separate issues. (The examples raised here are neither exclusive nor exhaustive and the growing body of operational experience in these areas will generate new issues as yet unidentified.) It would be easy to, and is equally important not to, conflate and confuse such issues. Sharing services is not necessarily the same thing as undertaking joint investigations. Any given joint investigation may be a one-off, ad hoc operation: collaborative working cannot be established on an ad hoc basis and must be pursuant to documented agreements between the collaborating authorities. Contracting out a function is not necessarily the same thing as delegating a power, nor is it likely ever to absolve organizational or individual statutory responsibility.

5.8 **Conclusion**

Failings and frustrations apparent within the undertaking of covert investigation are often proving to be management rather than legislative issues. The operationally advantageous, statutory self-authorization regime (with prior approval as required) will withstand legal challenge only so long as it is demonstrably well-managed, transparent in its accountability, and robust in review and self-reflection. Surveillance operatives have to be skilled and sophisticated; authorizing officers have defined and significant statutory obligations; those involved in the management of covert investigation (which will include individuals from the first two groups here identified) equally have a crucial role in successful covert investigation: an arena in which not only do the powers of the state have to be balanced against the rights of the individual, but in which also a plethora of (sometimes conflicting) organizational management issues have to be balanced against each other. That which the Law Lords have found to be a puzzling statute in reflective interpretation can be just as challenging in its frontline operational implementation and management.

PART TWO

Law and Procedure in Covert Investigation

6

Directed Surveillance

6.1 **Introduction**

Surveillance is defined at s 48(2) RIPA2000.

Definition of surveillance

Surveillance includes:

(a) monitoring, observing or listening to persons, their movements, their conversations or their other activities or communications;

(b) recording anything monitored, observed or listened to in the course of surveillance; and

(c) surveillance by or with the assistance of a surveillance device.

The definition is neither exclusive nor exhaustive, and the monitoring, observing, or listening do not have to be recorded and do not have to involve the use of technology in order to constitute surveillance.

Because they are subject to their own specific authority regimes (as will be discussed in later chapters), the conduct of covert human intelligence sources and interference with property under s 29 RIPA2000, Part III PA97, or s 5 Intelligence Services Act 1994 are not included in this definition (s 48(3) RIPA2000), notwithstanding that these tactics are deployed for exactly the same purposes.

A two-part hierarchy of surveillance is prescribed by law: directed and intrusive. Chapters 6 and 7 consider directed and intrusive surveillance separately because:

- not all public authorities empowered to conduct directed surveillance may also conduct intrusive surveillance; and
- the circumstances in which intrusive surveillance may be conducted are more restricted than those in which directed surveillance may take place.

The new Code of Practice for Covert Surveillance and Property Interference is available online for download from <https://www.gov.uk/government/collections/ripa-codes#current-codes-of-practice> (accessed 5 January 2018). In this volume 'CSPI Code' refers to this Code.

6.2 **Which Public Authorities May Deploy Directed Surveillance?**

Public authorities empowered to utilize directed surveillance are defined in Schedule 1 RIPA2000 as amended. This is accessible online via <http://www.legislation.gov.uk/ukpga/2000/23/schedule/1> (accessed 5 January 2018). Readers should be aware that although the online statutory database will have the latest available updated version of the Schedule (which has changed numerous times since original enactment), the online version may not have been amended to take account of all the most recent changes. The website provides information about which amendments have yet to be updated in the published version of the Schedule.

Some public authorities are empowered to use directed surveillance under s 28 RIPA2000 but not to deploy CHIS under s 29 RIPA2000. Other public authorities are empowered to do both. Authorizing officers will need to understand clearly what it is that their organization is empowered to do, and what conduct falls within and outside the definition of directed surveillance.

6.3 What Powers Does the Law Provide in Relation to Directed Surveillance?

Directed surveillance, subject to it being authorized, can be conducted if and only if necessary for the purpose of *preventing or detecting crime* or of *preventing disorder.* This means establishing by whom, for what purpose, by what means, and generally in what circumstances any criminal offence was committed (s 28(3)). It may also be conducted in order to apprehend the suspected offender (s 81(2) and 81(5) RIPA2000).

In limited circumstances certain specified agencies may conduct surveillance for other purposes (s 28(3) RIPA2000), namely:

- in the interests of national security
- in the interests of the economic well-being of the UK
- in the interests of public safety
- for the purpose of protecting public health
- for the purpose of assessing or collecting certain fiscal levies
- for any other purpose specified by order of the Secretary of State.

It should be noted, however, that although these additional statutory purposes have been enacted, they are not generally available. The Schedule to the Regulation of Investigatory Powers (Directed Surveillance and Covert Human Intelligence Sources) Order 2010 (SI 2010/521) (as amended—but note that, as of January 2018, only the version as originally made is available online) defines not only which staff can authorize directed surveillance but also the purposes for which such authorization can be given. Many organizations have only a restricted number of statutory purposes for which directed surveillance authority can be given. For example, local authorities can only undertake directed surveillance for the purpose of *preventing or detecting crime* or of *preventing disorder.*

Organizations and investigators intending to use directed surveillance and senior staff considering an application to authorize such activity will need to ensure that the intended activity is for a statutory purpose, for which they are entitled to give authorization.

6.3.1 **Definition of directed surveillance**

Directed surveillance is defined (s 26(2) RIPA2000) both by what it is not and by what it is. Surveillance will require a directed surveillance authority if:

- it comprises covert observation or monitoring by whatever means;
- it is for the purpose of a specific investigation or specific operation (any crime or any other offence);
- it will or is likely to obtain private information about *any* person, not just the subject of the operation (this is the key element that engages Article 8 ECHR); but
- it does not include observations conducted in an immediate response to spontaneous events.

Directed surveillance scenario

On patrol, investigators see a person acting suspiciously near a house. In order to maintain a view of the individual without raising their suspicions, the investigators conceal themselves behind a nearby wall.

Such a reactive intervention triggered by spontaneous events does not require an authority for directed surveillance as it is conduct consistent with normal patrol duties.

Directed surveillance can take place anywhere *except:*

- inside any premises at the time being used as a residence, no matter how temporary, including hotel accommodation, tents, caravans, a prison cell, or even railway arches;
- in any vehicle which is primarily used as a private vehicle either by the owner or the person having the right to use it (taxis are specifically excluded from this definition, s 48(7)(a) RIPA2000);
- outside such premises or vehicles if conducted by remote technical means (for instance, a long-range microphone) which enables events and conversations inside residential premises and private vehicles to be monitored from outside, producing a surveillance product of the same quality as would be obtained by devices or persons inside such premises or vehicles.

In these three circumstances such surveillance is considered to be *intrusive* and may be carried out only by certain public authorities (see Chapter 7).

Scenario illustrating action that goes beyond directed surveillance

Investigators wish to confirm whether a benefit claimant lives at a particular address identified to the social security department. At the address investigators are unable to get an answer to a knock at the door. They consider whether it would be appropriate to push open a window that is slightly ajar at the front of the house in order to look inside.

By opening the window investigators would be engaged in surveillance that is carried out on private premises, ie a dwelling house. This would constitute intrusive surveillance and property interference and therefore would not be lawful in these circumstances unless it was carried out by an investigating authority with such powers in circumstances that met the criteria for conducting intrusive surveillance and property interference.

(OSC *Annual Report 2005*, 4.18)

Surveillance conducted in offices or in business vehicles (including taxis and police vehicles) requires a directed surveillance authority, not an intrusive surveillance authority.

6.3.2 Definition of private information

Private information is defined (s 26(10) RIPA2000) as being:

- any information relating to a person's private or family life or personal relationships with others.

See also CSPI Code, paras 2.4–2.7.

> The totality of information gleaned may constitute private information even if individual records do not.
>
> (CSPI Code, para 2.6)

The fact that an individual happens to be located in a public space, for instance a car park, does not negate the obligation on public authorities to respect that individual's right to privacy and conduct surveillance only if duly authorized. A person present in a public space naturally will be casually observed by any other persons also present: that does not mean that any legitimate entitlement to privacy (in the sense of not being intruded upon or not being deliberately noticed) is negated or surrendered. Just because a person is present in a public space does not, in and of itself, entitle anyone else to know that person's business in being there. Once made a mental note of or recorded in any way, an observation ceases to be casual and private information has been gathered. (Recall the definition of surveillance in s 48(2) RIPA2000, discussed previously.)

Similar considerations would seem to apply when public authorities access social media sites. If the purpose of accessing social media is to observe and record information over a period of time, then consideration should be given to whether or not any authorization is required, the decision in each instance depending upon the nature of the circumstances. Initial individual social media access may not warrant authorization, but persistent monitoring may.

It is not only the rights of the investigation subject that have to be respected. Inevitably, there will be collateral intrusion into the privacy of third parties present in the surveillance arena and so investigators and authorizing officers must be able to demonstrate why it is both proportionate and necessary to infringe their Article 8 rights and what steps are to be taken to minimize the intrusion and the consequences thereof.

6.4 What Authority Regime Is Required for Directed Surveillance?

Individuals empowered within each public authority to grant authorities for directed surveillance have been defined in the Regulation of Investigatory Powers (Directed Surveillance and Covert Human Intelligence Sources) Order 2010 (SI 2010/521) and the Regulation of Investigatory Powers (Covert Human Intelligence Sources: Relevant Sources) Order 2013 (SI 2013/2788).

Thus authorizing officers include, amongst others, police superintendents, military Provosts Marshal, Lieutenant Colonels, Wing Commanders, or Commanders (Royal Navy), HMRC Senior Officers, and local authority Directors, Heads of Service, Service Managers, or their equivalent.

Authorizing officers can only authorize an application for directed surveillance made by members of their own organization. An exception to this principle exists when two or more *police forces* have entered into a collaborative working agreement pursuant to s 23 of the Police Act 1996 (for English and Welsh forces), *and* the collaboration agreement permits applicants and authorizing officers to be from different forces. Where a collaborative working agreement is established for the purpose (*inter alia*) of facilitating covert investigation for the signatory parties, such agreements must document specific arrangements for the management of covert investigation between the partners. 'Mere agreement to share resources is insufficient' (OSC *Annual Report 2010–11*, para 5.12; see also CSPI Code, paras 3.15–3.22).

6.5 **Which Authorizations for Directed Surveillance Require Judicial Approval?**

Section 38 of the Protection of Freedoms Act 2012 amended RIPA2000 by adding new ss 32A and 32B, the effect of which has been to introduce an additional element into the process for the authorization of directed surveillance to be undertaken by or on behalf of local authorities.

Once the prescribed authorizing officer for a local authority (SI 2010/521) has granted an authorization under s 28 RIPA2000, the authorization does not take effect—and so the surveillance cannot commence—until such time (if any) as a relevant judicial authority (a Justice of the Peace in England and Wales; a Sheriff in Scotland; or a magistrates' court district judge in Northern Ireland) makes an order approving the granting of the authorization.

The relevant judicial authority may approve the granting of the authority or renewal if, and only if:

- at the time the local authority authorizing officer granted the authorization, he or she had reasonable grounds for believing the authorization to be *necessary* for the purpose of preventing or detecting crime or of preventing disorder; *and*
- at the time the local authority authorizing officer granted the authorization, he or she had reasonable grounds for believing the authorized surveillance activity to be *proportionate* to what is sought to be achieved by carrying it out (that the methods to be used are proportionate to the product that will be derived); *and*
- at the time that approval for the granting of the authorization is sought, there remain reasonable grounds for believing that the authorization is *necessary* for the purpose of preventing or detecting crime or of preventing disorder and for believing that the authorized surveillance is *proportionate* to what is sought to be achieved by carrying it out; *and*
- that the local authority authorizing officer is so designated under s 28 RIPA2000; *and*
- that the grant of the authorization does not breach any restrictions imposed by an Order made under s 30(2) RIPA2000; *and*
- that any other conditions that may have been imposed by an Order made by a Secretary of State have been complied with.

Applications for approval may be made *ex parte*. The local authority does not have to give notice either to the person who is the subject of the proposed directed surveillance or to their legal representative when applying to the relevant judicial authority for an order approving the grant of the authorization.

If the magistrate (or other relevant judicial authority) refuses to approve the granting of the authorization, then he or she may make an order quashing the authorization.

> **Further information and reading**
>
> CSPI Code, Chapter 3 discusses general rules on authorizations.
>
> For the official guidance in relation to the amended authorization regime for local authorities, see the following:
>
> - Guidance to local authorities (England and Wales)
> - Guidance for magistrates' courts (England and Wales)
> - Guidance to local authorities (Scotland)
>
> These are accessible online at <https://www.gov.uk/government/ publications/ changes-to-local-authority-use-of-ripa> (accessed 5 January 2018).

6.6 What Information Is Required in an Application for Directed Surveillance?

Written applications for directed surveillance authority should describe both the *purpose* of the operation/investigation and the *conduct* for which authorization is sought.

The application should document in writing:

- the reasons why the authorization is *necessary* in the particular case and on the grounds (eg for the purpose of preventing or detecting crime) listed in s 28(3) of the 2000 Act;
- the nature of the surveillance (be it monitoring, observing, or listening to persons, their movements, conversations, or other activities and communications, including the recording of same, with or without the assistance of a surveillance device);
- the identities, where known, of those persons who will be the subject of the surveillance;
- a summary of the intelligence case and appropriate unique intelligence references where applicable (authorizing officers will quickly become aware of those applicants who attempt to strengthen their applications by including superfluous intelligence report reference numbers);
- an explanation of the information which it is desired to obtain as a result of the surveillance;
- the details of any potential collateral intrusion and why the intrusion is justified in the particular circumstances;
- the details of any confidential information that is likely to be obtained as a consequence of the surveillance and what steps have been taken to minimize the risk or manage the consequence (see 6.9);
- the reasons why the surveillance method proposed in each instance is considered *proportionate* to what it seeks to achieve;
- the level of authority required (or recommended, where that is different) for the surveillance; and

- a subsequent record of whether authorization was given or refused, by whom, and the time and date this happened (an elaboration of CSPI Code, para 5.8).

The authorizing officer considering the application should check the details therein and in writing record the grounds he or she has for believing that the authorization is *necessary* for one of the statutory purposes listed in s 28(2) RIPA2000, having first satisfied him- or herself that the purpose is one which he or she may lawfully authorize (see 6.3; also the Schedule to SI 2010/521). The authorizing officer should then record his or her reasons for believing that the proposed conduct is *proportionate* to the product that will be achieved from this particular use of a surveillance tactic. The mere assertion of such a belief, without reasoned argument supporting it, is insufficient.

If the application for authorization is urgent (due to spontaneous developments in the prevailing circumstances and not because the investigator has been tardy in planning and preparation), then the information above may be supplied orally by the applicant to the authorizing officer. In such cases both the applicant and the authorizing officer should document:

- the identities of those subject to surveillance;
- the nature of the surveillance (be it monitoring, observing, or listening to persons, their movements, conversations, or other activities and communications, including the recording of same, with or without the assistance of a surveillance device);
- the reasons why the authorizing officer considered the case so urgent that an oral instead of a written authorization was given; and
- where the officer entitled to act in urgent cases has given written authority, the reasons why it was not reasonably practicable for the application to be considered by the authorizing officer should also be recorded.

Urgent oral authorizations cease to have effect 72 hours from the time that they were granted. Should investigators wish to prolong the surveillance activity so authorized beyond the 72-hour limit, a normal written application must be made and then considered by an authorizing officer before the 72-hour period has elapsed.

Definition of urgent circumstances

Urgent circumstances are defined as instances in which to wait for an authorizing officer to become available to consider a written application would either:

- endanger life, or
- jeopardize the investigation concerned.

(CSPI Code, para 5.6)

Hint and tip: Negligence on the part of an applicant or conduct of the authorizing officer's own making does not constitute urgency.

Thus where an investigator forgets to apply for authorization until just before the operation is due to begin or where the authorizing officer does not or cannot attend to the application before the operation is due to start, the operation will have to be postponed until the full written application procedure is carried out.

There are two types of urgent authority procedure: one where an authorizing officer is available; and one where such an officer is unavailable.

In genuinely urgent cases an available authorizing officer may issue an *oral authority* (CSPI Code, para 5.9), recording the fact that this has been done as soon as is practicable. In the police service it is almost unheard of now for there not to be a duty on-call superintendent to deal with urgent PACE and RIPA2000 authorities.

In urgent cases in which there is no authorizing officer immediately available, specified individuals entitled to act in urgent cases (identified in the Schedule to SI 2010/521) may give a *written authorization* for directed surveillance for a period of 72 hours (CSPI Code, para 5.11). Such individuals cannot issue oral authorities.

Scenario illustrating issues around urgent authorization for directed surveillance

Intelligence came to light at 0300 one night about a burglary being planned for immediate execution. Police wished to maintain surveillance on the offender's house. Having tried unsuccessfully several times to contact the duty superintendent, officers thought it expedient to seek an urgent authority from the night duty inspector on the basis of an oral application. The inspector gave verbal authority for the surveillance to be conducted. However, the OSC confirmed that, absent an authorizing officer, an inspector could only consider a full written application upon which to base an authorization. In this particular instance, circumstances were such that there would not have been time to complete and submit such an application to the inspector before the burglary had been committed and the burglar had returned home. Thus alternative intervention strategies not involving surveillance, including perhaps disruption, such as the presence of a marked police vehicle patrolling in the immediate vicinity, should have been considered.

6.7 Review and Renewal of Authorities

The CSPI Code (para 3.23) stresses the need for *regular reviews of authorities* given for directed surveillance, the frequency of which reviews should be set by the authorizing officer when first authorizing the application. Where directed surveillance is likely to obtain confidential information or where there is a high degree of either direct or collateral intrusion it will be necessary to review the *necessity* and the *proportionality* of the authorized conduct more regularly. The authorizing officer granting a renewal of an authorization may amend such aspects of the authorization as seem appropriate on review. Reviews are the personal responsibility of the authorizing officer; they should be documented and retained for three years (see CSPI Code, Chapter 8).

Further information and reading

CSPI Code, paras 3.23–3.27 discuss the *reviewing* of covert investigation authorities.
CSPI Code, paras 5.12–5.16 discuss the *renewing* of directed surveillance authorities.

Written authorities for directed surveillance can be made for periods of up to three months. Applications for renewal of an authority would not normally be made until shortly before the current authorization period is due to end. An authorization may be renewed for a period up to three months (six months if the authorization was granted by a member of the intelligence services). CSPI Code, para 5.15 details the information to be recorded when seeking renewal of an authorization for directed surveillance.

6.8 Cancellation of Authorities

Authorizations must be cancelled as soon as the desired product is achieved or if circumstances change that require the application for and granting of a new authorization. The authorizing officer who granted or last renewed the authorization (or, if no longer available, the person who has succeeded him or her in that role) must cancel it if satisfied that the directed surveillance no longer meets the criteria upon which it was authorized (CSPI Code, paras 5.17–5.18). The time and date of cancellation must be recorded and instructions to cease surveillance issued immediately. Whether the surveillance had produced the planned objective should also be recorded.

6.9 Confidential Information and Legal Consultations

Special considerations and some restrictions apply to surveillance likely to acquire confidential information or information from a legal consultation, although RIPA2000 and the PA97 are inconsistent in the approaches adopted towards such material (see also Chapter 8.5).

Confidential information exists in four categories:

- Communications subject to legal privilege.
- Communication about constituency business between a Member of Parliament and another person.
- Personal information, expressly or by implication held in confidence, relating to the physical or mental health of an individual or to the spiritual counselling of an individual where that individual can be identified from the information concerned.
- Material held in confidence having been acquired or created for the purposes of journalism, including communications conveying information to be used for the purposes of journalism.

Confidential information that is acquired through directed surveillance and which is retained on record by the investigators must be reported to and made available to the OSC inspection team during the next inspection immediately following acquisition.

The case of *McE* [2009] UKHL 15 considered the issue of directed surveillance that captured *legal consultations*. Consequently the Regulation of Investigatory Powers (Extension of Authorization Provisions: Legal Consultations) Order 2010 (SI 2010/461) was made. What is a legal consultation, and is it covered by legal privilege?

'Legal consultation is a narrower concept than legal privilege, so a matter that is likely to cause confusion to an already confused area of the law': so warned Simon McKay, an expert in surveillance law shortly after the Order was made (*Covert Policing: Law and Practice*, Oxford University Press, Oxford, 2011, para 6.68). The subsequent new edition of the CSPI Code seeks to address such possible confusion by asserting (para 4.7) that the term 'legal consultations' should be understood to encompass both consultations protected by legal privilege, and consultations not so protected because they are for the purpose of committing crime.

Turner v R [2013] EWCA Crim 642, sheds further light on the issue. Suspecting Turner of having murdered his girlfriend, police obtained approval from the Surveillance Commissioner to conduct *intrusive* surveillance in Turner's home. Recordings of conversations between Turner and his parents captured clear evidence of Turner's guilt and his parents' complicity. On appeal it was contended that the surveillance evidence captured legal privilege material and so should have been excluded from trial.

The appeal was dismissed. The court held:

- the 2010 Order (SI 2010/461) permitted the use of surveillance even where such surveillance might capture matters subject to legal privilege;
- the surveillance was lawful;
- there was no basis for suspecting a deliberate breach of legal privilege on the part of the police;

- at trial the judge had not admitted any evidence which might have been subject to legal privilege; and
- 'Nothing which became known to the surveillance officers resulted in any further or wider investigations, or produced a single item of incriminating material to strengthen the case against T, other than properly recorded observations that he made to his parents' (case reported by Tom Rees in *Criminal Law Review* [2013] 12, 993–995; this quote from p 994 of the report).

In his commentary on this case report, Andrew Roberts observed:

> Covert recording, if it is to secure its underlying objective, will be conducted in places in which the suspect is expected to engage in conversations that are likely to produce incriminating statements. If a suspect has sufficient trust in those with whom he is conversing to incriminate himself, there is every reason to suppose that he will share with them details of conversations that he has had with his legal advisors as to what his case ought to be at trial and how it might be presented. Therefore, **the risk of a violation of the privilege accompanies *all* instances of covert recording following a suspect's arrest and consultation with a lawyer**.
>
> (Crim LR [2013] 12, 995, emphasis added).

Because of this risk, as the Court of Appeal noted: 'it is clear that arrangements for covert surveillance must focus attention on a need to preserve legal privilege, and where, for one reason or another, the relevant precautions have failed, to ensure that the interests of the potential defendant during the course of the investigation itself, or at any other subsequent trial, are not prejudiced in consequence', [2013] EWCA 642 at 24.

The 2010 Order requires (s 3(1)) that where directed surveillance on specified premises is likely to result in acquisition of legal consultation material, the surveillance must be regarded, treated, and accordingly authorized as *intrusive* surveillance.

Legal consultation is defined in the Order (s 2(a)) as:

(i) a consultation between a professional legal adviser and his client or any person representing his client, or

(ii) a consultation between a professional legal adviser or his client or any such representative and a medical practitioner made in connection with or in contemplation of legal proceedings and for the purposes of such proceedings.

The specified premises are detailed in s 3(2) of the Order as follows:

(a) any place in which persons who are serving sentences of imprisonment or detention, remanded in custody, or committed in custody for trial or sentence may be detained;

(b) any place in which persons may be detained under paragraph 16(1), (1A) or (2) of Schedule 2 or paragraph 2(2) or (3) of Schedule 3 to the Immigration Act 1971 or section 36(1) of the UK Border Act 2007;

(c) police stations;

(d) hospitals where high security psychiatric services are provided;

(e) the place of business of any professional legal adviser; and

(f) any place used for the sittings and business of any court, tribunal, inquest or inquiry.

Where planned directed surveillance is likely to capture legal consultation material, the surveillance must be regarded as being intrusive, and the appropriate authorization for *intrusive surveillance* sought accordingly (see Chapter 7).

The CSPI Code now devotes an entire chapter (Chapter 4) to discussion of issues concerning legally privileged and confidential information.

6.10 General Principles and Practicalities in Authorization

Authorizing officers should not authorize covert surveillance in investigations in which they have direct involvement, although this may sometimes be unavoidable (CSPI Code, para 5.7).

Authorizing officers must apply two tests when considering whether to grant an authorization. These are set out in s 28(2) RIPA2000 and are explained in the OSC *Annual Report 2000–2001*, para 4.13: 'When giving an authorization for directed surveillance ... the authorizing officer must *believe* that the authorized surveillance is *proportionate* to what is sought to be achieved by carrying it out, and that the action is *necessary* for' one of the purposes defined in s 28(3) RIPA2000 (emphasis added). The seriousness of the crime under investigation will not, in and of itself, provide a basis for meeting the proportionality test. Authorizing officers must articulate and document *why* the proposed method is proportionate to the product it is intended to produce and not merely assert a belief that it is proportionate (see Chapter 2.2).

Section 28(4) makes it clear that only conduct and circumstances specified in the authority will be authorized and therefore lawful. This important subsection obliges investigators and authorizing officers to be very precise in the wording of their applications and authorities.

For example, investigators conducting surveillance decide to secure photographic and video evidence. If the use of still photography and video cameras is not specified in the authority, then any evidence so secured will have been obtained in an unauthorized way and therefore vulnerable to exclusion under s 78 PACE. Lack of precision in the wording of authorities, resulting in unlawful or unauthorized activity by investigators, is a recurring deficiency identified by the OSC (for example, *Annual Report 2003–04*, 12).

Thus investigators must seek detailed authority for all the conduct in which they wish to engage, and authorizing officers must ensure that their authorities specify in detail all conduct that they are content to authorize. Where authorizing officers authorize more than has been applied for, they must state their reasons for doing so. Similarly they must record their reasons for not authorizing all or any of the conduct detailed in an application.

In relation to town-centre CCTV systems, the CSPI Code (paras 2.27–2.28) provides that, *except when used for pre-planned surveillance operations*, the use of such systems does not require a directed surveillance authority.

Further information and reading

The Information Commissioner has published a Code of Practice on the use of CCTV systems which is available online at <https://ico.org.uk/for-organisations/guide-to-data-protection/cctv/> (accessed 5 January 2018).

6.11 Surveillance and Social Media

The same principles apply to covert investigation in the virtual world as in the real world. Will the proposed activity engage Article 8 rights? Is it being conducted covertly, without the knowledge of the person being investigated? Will private information about any person be acquired or accumulated over time?

The fact that, through their use of social media, individuals may render themselves more susceptible to being surveilled does not negate the need for covertly conducted investigation of such individuals to be appropriately authorized. The internet and social media, to varying degrees, are the virtual equivalent of real-world public spaces.

Where investigators propose to communicate with others and intend to use assumed or disguised identities to do so, then a CHIS authority may be required if a relationship is to be established or maintained, in a manner calculated to ensure that one party is unaware of the real purpose to which the relationship is being put, and the relationship is being used to obtain, facilitate access to, or disclose information without the knowledge of one of the parties in the relationship (CSPI Code, para 2.29; CHIS Code, para 4.32).

In his 2011–12 Annual Report, the Chief Surveillance Commissioner observed (para 5.18): 'The internet is a surveillance device as defined by RIPA2000 section 48(1) ... The ease with which an [investigation] activity meets the legislative threshold demands improved supervision.'

In his 2013–14 Annual Report, the Chief Surveillance Commissioner cautioned (para 5.30) that 'repeat viewing of individual "open source" sites for the purpose of intelligence gathering and data collection should be considered within the context of the protection that RIPA2000 affords to such activity'. He went on (para 5.33) to 'strongly advise all public authorities empowered to use RIPA2000 to have in place a corporate policy on the use of social media in investigations'. In connection with the management of CHISs, it is the role of the Senior Responsible Officer in each relevant public authority to have in place a strategic approach to such issues: it seems relatively little extra effort (for the potential benefit to be gained) for the same individual to drive policy in the directed surveillance arena also.

6.12 What Significant Case Law Has Been Decided in Relation to Directed Surveillance?

Key principles have been established or confirmed in case law both pre-RIPA2000 and post-RIPA2000 and from case law not directly concerning criminal investigations.

6.12.1 Private life

An initial issue for investigators and authorizing officers is the determination of whether surveillance will or is likely to obtain information about anyone's private life. Strasbourg has interpreted 'private life' and what might constitute information about private life very broadly.

In *Peck v UK* (2003) 36 EHRR 41, in which CCTV footage of the aftermath of Peck's suicide attempt in a town centre was released to TV broadcasters by the local council whose CCTV system had captured the images, the court held: 'Private life is a broad term not susceptible to exhaustive definition ... There is a zone of interaction of a person with others, even in a public context, which may fall within the scope of "private life"' (at 730, para H5).

In *Von Hannover v Germany* [2006] 43 EHRR 7, the court held that private life can take place in the public domain; just because something happens in the public domain does not mean it is not private. Reinforcement for the notion that privacy still exists within a public environment is also found in UK case law. In *Campbell v MGN* [2004] 2 AC 457 at 458, the court held that 'although the photographs of the claimant were taken in a public place, the context in which they were used ... added to the overall intrusion into the claimant's life'.

Collateral intrusion of third-party privacy must also be considered and addressed. In *XXX & YYY v ZZZ* [2004] EWCA Civ 231, an au pair set up covert cameras in the home where she worked to record sexual advances from her male employer. The cameras also recorded the children, which was considered a breach of their privacy.

Further information and reading

For a further discussion around the case law enforcement interpreting private life, see K Starmer, *European Human Rights Law* (Legal Action Group, London, 1999) paras 3.109–3.111 (a little dated now in terms of case law, but still a very useful guide to rights jurisprudence); *Niemitz v Germany* (1993) 16 EHRR 97; *Costello-Roberts v UK* (1995) 19 EHRR 112; *Friedl v Austria* (1996)

---

21 EHRR 83; *Halford v UK* (1997) 24 EHRR 523; *Perry v UK* (2004) 39 EHRR 3 (although a case involving a breach of PACE, it has been applied by OSC inspectors when interpreting private life). See also OSC *Annual Report 2003–04*, 8. S McKay, *Covert Policing: Law and Practice* (Oxford University Press, Oxford, 2011) devotes Chapter 2 to the issues of privacy, proportionality, and other human rights issues. CSPI Code, paras 2.4–2.7 consider private information.

6.12.2 Protection of observation posts

Recognizing that failure to secure observation posts from which to conduct surveillance could seriously impede legitimate investigations, the Court of Appeal applied, in *R v Rankine* [1986] 1 QB 861, the same presumption of protection applied to human sources of information, namely that the identity of locations used should be protected unless doing so would lead to a miscarriage of justice. Minimum evidential standards were applied to this principle in *R v Johnson* [1988] 1 WLR 1377, confirmed by *R v Hewitt and Davis* [1992] 95 Cr App R 81, and *R v Grimes* [1994] Crim LR 213.

....

Case law criteria: *R v Johnson* [1988] 1 WLR 1377

The criteria set out in *R v Johnson* are reproduced in the ACPO *Practice Advice on Core Investigative Doctrine* (2005) 104:

The police officer in charge of observations of a rank not lower than sergeant must be able to testify that beforehand he or she visited all the observation places to be used and ascertained the attitude of the occupiers of the premises:

- as to the use of the premises;
- to the disclosure of the use of the premises;
- to the possible identification of the premises or the occupiers.

The difficulties, if any are encountered, are in obtaining observation posts in the area.

In addition, immediately prior to the trial, an officer of a rank not lower than chief inspector must be able to testify that he or she visited the premises used for observations and ascertained if the occupiers are the same as when the observations were conducted and, whether they are or not, what their attitude is to:

- the possible disclosure of the use made of the premises;
- the disclosure of facts which would lead to the identification of those premises and their occupiers.

This evidence will be given in the absence of the jury when the application to exclude the material evidence is made. The judge should explain to the jury the effect of his or her ruling regarding the disclosure of the premises.

....

Because exposure of unmarked police vehicles would not necessarily involve the same threat of harassment or fear of violence for members of the public (*Blake and Austin v DPP* (1993) 97 Cr App R 169), the presumption of protection for private premises used as observation points would not, as a matter of policy, be applied to police vehicles from which observations were conducted (*R v Brown and Daley* (1988) 87 Cr App R 52).

6.12.3 Disclosure of surveillance authorizations

The statutory presumption of disclosure is founded in the Criminal Procedure and Investigations Act 1996 (CPIA). Because surveillance authorities may contain sensitive detail, exposure of which would be against the public interest, such authorities may be scheduled as sensitive unused material. Unless the requirements of the disclosure regime are directly engaged (for example, the authorization documentation contains material that tends to undermine the prosecution case or will assist the defence case), authorization documentation will not normally be disclosed (*R v GS* [2005] EWCA Crim 887; see also *R v Jones* [2010] EWCA Crime 925).

It is the prosecutor's responsibility to ensure proper disclosure of any material falling within the disclosure regime, including authorization material (*R v GS* [2005] EWCA Crim 887). If the prosecutor recognizes contentious issues regarding the authorization process, a redacted version of the authority should be disclosed and an unedited version supplied to the judge for determination that the defendant is not vulnerable to a miscarriage arising from non-disclosure (*R v Hardy and Hardy* [2002] EWCA Crim 3012). The defence cannot go on fishing trips and, if seeking to challenge admissibility and a ruling under s 78 PACE, must have convincing reasons for doing so (*R v GS* [2005] EWCA Crim 887). Where the defence declares specific issues with the authorization process, as in *R v Grant* [2005] EWCA Crim 1089, full disclosure of all documentation related to a covert investigation authorization may be ordered. Although in cases involving *intrusive* surveillance a court may rely on the approval forms signed by the Surveillance Commissioner as independent evidence of lawful authorization (*R v GS* [2005] EWCA Crim 887), in matters concerning *directed* surveillance the court may wish to inspect the authorization documentation for itself. In *R v Harmes* [2006] EWCA Crim 928 the court considered the authorization documentation in detail, noting (at para 22) that renewals of the authorization had failed to detail either changes in circumstances or changes in planned police activity, and concluding (at para 42) that 'there were serious breaches of the Act and the Code in the process of authorization'.

6.12.4 Police vehicles and police cells

In *R v Plunkett (Daniel Michael)* [2013] EWCA Crim 261; [2013] 1 WLR 3121 (CA (Crim Div)), the court held that a police vehicle was not a private vehicle because it was owned and used solely for police purposes. Consequently the covert audio recording of conversations between suspects in the back of a police van did not require an intrusive surveillance authorization: an authorization for directed surveillance sufficed.

Whereas a prison cell is considered to be a residential premises, a police cell is not considered to be residential premises (unless it is being used as temporary prison accommodation) (CSPI Code, para 2.16).

6.13 **Considerations in Respect of Authorizing Directed Surveillance**

Concern exists that example scenarios may tempt authorizing officers to construct an authorization better suited to the example scenario than to the facts of the application before them (see OSC *Annual Report 2008–09*, para 3.15; OSC *Annual Report 2009–10*, paras 3.8 and 5.3). Accordingly, whereas previous editions of this book have used scenarios to suggest courses of action, this approach has been modified in this edition to highlight certain practicalities to which applicants and authorizing officers should give consideration. The decision whether or not to authorize a specific application for covert investigation remains the responsibility of the authorizing officer: 'the law obliges an Authorizing Officer to satisfy his [or her] own mind[;] he [or she] is not to be dictated to or obliged to follow any particular interpretation' (OSC *Annual Report 2009–10*, para 3.8). Authorizing officers may be required to account for any decision made either to the OSC or in cross-examination at trial. The following considerations are neither exclusive nor exhaustive. They are intended to illustrate issues that applicant investigators and authorizing officers might wish to consider when being asked to authorize directed surveillance.

Example 1

A uniformed police officer wishes to record covertly a conversation with a member of the public in order to have an accurate record of the meeting which is due to take place at the police station.

A directed surveillance authority may be considered even though the officer is in uniform, as a member of the public would not be aware of the recording. This might be considered a higher level of intrusion than would normally be expected in such an encounter. An investigator may still be capable of executing some actions covertly even if those with whom the investigator is interacting are aware of who and what the investigator is. In some jurisdictions, New South Wales (Australia) for instance, police officers are equipped routinely to record conversations with the public and announce this fact to the member of the public when first introducing themselves. Such a declaration renders the recording overt rather than covert.

Example 2

A local authority has installed CCTV in an area subject to frequent crime and disorder. Investigators intend to carry out an operation where CCTV operators identify those responsible for committing offences so that officers can attend and make arrests.

When CCTV is monitored in order to trigger immediate reactive intervention to a spontaneous crime observed, this would seem to amount to routine observations as part of the normal duty of the CCTV operator. Where the use of CCTV is planned as part of a targeted covert investigation based on specific intelligence about ongoing criminality, the investigation being conducted in a manner which is likely to produce private information about persons observed (either the subject of the investigation or unassociated third parties), then consideration must be given to authorizing such use as directed surveillance.

Note: In May 2015, the Information Commissioner updated the Code of Practice in relation to the use of CCTV systems that monitor public spaces. It is accessible online at <https://ico.org.uk/media/for-organisations/documents/1542/cctv-code-of-practice.pdf> (accessed 29 July 2015).

Example 3

A commercial catering premises has been the subject of early-morning thefts of its milk supply. The thefts occur in the early hours after the milk delivery but before the premises open. An officer wishes to set up an observation point in premises opposite those where the thefts occur. If it is likely that this operation will capture private information about persons frequenting or passing through the area, whether suspects or innocent third parties, then an authority for directed surveillance should be considered. Investigators operating an observation post must comply with *R v Johnson*. Successful observations may trigger a successful prosecution for the single occasion of theft observed. Absent a corroborated confession, no prosecution of the previous offences is likely. Is covert investigation justified in this context? Is the object to secure a prosecution for one instance of theft or to prevent future thefts? Would enhanced visible patrolling of the area (with perhaps recourse to PACE stop and search powers) achieve the same purpose?

Example 4

Local residents are complaining about young people drinking alcohol in the park in the evenings. Residents believe that those drinking in the park are under 18 years of age and are obtaining their alcohol from a local shop which has previously been visited by officers outlining the problems in the local area. The shop owner denies selling alcohol to anyone under age. Investigators wish to set up surveillance to establish a pattern of business in the store and identify anyone under age being sold alcohol.

Whether these observations are conducted by police or other licensing/regulatory bodies, if it is likely that private information (such as a pattern of behaviour exhibited by an identifiable individual) will be obtained as a consequence of the planned observations, then consideration must be given to authorizing the operation as directed surveillance. Such an operation may obtain evidence to support a prosecution against the shop owner, but will such intervention resolve the underlying problem? Is the real problem one of unlawful retailing (arguably a symptom) or underage drinking (arguably a symptom or the cause)? Will prosecution of the shopkeeper resolve the problem of underage misuse of alcohol in this local authority area? Can covert investigation of a shopkeeper, with its concomitant collateral intrusion against the privacy of lawful customers, be justified if social and educational intervention alternatives (which may not engage Article 8 rights) could also be applied? In the context of alternative interventions, can covert investigation be justified by the authorizing officer as necessary?

Example 5

As part of an operational order in which a search warrant is to be executed on premises, investigators wish to set up observations in order to establish who is on the premises prior to the execution of the warrant. Intelligence suggests a number of potentially violent individuals use and stay at the address and the intention is to execute the warrant when such persons are away from the premises in order to minimize risk.

A directed surveillance authority should be considered if covert observation of the premises is likely to capture private information of persons on or near the premises. The fact that such observations are to facilitate the safe execution of a subsequent overt intervention does not of itself automatically absolve investigators from considering whether an authority for directed surveillance is required for this part of the overall process. Where such an authority is deemed not necessary, those responsible for taking the decision may wish to document the reasons upon which it is based. If visual equipment planned to be used by the officers for the purposes of such observations from outside the premises were capable of providing information on activities inside the dwelling of the same quality as if the surveillance devices were inside the dwelling, then an intrusive surveillance authority should be considered.

It is not suggested that any of these example considerations is typical. Indeed, that is the point. No matter how similar individual investigations may be in terms of *circumstance*, the *facts* of each investigation will differ. It is upon the particular facts of each case that authorizing officers must determine whether or not to authorize directed surveillance.

Checklist of key issues when considering whether or not to deploy covert investigation techniques

- What evidence or intelligence is being sought?

- How is it relevant to the operation under consideration?

- What is the least intrusive means of securing such evidence or information?

- Has the least intrusive means of securing the evidence or information been attempted? If not, why not?

- What is the likelihood of collateral intrusion against the privacy of persons not being investigated? How will collateral intrusion be prevented (or if not, minimized) and how will the product of collateral intrusion be managed?

- What are the risks to the organization of such tactics? (Chapter 4)

- What are the risks to the organization's staff of such tactics? (Chapter 4)

- What are the risks to the public or specific third parties when such tactics are deployed? (Chapter 4)

- What are the risks to the subject of the investigation? (Chapter 4)

- Will the proposed methods breach Article 8(1)? (Chapter 2.2)

- Is there justification for doing so provided by Article 8(2)? (Chapter 2.2)

- How is the legality test met? (Chapter 2.2.3)

- How is the legitimacy test met? (Chapter 2.2.4)

- How is the necessity test met? (Chapter 2.2.5)

- How is the proportionality test met? (Chapter 2.2.5)

- Are the arguments justifying the application to use covert investigation based on reliable information/intelligence, or has the applicant adopted a 'tick-the-box' approach to completing the application without giving full consideration to the facts of the case and the issues arising?

- Have the arguments justifying the granting of authorization to use covert investigation been fully articulated, or has the authorizing officer merely paid lip service to the pro forma authorization template via which authority is granted?

- When should this authority be reviewed? What circumstances will or may arise that will necessitate review before then?

- How are the methods by which the evidence/intelligence will be obtained to be protected at trial? (Chapter 5)

- How will the product of the surveillance be managed? (Chapter 5)

Planning covert investigation actions

Remember to include the PLAN for covert investigation tactics in all investigation policy-book entries relating to covert investigation considerations and decisions.

P Proportionality

Why is it proportionate to obtain the intended product of this surveillance in the manner proposed? (Chapter 2.2.5)

L Legitimacy

What is the legitimate purpose of the proposed action: the prevention of disorder or crime; the interests of national security; the interests of public safety; the interests of the economic well-being of the country; the protection of health or morals; the protection of the rights and freedoms of others? (Chapter 2.2.4)

A Authority to Undertake Proposed Action

What is the lawful foundation and authority for the proposed action? From whom must authorization be sought? (Chapter 2.2.3)

N Necessity of Proposed Action

Why is the proposed action necessary? (Chapter 2.2.5)

7

Intrusive Surveillance

7.1 **Introduction**

Surveillance is defined at s 48(2) RIPA2000.

Definition of surveillance

Surveillance includes:

(a) monitoring, observing or listening to persons, their movements, their conversations or their other activities or communications;

(b) recording anything monitored, observed or listened to in the course of surveillance; and

(c) surveillance by or with the assistance of a surveillance device.

The definition is neither exclusive nor exhaustive, and the monitoring, observing, or listening do not have to be recorded and do not have to involve the use of technology in order to constitute surveillance.

Because they are subject to their own specific authority regimes (as will be discussed in later chapters), the conduct of CHISs and interference with property under either Part III PA97 or s 5 Intelligence Services Act 1994 are not included in this definition (s 48(3) RIPA2000), notwithstanding that these tactics are deployed for exactly the same purposes.

A two-part hierarchy of surveillance is prescribed by law: directed and intrusive. Chapters 6 and 7 consider directed and intrusive surveillance separately because:

• not all public authorities empowered to conduct directed surveillance may also conduct intrusive surveillance; and

• the circumstances in which intrusive surveillance may be conducted are more restricted than those in which directed surveillance may take place.

The new Code of Practice for Covert Surveillance and Property Interference is available online for download from <https://www.gov.uk/government/collections/ripa-codes> (accessed July 2015). In this volume 'CSPI Code' refers to this Code.

7.2 **Which Public Authorities May Deploy Intrusive Surveillance?**

Public authorities empowered to utilize intrusive surveillance are defined by reference to senior authorizing officers within each organization able to grant an intrusive surveillance authority (s 32(6) and s 41(1) RIPA2000). Fewer organizations may conduct intrusive surveillance than those empowered to conduct directed surveillance. Those organizations are:

- Any police force maintained under s 2 Police Act 1996
- The Police Service of Scotland (also known as Police Scotland)
- The Metropolitan Police Service
- The City of London Police
- The Police Service of Northern Ireland
- The Ministry of Defence Police
- The British Transport Police
- The National Crime Agency
- The Army, Royal Navy, and Royal Air Force
- HM Revenue and Customs
- Competition and Markets Authority
- MI5, MI6, and GCHQ.

7.3 What Powers Does the Law Provide in Relation to Intrusive Surveillance?

Definition of intrusive surveillance

Intrusive surveillance is (s 26(3) RIPA2000):

- covert surveillance
- carried out on any residential premises or in any private vehicle and which involves
- the presence of an individual on the premises or in the vehicle or
- the use of a surveillance device (ie audio or visual monitoring and/or recording device).

Hint and tip: A stolen vehicle is not a private vehicle for the purposes of RIPA2000 authorization as the necessity for authorization relates to the rightful owner or user of the vehicle.

Intrusive surveillance, subject to it being authorized, may be conducted for the purpose of *preventing or detecting serious crime*. Which means establishing by whom, for what purpose, by what means, and generally in what circumstances any *serious crime* was committed and apprehending the suspected offender (ss 32(3) and 81(5) RIPA2000). Note that there is a higher threshold for intrusive surveillance—serious crime—than for directed surveillance (any crime or offence).

Other purposes for which intrusive surveillance is permitted are (s 32(3) RIPA2000):

- in the interests of national security; and
- in the interests of the economic well-being of the UK.

The Regulation of Investigatory Powers (Extension of Authorization Provisions: Legal Consultations) Order 2010 (SI 2010/461) requires (s 3(1)) that where directed surveillance on specified premises is likely to result in acquisition of legal consultation material, the surveillance must be regarded, treated, and accordingly authorized as intrusive surveillance.

7.3.1 Definition of serious crime

Serious crime is defined as (ss 81 (2)(b) and 81(3) RIPA2000, following s 93(4) PA97):

(a) An offence for which, on first conviction, a person aged 21 years or over with no previous convictions might receive three years' imprisonment, or
(b) The conduct:
  • involves the use of violence;
  • results in substantial financial gain; or
  • is engaged in by a large number of persons for a common purpose.

(Section 81 RIPA2000 does not reproduce that part of s 93(4) PA97 which refers to matters assigned under s 1(1) Customs and Excise Management Act 1979.)

If a technical device deployed outside the premises or the vehicle nevertheless produces a product of the same quality as would have been obtained by a device inside the premises or vehicle, then this also requires authority for intrusive surveillance; for instance, a long-range microphone capable of hearing conversations inside a building (s 26(5) RIPA2000; CSPI Code, para 2.19).

The meaning of residential premises is discussed in the CSPI Code, paras 2.13–2.16. 'Residential premises are considered to be so much of any premises as is for the time being occupied or used by any person, however temporarily, for residential purposes or otherwise as living accommodation', CSPI Code, para 2.13. This includes hotel rooms and prison accommodation, although not communal areas if no one is using these areas as a personal residence. Unless being used as temporary prison accommodation, a police cell is not included in this definition. Outside locations in public space where homeless persons sleep can be included in the protections provided by the concept of residential premises.

A private vehicle is defined (s 48(1) RIPA2000) as 'any vehicle which is used primarily for the private purposes of the person who owns it or of a person otherwise having the right to use it'. This does not include instances where an individual has hired the use of the vehicle and its driver for a particular journey, for example a taxi (s 48(7) RIPA2000).

A tracking device attached to a vehicle that reveals only its location does not constitute intrusive surveillance (s 26(4)(a) RIPA2000), but will comprise directed surveillance and interference with property (s 26(2) RIPA2000 in conjunction with s 93 PA97). Where both a surveillance authority and a property interference authority is required, a combined authority may be issued (s 33(5) RIPA2000). The relevant provisions of each Act apply in a combined authority and so in practice the different authority levels mean that whoever is the senior appropriate authorizing officer under the two regimes will consider combined applications.

Surveillance conducted in offices or in business vehicles (including taxis) requires a directed surveillance authority, not an intrusive surveillance authority.

7.4 When Does Directed Surveillance Require an Intrusive Surveillance Authority?

Where directed surveillance is carried out in premises that are specified in Article 3(2) of the Regulation of Investigatory Powers (Extension of Authorization Provisions: Legal Consultations Order (SI 2010/461), and at the time the surveillance is being conducted the premises are being used for the purpose of legal consultation, then such surveillance must be treated for the purposes of authorization as being intrusive surveillance.

'Legal consultation is a narrower concept than legal privilege, so a matter that is likely to cause confusion to an already confused area of the law': so warned Simon McKay, an expert in surveillance law, shortly after the Order was made (*Covert Policing: Law and Practice*, Oxford University Press, Oxford, 2011, para 6.68). The subsequent new edition of the CSPI Code seeks to address such possible confusion by asserting (para 4.7) that the term 'legal consultations' should be understood to encompass both consultations protected by legal privilege, and consultations not so protected because they are for the purpose of committing crime.

Turner v R [2013] EWCA Crim 642 sheds further light on the issue. Suspecting Turner of having murdered his girlfriend, police obtained approval from the Surveillance Commissioner to conduct *intrusive* surveillance in Turner's home. Recordings of conversations between Turner and his parents captured clear evidence of Turner's guilt and his parents' complicity. On appeal it was contended that the surveillance evidence captured legal privilege material and so should have been excluded from trial.

The appeal was dismissed: the court held:

- the 2010 Order (SI 2010/461) permitted the use of surveillance even where such surveillance might capture matters subject to legal privilege;
- the surveillance was lawful;
- there was no basis for suspecting a deliberate breach of legal privilege on the part of the police;
- at trial the judge had not admitted any evidence which might have been subject to legal privilege; and

- 'Nothing which became known to the surveillance officers resulted in any further or wider investigations, or produced a single item of incriminating material to strengthen the case against T, other than properly recorded observations that he made to his parents' (case reported by Tom Rees in the Criminal Law Review [2013] 12, 993–995; this quote from p 994 of the report).

In his commentary on this case report Andrew Roberts observed:

> Covert recording, if it is to secure its underlying objective, will be conducted in places in which the suspect is expected to engage in conversations that are likely to produce incriminating statements. If a suspect has sufficient trust in those with whom he is conversing to incriminate himself, there is every reason to suppose that he will share with them details of conversations that he has had with his legal advisors as to what his case ought to be at trial and how it might be presented. Therefore, **the risk of a violation of the privilege accompanies *all* instances of covert recording following a suspect's arrest and consultation with a lawyer**.
>
> (*Crim LR* [2013] 12, 995, emphasis added)

Because of this risk, as the Appeal Court noted: 'it is clear that arrangements for covert surveillance must focus attention on a need to preserve legal privilege, and where, for one reason or another, the relevant precautions have failed, to ensure that the interests of the potential defendant during the course of the investigation itself, or at any other subsequent trial, are not prejudiced in consequence', [2013] EWCA 642 at 24.

The 2010 Order requires (s 3(1)) that where directed surveillance on specified premises is likely to result in acquisition of legal consultation material, the surveillance must be regarded, treated, and accordingly authorized as *intrusive* surveillance.

Legal consultation is defined in the Order (s 2 (a)) as:

(i) a consultation between a professional legal adviser and his client or any person representing his client, or

(ii) a consultation between a professional legal adviser or his client or any such representative and a medical practitioner made in connection with or in contemplation of legal proceedings and for the purposes of such proceedings.

The specified premises are detailed in s 3(2) of the Order as follows:

(a) any place in which persons who are serving sentences of imprisonment or detention, remanded in custody or committed in custody for trial or sentence may be detained;

(b) any place in which persons may be detained under paragraph 16(1), (1A) or (2) of Schedule 2 or paragraph 2(2) or (3) of Schedule 3 to the Immigration Act 1971 or section 36(1) of the UK Border Act 2007;

(c) police stations;

(d) hospitals where high security psychiatric services are provided;

(e) the place of business of any professional legal adviser; and

(f) any place used for the sittings and business of any court, tribunal, inquest or inquiry.

Where planned directed surveillance is likely to capture legal consultation material, the surveillance must be regarded as being intrusive, and the appropriate authorization for *intrusive surveillance* sought accordingly.

The CSPI Code now devotes an entire chapter (Chapter 4) to discussion of issues concerning legally privileged and confidential information.

7.5 What Authority Regime Is Required for Intrusive Surveillance?

Authorizations for intrusive surveillance may be given by:

- Chief Constable or Commissioner of a police force as defined at 7.2, including the Ministry of Defence Police and British Transport Police
- Director General of the National Crime Agency
- The Chief Constable and Deputy Chief Constable, Police Service of Northern Ireland
- Any Assistant Commissioner of the Metropolitan Police Service
- A designated senior officer of HM Revenue and Customs
- A Provost Marshal in the Army, Royal Air Force, or Royal Navy
- The Secretary of State in relation to the intelligence agencies
- The Chair of the Competition and Markets Authority.

Section 34(2) RIPA2000 allows for a designated deputy to consider an application to authorize intrusive surveillance if it is not reasonably practicable for the senior authorizing officer to consider the application. It will only be considered not reasonably practicable for the senior authorizing officer to consider such an application if that individual is on annual leave, away from both home and the office, or cannot within a reasonable time access a secure telephone and fax machine.

Authorizations must generally be in writing but where the time taken to secure the appropriate written authorization would place life in danger or the investigation in jeopardy, then limited urgency provisions apply and these are outlined in paras 6.6–6.8 of the CSPI Code.

Authorizations last for three months and can be renewed for three months. They should be reviewed at monthly intervals or whenever there is a material change in circumstances affecting the validity of the authority. An urgent authority ceases to have effect 72 hours after it was granted (CSPI Code, paras

6.23–6.24); warrants issued to the intelligence agencies by the Secretary of State last for six months (CSPI Code, paras 6.21–6.22, see also paras 6.25–6.26).

Applications to conduct intrusive surveillance may only be made to, and considered by, investigators and authorizing officers working in the same organization or agency. Thus a police officer may only seek authority from, or grant authority to, a member of the same force. An exception to this general principle is made when two or more *police forces* have entered into a collaborative working agreement pursuant to s 23 of the Police Act 1996 (for English and Welsh forces), *and* the collaboration agreement permits applicants and authorizing officers to be from different forces. Where a collaborative working agreement is established for the purpose (*inter alia*) of facilitating intrusive surveillance or other forms of covert investigation, such agreements must document specific arrangements for the management of covert investigation between the partners. Authorizations granted by Her Majesty's Revenue and Customs (HMRC) or by the Competition and Markets Authority (CMA) can only be granted to an applicant from HMRC and CMA respectively (CSPI Code, para 6.9).

KEY POINT ON PROPORTIONALITY

The seriousness of the crime under investigation will not, in and of itself, provide a basis for meeting the proportionality test. Authorizing officers must articulate and document why the proposed method is *proportionate to the product it is intended to produce* (see Chapter 2.3.5). It is particularly important to consider whether the information sought could be obtained by less intrusive means, and to document such consideration.

KEY POINTS FOR AUTHORIZATIONS

- When considering combined authorities (s 33(5) RIPA2000) first identify whether this will lead to complications as a result of disclosure requirements.
- To ensure precision of applications (and therefore lawful authority), be careful to use words that are not ambiguous (for instance, 'monitor' is open to varied interpretation while 'listen' and 'watch' are more precise; use both if both are required).
- Do not use the term 'subject' without identifying the person.
- If an authorization is no longer necessary it must be cancelled and notice given to the OSC [now the IPCO] within four hours of signing the cancellation.
- Rank or position of the authorizing officer must be indicated on the authority and if the authorizing officer is a designated deputy this must also be indicated on the authority, as must the reason why the deputy has given the authority.
- Designated deputies can only authorize if the authorizing officer is too ill, on annual leave, or absent from their office or home and so not able to access a secure

---

telephone or fax machine within a reasonable time. The reason for the absence of the authorizing officer must be included in the application.

- The scope of an authority may not be expanded on renewal but it may be reduced. A new authority is required if the scope of the surveillance is to increase.

Authorizing officers must review and renew the authorities they gave.

OSC Annual Report 2005, section 4

(Although the OSC has been replaced by the ICPO, the considerations above remain valid and relevant.)

7.6 The Need for Prior Approval from the Investigatory Powers Commissioner's Office

Before any investigative action pursuant to the authority can be carried out, the authorizing officer must notify the IPCO in writing (s 35 RIPA2000). To make the authorization effective, *prior approval* is required from the IPCO *and* written notice of the IPCO approval has to be given to the person who granted the authorization (s 36(2) RIPA2000).

Surveillance cannot commence until the authorizing officer has received written approval from the IPCO.

If the authorizing officer considers the matter to be so urgent that prior approval cannot be sought, the authority will be effective upon written notification to the IPCO (s 36(3) RIPA2000), subject to the IPCO confirming or quashing the authority, having considered both whether it is an authority that would have received prior approval in normal circumstances *and* whether the circumstances in this case were really urgent.

Where the IPCO decides not to approve an authority or to quash an authority, the decision will be conveyed to the most senior relevant person in the organization concerned.

Prior approval has been withheld in cases where:

- the matter under investigation failed to meet the serious crime criteria;
- the proposed action was not necessary; or
- the proposed action would not have been of substantial value to the investigation (OSC *Annual Report 2001–02*, 8–9).

7.7 What Information Is Required in an Application for Intrusive Surveillance?

Written applications for intrusive surveillance authority should describe both the purpose of the operation/investigation and the conduct for which authorization is sought. CSPI Code, para 6.19 details further information that should be included in applications.

Further information and reading

Applications should be in writing and describe the conduct to be authorized and the purpose of the investigation or operation. The following matters must be covered in an application:

- an explanation of the *information or evidence* which it is desired to obtain as a result of the surveillance;
- the reasons why the authorization is *necessary* in the particular case and on the grounds listed in s 32(3) RIPA2000;
- the reasons why the surveillance is considered *proportionate* to what it seeks to achieve;
- an explanation as to why the information sought cannot reasonably be acquired by other means;
- the nature of the surveillance (ie precisely what actions investigators intend to take);
- precise details of the residential premises or private vehicle in relation to which the surveillance will take place;
- details of any potential *collateral intrusion* and why the collateral intrusion is justified (that which justifies the intrusive surveillance may not necessarily justify collateral intrusion);
- details of any *confidential information* that is likely to be obtained as a consequence of the surveillance.

A subsequent record should be made of whether authority was given or refused, by whom and the time and date.

In urgent cases the following should be recorded in writing as soon as practicable:

- the identities, where known, of those subject to surveillance;
- the nature and location of the surveillance;
- the reasons why the *authorizing officer* or the *officer* entitled to act in urgent cases considered the case so urgent that an oral instead of a written *authorization* was given; and/or
- the reasons why it was not reasonably practicable for the *application* to be considered by the *authorizing officer*.

CSPI Code, Chapter 6 deals with authorization procedures for intrusive surveillance. It should be read in conjunction with Chapter 2 (definitions) and Chapter 3 (general rules on authorizations).

Hint and tip: *In relation to confidential information (communications subject to legal privilege; confidential personal information; or confidential journalistic material), special rules of authorization exist when such material is likely to be gathered by a CHIS or as a consequence of property interference (including variously the need for authorization by more senior staff and IPCO prior approval). These rules are not reproduced for intrusive surveillance because such actions must have IPCO prior approval, regardless of whether confidential information is likely to be acquired. Nevertheless the likelihood of doing so must be brought to the attention of the IPCO in the application and authority.*

7.8 **Review and Renewal of Authorities**

The CSPI Code (para 3.23) stresses the need for regular reviews of intrusive surveillance authorities, the frequency of which should be set by the authorizing officer when first authorizing the application. Where intrusive surveillance is likely to obtain confidential information or there is a high degree of either direct or collateral intrusion it will be necessary to review relevant authorities more regularly. Reviews are the responsibility of the authorizing officer; they should be documented and retained for three years (see CSPI Code, Chapter 8).

Further information and reading

CSPI Code, paras 3.23–3.27 discuss the reviewing of covert investigation authorities. CSPI Code, paras 6.27–6.31 discuss the renewing of intrusive surveillance authorities.

7.9 **Cancellation of Authorities**

'The senior authorizing officer who granted or last renewed the authorization must cancel it, or the person who made the application to the Secretary of State must apply for its cancellation, if he is satisfied that the authorization no longer meets the criteria upon which it was authorized.' If this individual is no longer available, this statutory duty will fall to the person who has succeeded them in the relevant role (s 45 RIPA2000; CSPI Code, paras 6.32–6.34; Regulation of Investigatory Powers (Cancellation of Authorisations) Regulations 2000 (SI 2000/2794)).

The IPCO must be notified where authorities are cancelled.

KEY POINTS ON PROPORTIONALITY

Authorities and renewals last for a period of *three months* from when authorization is given. For *prior approval* this means authority from the Commissioner; thus if an authority was given at 0900 hours on 10 May, it expires at 2359 hours on 9 August. Authorities given under the urgency provisions last only *seventy-two hours.*

7.10 **Confidential Information**

Special considerations and some restrictions apply to surveillance likely to acquire confidential information or information from a legal consultation, although RIPA2000 and the PA97 are inconsistent in the approaches adopted towards such material.

Confidential information exists in four categories:

- Communications subject to legal privilege.
- Communication about constituency business between a Member of Parliament and another person.
- Personal information, expressly or by implication held in confidence, relating to the physical or mental health of an individual or to the spiritual counselling of an individual where that individual can be identified from the information concerned.
- Material held in confidence having been acquired or created for the purposes of journalism, including communications conveying information to be used for the purposes of journalism.

Confidential information that is acquired through surveillance and which is retained on record by the investigators must be reported to and made available to the OSC inspection team during the next inspection immediately following acquisition.

Any surveillance that is likely to capture information from legal consultations, including such information subsequently reported by one of the parties involved to third parties, is surveillance that must be authorized as intrusive surveillance (see also 7.4).

7.11 What Significant Case Law Has Been Decided in Relation to Intrusive Surveillance?

Key principles have been established or confirmed in case law both pre-RIPA2000 and post-RIPA2000 and from case law not directly concerning criminal investigations.

7.11.1 Private life

An initial issue for investigators and authorizing officers is the determination of whether surveillance will or is likely to obtain information about anyone's private life. Strasbourg has interpreted 'private life' and what might constitute information about private life very broadly. It is difficult to envisage any circumstances in which intrusive surveillance will not involve acquiring private information.

In *Peck v UK* (2003) 36 EHRR 41, in which CCTV footage of the aftermath of Peck's suicide attempt in a town centre was released to TV broadcasters by the local council whose CCTV system had captured the images, the court held: 'Private life is a broad term not susceptible to exhaustive definition ...

There is a zone of interaction of a person with others, even in a public context, which may fall within the scope of "private life"' (at 730, para H5).

In *Von Hannover v Germany* [2006] 43 EHRR 7, the court held that private life can take place in the public domain; just because something happens in the public domain does not mean it is not private. Reinforcement for the notion that privacy still exists within a public environment is also found in UK case law. In *Campbell v MGN* [2004] 2 AC 457 at 458, the court held that 'although the photographs of the claimant were taken in a public place, the context in which they were used … added to the overall intrusion into the claimant's life'.

Collateral intrusion of third-party privacy must also be considered and addressed. In *XXX & YYY v ZZZ* [2004] EWCA Civ 231, an *au pair* set up covert cameras in the home where she worked to record sexual advances from her male employer. The cameras also recorded the children, which was considered a breach of privacy.

Further information and reading

For a fuller discussion around the case law enforcement interpreting private life, see K Starmer, *European Human Rights Law* (Legal Action Group, London, 1999) paras 3.109–3.111; *Niemitz v Germany* (1993) 16 EHRR 97; *Costello-Roberts v UK* (1995) 19 EHRR 112; *Friedl v Austria* (1996) 21 EHRR 83; *Halford v UK* (1997) 24 EHRR 523; *Perry v UK* (2004) 39 EHRR 3 (although a case involving a breach of PACE, it has been applied by OSC inspectors when interpreting private life). See also OSC *Annual Report 2003–04*, 8. S McKay, *Covert Policing: Law and Practice* (Oxford University Press, Oxford, 2011) devotes Chapter 2 to the issues of privacy, proportionality, and other human rights issues.

7.11.2 Audio devices in police cells, exercise yards, and police vehicles

Several cases provide guidance about this intrusive surveillance tactic, two of which pre-date RIPA2000. Covert recording of suspects in custody for serious offences was held not to be contrary to PACE in *R v Mason and others* [2002] 2 Cr App R 38 at 648, para 77, in which Woolf LCJ determined:

> The police did no more than arrange a situation which was likely to result in the appellants volunteering confessions. The appellants were not tricked into saying what they did even though they were placed in a position where they were likely to do so. If evidence of a satisfactory nature could be obtained by other means, it is preferable that it is obtained by those means rather than covertly. Here, it was not unreasonably considered by the Chief Constable that the evidence would not be obtained by more conventional means.

R v Bailey and Smith [1993] 3 All ER 513 established the principle that conversations between co-defendants placed in the same cell after charge, which were recorded by police, could be admitted in evidence. Such admissibility was reconsidered in *R v Roberts (Stephen Paul)* [1997] 1 Cr App R 217, in which the Court of Appeal held that it was for the trial judge to determine admissibility on the merits of each case. The crucial test would be the conduct of the investigators and whether such conduct would result in an unfair trial.

The conduct of investigators was a key determining factor in three cases—*Sutherland*, *Sentence*, and *Grant*—arising from the deployment of audio surveillance devices in police station exercise yards by Lincolnshire Police. In each case the surveillance devices recorded conversations between suspects and their legal representatives—conversations that were legally privileged. In each case Lincolnshire police asserted that the capture of such conversations had been inadvertent.

In *R v Sutherland* the judge stayed proceedings to prevent abuse of process because he concluded that the police had acted in bad faith and that the recording of privileged conversations had been deliberate, not inadvertent (unreported, Nottingham Crown Court, 29 January 2002; discussed in *Archbold's Criminal Pleading, Evidence and Practice* (revd edn, Sweet & Maxwell, London, 2005) para 15–532, at 1626; cited in *R v Mason and others* [2002] 2 Cr App R 38 at 643, para 60).

In *R v Sentence* a defence application to stay proceedings due to a breach of process was also successful, the judge determining that the circumstances were identical to those in *Sutherland* and concluding:

> It is plain that I have not been told the whole truth by several police officers, namely ... I am driven by all the evidence in this case to the clear conclusion on the balance of probabilities that there was a planned and deliberate capture of privileged conversation between a solicitor and his client [...]. This is not a case of a chapter of accidents or a comedy of errors.
>
> (Transcript 64E–65A, 1 April 2004, HH Judge Heath, Lincoln Crown Court)

In quashing Grant's conviction the Court of Appeal, *R v Grant* [2005] EWCA Crim 1089, rejected the trial judge's acceptance of such police tactics and doubted his acceptance from police officers at the *voir dire*, *Sutherland* and *Sentence* notwithstanding, that the possibility of privileged conversations being recorded in such circumstances had not crossed their minds. The Court of Appeal found that police investigators had deliberately interfered with the appellant's rights so acting in bad faith.

Where the content of legal consultations is likely to be captured through surveillance, that surveillance is to be treated as intrusive and authorized accordingly. Whereas a prison cell is considered to be a residential premises, a police cell is not considered to be residential premises (unless it is being used as temporary prison accommodation) (CSPI Code, para 2.16).

In *R v Plunkett (Daniel Michael)* [2013] EWCA Crim 261; [2013] 1 WLR 3121 (CA (Crim Div)), the court held that a police vehicle was not a private vehicle because it was owned and used solely for police purposes. Consequently the covert audio recording of conversations between suspects in the back of a police van did not require an intrusive surveillance authorization: an authorization for directed surveillance sufficed.

7.11.3 **Protection of observation posts**

Recognizing that failure to secure observation posts from which to conduct surveillance could seriously impede legitimate investigations, the Court of Appeal applied, in *R v Rankine* [1986] 1 QB 861, the same presumption of protection applied to human sources of information, namely that the identity of locations used should be protected unless doing so would lead to a miscarriage of justice. Minimum evidential standards were applied to this principle in *R v Johnson* [1988] 1 WLR 1377, confirmed by *R v Hewitt and Davis* (1992) 95 Cr App R 81 and *R v Grimes* [1994] Crim LR 213.

....

Case law criteria: *R v Johnson* [1988] 1 WLR 1377

The criteria set out in *R v Johnson* are reproduced in the ACPO *Practice Advice on Core Investigative Doctrine* (2005) 104:

The police officer in charge of observations of a rank not lower than sergeant must be able to testify that beforehand he or she visited all the observation places to be used and ascertained the attitude of the occupiers of the premises:

- as to the use of the premises;
- to the disclosure of the use of the premises;
- to the possible identification of the premises or the occupiers;
- the difficulties, if any are encountered, in obtaining observation posts in the area.

In addition, immediately prior to the trial, an officer of a rank not lower than chief inspector must be able to testify that he visited the premises used for observations and ascertained if the occupiers are the same as when the observations were conducted and, whether they are or not, what their attitude is to:

- the possible disclosure of the use made of the premises;
- the disclosure of facts which would lead to the identification of those premises and their occupiers.

This evidence will be given in the absence of the jury when the application to exclude the material evidence is made. The judge should explain to the jury the effect of his or her ruling regarding the disclosure of the premises.

....

Because exposure of unmarked police vehicles would not necessarily involve the same threat of harassment or fear of violence that members of the public who make premises available for observation posts might face (*Blake and Austin v DPP* (1993) 97 Cr App R 169), the same presumption of protection would not, as a matter of policy, be applied to police vehicles from which observations were conducted (*R v Brown and Daley* (1988) 87 Cr App R 52).

7.11.4 Disclosure of surveillance authorizations

The statutory presumption of disclosure is founded in the CPIA. Because surveillance authorities may contain sensitive detail exposure of which would be against the public interest, such authorities may be scheduled as sensitive unused material. Unless the requirements of the disclosure regime are directly engaged, for example, the authorization documentation contains material that tends to undermine the prosecution case or will assist the defence case, authorization documentation will not normally be disclosed (*R v GS* [2005] EWCA Crim 887; see also *R v Jones* [2010] EWCA Crime 925).

It is the prosecutor's responsibility to ensure proper disclosure of any material falling within the disclosure regime, including authorization material (*R v GS* [2005] EWCA Crim 887). It is the investigator's responsibility to *reveal* all information to the prosecutor so that the prosecutor can properly discharge his or her duties in relation to what information should be *disclosed*.

If the prosecutor recognizes contentious issues regarding the authorization process, a redacted version of the authority should be disclosed and an unedited version supplied to the judge for determination that the defendant is not vulnerable to a miscarriage arising from non-disclosure (*R v Hardy and Hardy* [2002] EWCA Crim 3012). The defence cannot go on fishing trips and, if seeking to challenge admissibility and a ruling under s 78 PACE, must have convincing reasons for doing so (*R v GS* [2005] EWCA Crim 887). Where the defence declare specific issues with the authorization process, as in *R v Grant* [2005] EWCA Crim 1089, full disclosure of all documentation related to a covert investigation authorization may be ordered. In cases involving *intrusive* surveillance, a court may rely on the approval forms signed by the Surveillance Commissioner as independent evidence of lawful authorization (*R v GS* [2005] EWCA Crim 887). In *R v Harmes* [2006] EWCA Crim 928, the court considered the authorization documentation in detail, noting (at para 22) that renewals of the authorization had failed to detail either changes in circumstances or changes in planned police activity, and concluding (at para 42) that 'there were serious breaches of the Act and the Code in the process of authorization'.

Checklist of key issues when considering whether or not to deploy covert investigation techniques

- What evidence or intelligence is being sought?

- How is it relevant to the operation under consideration?

- What is the least intrusive means of securing such evidence or information?

- Has the least intrusive means of securing the evidence or information been attempted? If not, why not?

- What is the likelihood of collateral intrusion against the privacy of persons not being investigated? How will collateral intrusion be prevented (or if not, minimized) and how will the product of collateral intrusion be managed?

- What are the risks to the organization of such tactics? (Chapter 4)

- What are the risks to the organization's staff of such tactics? (Chapter 4)

- What are the risks to the public or specific third parties when such tactics are deployed? (Chapter 4)

- What are the risks to the subject of the investigation? (Chapter4)

- Will the proposed methods breach Article 8(1)? (Chapter 2.2)

- Is there justification for doing so provided by Article 8(2)? (Chapter 2.2)

- How is the legality test met? (Chapter 2.2.3)

- How is the legitimacy test met? (Chapter 2.2.4)

- How is the necessity test met? (Chapter 2.2.5)

- How is the proportionality test met? (Chapter 2.2.5)

- Are the arguments justifying the application to use covert investigation based on reliable information/intelligence, or has the applicant adopted a 'tick-the-box' approach to completing the application without giving full consideration to the facts of the case and the issues arising?

- Have the arguments justifying the granting of authorization to use covert investigation been fully articulated, or has the authorizing officer merely paid lip service to the pro forma authorization template via which authority is granted?

- When should this authority be reviewed? What circumstances will or may arise that will necessitate review before then?

- How are the methods by which the evidence/intelligence will be obtained to be protected at trial? (Chapter 5)

- How will the product of the surveillance be managed? (Chapter 5)

Planning covert investigation actions

Remember to include the PLAN for covert investigation tactics in all investigation policy-book entries relating to covert investigation considerations and decisions.

P Proportionality

Why is it proportionate to obtain the intended product of this surveillance in the manner proposed? (Chapter 2.2.5)

L Legitimacy

What is the legitimate purpose of the proposed action: the prevention of disorder or crime; the interests of national security; the interests of public safety; the interests of the economic well-being of the country; the protection of health or morals; the protection of the rights and freedoms of others? (Chapter 2.2.4)

A Authority to Undertake Proposed Action

What is the lawful foundation and authority for the proposed action? From whom must authorization be sought? (Chapter 2.2.3)

N Necessity of Proposed Action

Why is the proposed action necessary? (Chapter 2.2.5)

8

Interference with Property and Entry onto Land or Equipment

8.1 **Introduction**

Certain tactics that facilitate covert investigation, particularly intrusive surveillance, involve actions that constitute crimes or torts. The deployment of a
listening device at private residential premises or the attachment of a location-
tracking device to a vehicle, for instance, will certainly involve trespass and could
involve criminal damage being caused. Part III PA97 and Part 5 IPA2016 provide
the statutory regimes under which such actions may be authorized and so *rendered lawful within the context of the authorized action*. The IPA2016 has the effect
of reducing the scope of Part III PA97. Part 5 IPA2016 specifically provides an
authority regime for interfering with any equipment producing 'electromagnetic, acoustic or other transmissions and any device capable of being used with
such equipment'. Examples of such equipment include computers, tablets, smart
phones, data storage devices and associated peripherals such as cabling and wires
(Equipment Interference Code of Practice, paras 2.1–2.2). Interference with such
equipment can no longer be authorized under Part III PA97 (see Chapter 9).

Authorizations for property interference or entry onto land should be sought
wherever members of the empowered organizations 'or persons acting on their
behalf, conduct entry on, or interference with, property that would be otherwise unlawful' (CSPI Code, para 7.1). The 1997 Act, enacted to address the
issues raised in *Khan* in which existing Home Office guidelines were held to fail
the ECHR legality test, did not make provision for surveillance itself, hence the
need to provide an additional statutory regime for surveillance in RIPA2000.

Because property interference will often be a prerequisite for intrusive surveillance under RIPA2000, provision is made for combined authorizations to
be made where authority is required for property interference and for intrusive
surveillance in order to complete a single operation within an investigation.
For combined authorizations, all the authorization criteria, both for property
interference and for intrusive surveillance, must be considered separately by the
authorizing officer (CSPI Code, para 7.3). The arguments justifying the necessity and the proportionality of an intrusive surveillance tactic may not found
justification for the necessity or the proportionality of interfering with property
in order to conduct the intrusive surveillance: for example, if in the particular
circumstances an externally located audio sensor will capture conversations inside a dwelling, there will be no justification for interfering with the property
in order to deploy an audio sensor within the dwelling.

Further information and reading

R v Khan [1997] AC 558; *Khan v UK* (2001) 31 EHRR 45; see also K Starmer,
European Human Rights Law (Legal Action Group, London, 1999).

    M Strange and Q Whitaker, *Criminal Justice, Police Powers and Human Rights*
(Blackstone Press, London, 2001), 37.

    B Emmerson and D Friedman, *A Guide to the Police Act 1997* (Butterworths,
London, 1998), 4.

A revised Code of Practice for Covert Surveillance and Property Interference has been published. The new Code of Practice for Covert Surveillance and Property Interference is available online at <https://www.gov.uk/government/collections/ripa-codes> (accessed July 2015). In this volume 'CSPI Code' refers to this Code.

Applicants and authorizing officers, when considering property interference and the need for an authorization, should consider:

- whether anyone is in a position to consent to the interference, and whether such consent can be obtained without compromising the operation;
- whether the proposed action can be reconfigured so as to avoid property interference; and
- whether the interference is so minor as to be insignificant and is therefore rendered lawful by virtue of s 27(2) RIPA2000.

Section 27(2) RIPA2000 states that a person shall not be subject to *civil* liability in respect of any conduct that is incidental to the authorized conduct and which cannot be otherwise authorized and might reasonably not have been anticipated when seeking the original authorization.

8.2 Which Public Authorities May Interfere with Property and Enter onto Land?

The following organizations may carry out these aspects of covert investigation:

- Police forces in England and Wales maintained under s 2 Police Act 1996
- The Metropolitan Police
- The City of London Police
- The Police Service of Scotland
- The Police Service of Northern Ireland
- HM Revenue and Customs
- The National Crime Agency
- The Competition Markets Authority.

The organizations are defined by reference to who may authorize such interference and entry (s 93(5) PA97) and, in the case of the intelligence agencies, by virtue of s 5 Intelligence Services Act 1994.

8.3 What Powers Does the Law Provide in Relation to Interference with Property and Entry onto Land?

Investigators can take such action, in respect of property or wireless telegraphy in the relevant area, as is specified in the authorization (s 93(1) PA97). Authorizing officers must document explicitly what is being authorized. Thus in relation to the placing of an audio sensor inside residential premises, for example, *every action required to achieve this objective* must be specifically authorized: separate reconnoitring operations to determine feasibility prior to the actual deployment and subsequent operations to retrieve the device may require separate authorizations.

Certain criteria must be present for the power to be applied.

KEY POINT FOR AUTHORIZING OFFICERS

Before authorizing such action as may be required, the authorizing officer must believe:

(a) that the taking of the action specified is *necessary* for the purpose of preventing or detecting *serious crime* (or, where the authorizing officer is the Chair of the CMA, that the taking of the action specified is necessary for preventing or detecting an offence under s 188 Enterprise Act 2002); and

(b) that the taking of such action is *proportionate* to what the action seeks to achieve (s 93(2) PA97).

When considering proportionality, applicants and authorizing officers will have to take into account that increasingly sophisticated surveillance technology may negate the need for property interference: for instance, external monitoring of conversations within a premises rather than internal monitoring.

Section 93(2A) PA97 provides that where the authorizing officer is the Chief Constable or Deputy Chief Constable of the Police Service of Northern Ireland, the reference to serious crime is taken to include the interests of national security, but note that:

An authorizing officer in a public authority other than the Security Service shall not issue an authorization under Part III of the 1997 Act where the investigation or operation falls within the responsibilities of the Security Service.

CSPI Code, para 7.10, footnote 46

8.3.1 Definition of serious crime

Conduct will constitute serious crime if:

(a) it involves the use of violence, or it results in substantial financial gain, or it is conducted by a large number of persons in pursuit of a common purpose; or

(b) the offence, or one of the offences, is an offence for which a person who has attained the age of twenty-one and has no previous convictions could reasonably be expected to be sentenced to imprisonment for a term of three years or more (s 93(4) PA97).

Note: This statutory definition is worded slightly differently from, but appears to have influenced, the definition of serious crime in ss 81(2)(b) and 81(3) RIPA2000 which sets the threshold for recourse to intrusive surveillance.

8.4 What Authority Regime Is Required for Interference with Property and Entry onto Land?

Where the criteria in 8.3 are met, the following may authorize such interference (s 93(5) PA97), in some circumstances (described at 8.5) subject to the prior approval of the OSC:

- Chief Constable (police forces in England, Wales, and Scotland)
- Commissioner or Assistant Commissioner (Metropolitan Police)
- Commissioner (City of London Police)
- Chief Constable and Deputy Chief Constable Police Service of Northern Ireland
- A designated authorizing officer within the National Crime Agency
- Chief Constable British Transport Police
- Chief Constable Ministry of Defence Police
- Provost Marshals in the Army, Royal Navy, and Royal Air Force
- Any customs officer designated by the Commissioners of Revenue and Customs for this purpose.

Where it is not reasonably practicable to obtain the authority of the authorizing officer identified above, the Act specifies that designated deputies may make such authorizations (s 94 PA97).

The default position set out in RIPA2000 and PA97 is that authorizations may only be given to applicants from the same organization as the authorizing officer. However, pursuant to ss 1 and 157 Police and Crime Act 2017, which consolidate and enhance public service collaboration arrangements, all 43 police forces and Police and Crime Commissioners have signed a National Collaboration Agreement that permits a Senior Authorizing Officer authorizing interference with property under s 93 PA97 to issue authorities 'not only in relation to their own force area but, where necessary and proportionate, in relation to other force areas' (OSC *Annual Report 2016–17*, para 5.1).

KEY POINTS ON PROPERTY INTERFERENCE AUTHORIZATION TIMESCALES

Property interference authorities are effective from the time of signing, but authorizations are notified to the Commissioner for scrutiny. Those categories of property interference authorities requiring prior approval (see 8.5) are only effective from the time the authorizing officer receives written approval from the IPC.

Authorizations, renewals, and cancellations should be notified to the IPC within *four working hours* of being given. In the case of *prior approval* authorizations, notifications should be sent to the IPC *at least sixteen working hours* before surveillance is due to start. Decisions on *prior approval* applications from Commissioners should be received within eight working hours.

KEY POINTS ON DRAFTING APPLICATIONS AND AUTHORITIES

- When considering combined authorities (s 33(5) RIPA2000), first identify whether this will lead to complications as a result of disclosure requirements.
- To ensure precision of applications (and therefore lawful authority), be careful to use words that are not ambiguous (for instance, 'monitor' is open to varied interpretation, while 'listen' and 'watch' are more precise; use both if both are required).

KEY POINTS FOR AUTHORIZING OFFICERS

- Do not use the term 'subject' without identifying the person.
- If an authorization is no longer necessary it must be cancelled and notice given to the IPC within four hours of signing the cancellation.
- Rank or position of the authorizing officer must be indicated on the authority and if the authorizing officer is a designated deputy, this must also be indicated on the authority, as must the reason why the deputy has given the authority.
- Designated deputies can only authorize if the authorizing officer is too ill, on annual leave, or absent from their office or home and so not able to access a secure telephone or fax machine within a reasonable time. The reason for the absence of the authorizing officer must be included in the application.
- The scope of an authority may not be expanded on renewal but it may be reduced. A new authority is required if the scope of the surveillance is to increase.

Authorizing officers must review and renew the authorities they gave.

(OSC *Annual Report* 2005, section 4)

The seriousness of the crime under investigation will not, in and of itself, provide a basis for meeting the proportionality test. Authorizing officers must articulate and document why the proposed method is proportionate to the product it is intended to produce (see Chapter 2.2.5).

Authorizations for such interference with or entry onto property must be in writing and will last for three months (s 95 PA97). Authorities issued orally in matters of urgency have effect for seventy-two hours only.

Authorizing officers may only authorize applications made by members of their organization (s 93(3)) and may only authorize activity with the relevant area over which they have jurisdiction (s 93(6)). In each case this includes, where appropriate, the twelve nautical miles of territorial waters adjacent to the relevant area.

Section 96 imposes on authorizing officers the obligation to notify the IPC as soon as reasonably practicable when granting, renewing, or cancelling any authority.

It is accepted that occasionally incidental property interference will occur. No civil liability arises where such conduct is 'incidental to correctly authorized, directed or intrusive surveillance activity and for which an authorization or warrant is not capable of being granted or might not reasonably have been expected to be sought under any existing legislation' (CSPI Code, para 7.6). Authorization should be sought whenever it might be reasonably expected to do so and the public authority concerned is capable of doing so (CSPI Code, para 7.7).

The acquisition of samples (DNA, fingerprints, footwear impressions) is not itself unlawful interference with property if no damage is caused during the acquisition. Authorization will be required where it is necessary to interfere with property in order 'to access and obtain the samples' (CSPI Code, para 7.8).

8.5 The Need for Prior Approval from the Investigatory Powers Commissioner

Prior approval must be sought from the IPC before the authorized activity can take place when the property specified in the authority (s 97(2) PA97):

- is wholly or mainly used as a dwelling
- is a hotel bedroom
- constitutes office premises

or when the action authorized is likely to result in the acquisition of knowledge about:

- matters subject to legal privilege (defined in s 98)
- confidential personal information (defined in s 99)
- confidential journalistic material (defined in s 100).

In such circumstances the authorized action can only commence once the authorizing officer has received written approval from the IPC (CSPI Code, para 7.25), which will only be given if the Commissioner holds the beliefs specified at s 93(2) (see 'Key points for authorizing officers' box on p 139). Where prior approval is refused, the authorizing officer shall be given a report explaining why. Appeals against a refusal may be made to the Chief Commissioner in the manner prescribed in s 104.

The interference may not take place until the approval has been communicated by the IPC to the authorizing officer.

An authority granted by an authorizing officer to interfere with property that is not a dwelling, a hotel bedroom, or office premises does not require prior approval from the Surveillance Commissioner.

A combined property interference and intrusive surveillance authority will always require prior approval because of the intrusive surveillance element.

8.6 What Information Is Required in an Application for Interference with Property?

Written applications for authority to interfere with property should describe both the purpose of the operation/investigation and the conduct for which authorization is sought. CSPI Code, para 7.18 details further information that should be included in applications.

Further information and reading

Applications should be in writing and describe the conduct to be authorized and the purpose of the investigation or operation. The following matters must be covered in an application:

- the identity or identities, where known, of those who possess the property that is to be subject to the interference;
- sufficient information to identify the property which the entry or interference will affect;
- the nature and extent of the proposed interference; the details of any collateral intrusion, including the identity of individuals and/or categories of people, where known, who are likely to be affected, and why the intrusion is justified;
- details of the offence suspected or committed;
- how the authorization criteria (as set out above) have been met;
- any action which may be necessary to maintain any equipment, including replacing it;
- any action which may be necessary to retrieve any equipment;
- in case of a renewal, the results obtained so far, or a full explanation of the failure to obtain any results; and
- whether an authorization was given or refused, by whom and the time and date on which this happened.

In urgent cases the above information should be supplied orally, but as soon as reasonably practicable the applicant and the authorizing officer should record in writing:

- the identity or identities, where known, of those owning or using the property;
- sufficient information to identify the affected property;
- details of the offence suspected or committed;
- the reasons why the authorizing officer considered the case so urgent that an oral authority was issued instead of a written authority; and

---

> • if relevant, the reason why it was not reasonably practicable for the application to be considered by the authorizing officer or designated deputy.
>
> See CSPI Code, paras 7.18–7.19.

8.7 Review and Renewal of Authorities

The CSPI Code (para 3.23) stresses the need for regular reviews of intrusive surveillance authorities, the frequency of which should be set by the authorizing officer when first authorizing the application. Where intrusive surveillance is likely to obtain confidential information or there is a high degree of ether direct or collateral intrusion it will be necessary to review relevant authorities more regularly. Reviews are the responsibility of the authorizing officer; they should be documented and retained for three years (see CSPI Code, Chapter 8).

> **Further information and reading**
>
> CSPI Code, paras 3.23–3.27 discuss the reviewing of covert investigation authorities.
>   CSPI Code, paras 7.27–7.29 discuss the renewing of property interference authorities.

8.8 Cancellation of Authorities

'The senior authorizing officer who granted or last renewed the authorization must cancel it, or the person who made the application to the Secretary of State must apply for its cancellation, if he is satisfied that the authorization no longer meets the criteria upon which it was authorized.' If this individual is no longer available, this statutory duty will fall to the person who has succeeded them in the relevant role (s 95(5) PA97; CSPI Code, paras 7.30–7.32; the Police Act 1997 (Notification of Authorisations etc) Order 1998 (SI 1998/3241)).

8.9 What Significant Case Law Has Been Decided in Relation to Property Interference and Entry onto Land?

In September 1992 Khan, together with his cousin N, entered the UK at Manchester airport. They were detained by HMCE. N was found to be in possession of heroin with a street value of £100,000 and was prosecuted. In interview

Khan made no admissions and, in the absence of other evidence, was not proceeded against.

In January 1993 police deployed a listening device at the house of B in Sheffield who was under separate suspicion of heroin dealing. Deployment of the device involved trespass and minor criminal damage. Unknown to police at the time, B was an associate of Khan. Khan visited B whilst the listening device was deployed and recording. The listening device recorded a casual conversation between B and Khan, in which the latter described his involvement in the heroin shipment the previous September for which N had been convicted. This recording was relied upon in evidence in the prosecution of Khan for importation.

Khan sought exclusion of the recording in a *voir dire* arguing that the Home Office Guidelines (deposited in the library of the House of Commons and available on application from the Home Office) under which the surveillance had been conducted did not constitute law and so breached Article 8(2). The judge admitted the evidence as being relevant regardless of any ECHR breach. The Court of Appeal subsequently held he was right to do so (*R v Khan* [1997] AC 558).

The ECtHR subsequently held that the deployment of the device in the absence of a statutory regime constituted a violation of Article 8(2), but the use of the evidence obtained thereby did not constitute a violation of Article 6, nor had the investigators acted in bad faith because they had complied with the prevailing regime even though it subsequently was held to be unlawful (*Khan v UK* (2001) 31 EHRR 45). This decision followed the principles previously asserted in *Govell v UK* (1997) 23 EHRR CD101 and was reasserted in *Lewis v UK* (2004) 39 EHRR 9.

This finding highlighted the need for the statutory regime subsequently established in Part III PA97 and reaffirmed the principle that relevant evidence unlawfully obtained may yet be admitted by the court.

Interference with property scenario

Mr Leonard is believed to be a money-launderer from a group involved in people trafficking. His refuse is collected weekly from the front drive of his house. It is desired to examine the contents of the refuse to ascertain details of any bank accounts he may have. In order to do this investigators will need to enter the front drive of Mr Leonard's house and remove the refuse bags.

In order to enter the driveway of the house (a private property), a property interference authority will be required. The refuse bags, although abandoned by the owner, still remain property because they have only been abandoned in favour of the refuse collector. Therefore, investigators will also require an authority to interfere with the refuse bags. This would also be true if the refuse bags were left outside the perimeter of the premises on the public highway.

(OSC *Annual Report* 2005, 4.7)

Checklist of key issues when considering whether or not to deploy covert investigation techniques

- What evidence or intelligence is being sought?

- How is it relevant to the operation under consideration?

- What is the least intrusive means of securing such evidence or information?

- Has the least intrusive means of securing the evidence or information been attempted? If not, why not?

- What is the likelihood of collateral intrusion against the privacy of persons not being investigated? How will collateral intrusion be prevented (or if not, minimized) and how will the product of collateral intrusion be managed?

- What are the risks to the organization of such tactics? (Chapter 4)

- What are the risks to the organization's staff of such tactics? (Chapter 4)

- What are the risks to the public or specific third parties when such tactics are deployed? (Chapter 4)

- What are the risks to the subject of the investigation? (Chapter 4)

- Will the proposed methods breach Article 8(1)? (Chapter 2.2)

- Is there justification for doing so provided by Article 8(2)? (Chapter 2.2)

- How is the legality test met? (Chapter 2.2.3)

- How is the legitimacy test met? (Chapter 2.2.4)

- How is the necessity test met? (Chapter 2.2.5)

- How is the proportionality test met? (Chapter 2.2.5)

- Are the arguments justifying the application to use covert investigation based on reliable information/intelligence, or has the applicant adopted a 'tick-the-box' approach to completing the application without giving full consideration to the facts of the case and the issues arising?

- Have the arguments justifying the granting of authorization to use covert investigation been fully articulated, or has the authorizing officer merely paid lip service to the pro forma authorization template via which authority is granted?

- When should this authority be reviewed? What circumstances will or may arise that will necessitate review before then?

- How are the methods by which the evidence/intelligence will be obtained to be protected at trial? (Chapter 5)

- How will the product of the surveillance be managed? (Chapter 5)

Planning covert investigation actions

Remember to include the PLAN for covert investigation tactics in all investigation policy-book entries relating to covert investigation considerations and decisions.

P Proportionality

Why is it proportionate to obtain the intended product of this surveillance in the manner proposed? (Chapter 2.2.5)

L Legitimacy

What is the legitimate purpose of the proposed action: the prevention of disorder or crime; the interests of national security; the interests of public safety; the interests of the economic well-being of the country; the protection of health or morals; the protection of the rights and freedoms of others? (Chapter 2.2.4)

A Authority to Undertake Proposed Action

What is the lawful foundation and authority for the proposed action? From whom must authorization be sought? (Chapter 2.2.3)

N Necessity of Proposed Action

Why is the proposed action necessary? (Chapter 2.2.5)

Covert Investigation Involving Computers

Computers can be the scene of a crime (victim evidence), the means by which a crime is planned or committed (offender evidence; intelligence), a means of communication when facilitating a conspiracy (offence and offender evidence; intelligence), and a means of (covertly) investigating crime. Consequently, covert investigation engages computers both as the object under investigation and as a tool used by investigators (to intercept communications, to identify and secure digital evidence/intelligence, or to engage in an interactive relationship for a covert purpose). Precision in the drafting of applications and authorities relating to computers is thus very important, especially so given the multiple roles of the computer within covert investigation.

This remains an area of fast-developing technology and slowly evolving law; an area in which investigators without expertise in hi-tech crime investigation would be well advised to seek up-to-date advice from computer crime investigators when planning covert operations. This chapter, which focuses on law enforcement investigations rather than on intelligence community matters, should be seen as a general introduction to a rapidly evolving arena.

This is also an area in which particular attention must be made to collateral intrusion since the surveillance can be focused on the use made of a computer rather than direct surveillance of a person. Since in any given household more than one person might use any given computer, the potential for collateral intrusion when monitoring computer use is particularly high and careful consideration to the potential for and management of such intrusion will be required in both applications and authorities. No intrusion can be authorized that is disproportionate to the information that is expected to be obtained as a result of this particular investigation tactic.

Further information and reading

A new Equipment Interference Code of Practice has been published, pursuant to s 7 IPA2016. It is available online at <https://www.gov.uk/government/publications/equipment-interference-code-of-practice> (accessed 23 January 2018). In this volume 'EI Code' refers to this Code.

9.1 Computers as the Object of Covert Investigation

The covert examination of computers will involve some form of interference with the target computer, which conduct is likely to constitute an offence under the Computer Misuse Act 1990. To render lawful conduct that would otherwise be criminal, precise and proper authorization must exist and the IPA2016 establishes a new equipment interference authority regime that removes such conduct from the auspices of Part III PA97, the scope of which is consequently narrowed.

Equipment is defined as comprising any equipment producing or capable of producing 'electromagnetic, acoustic or other emissions'. This definition is intended to be technology neutral. The definition encompasses all types of computers, tablets, smart phones, any device that is internet-enabled (thus all devices networked to form part of the 'internet of things'), digital data storage devices, and peripherals such as cabling and wires (EI Code, paras 2.1–2.2).

Equipment data is defined as 'systems data' and 'identifying data' (the latter being data logically associated with a communication but which is capable of being logically separated from the communication so as to be amenable for investigation without the contents and meaning of the communication being known) (s 263 IPA2016).

Part 5 IPA2016 provides for three types of warrant:

- A targeted equipment interference warrant (s 99(2) IPA2016);
- A targeted examination warrant (s 99(9) IPA2016); and
- A bulk equipment interference warrant (s 176 IPA2016, which provisions falls under Part 6 IPA2016).

The last of these is restricted to the use of the intelligence and security services and will not be considered further here.

9.1.1 When may an equipment interference warrant be issued to law enforcement investigators?

A law enforcement chief may issue a targeted equipment interference (EI) warrant for a period up to six months (s 116 IPA2016; five days if issued as an urgent warrant) to an appropriate law enforcement officer in relation to the chief if the following criteria are met:

(a) The law enforcement chief considers that the warrant is necessary for the purposes of preventing or detecting serious crime;
(b) The law enforcement chief considers that the conduct authorized by the warrant is proportionate to what is sought to be achieved by that conduct;
(c) The law enforcement chief considers that satisfactory arrangements have been made relating to safeguarding the retention and disclosure of material;
(d) Prior approval of the decision to issue the warrant has been granted by the IPC or a Judicial Commissioner before the warrant is issued (except in cases of urgency) (s 106 IPA2016; see also ss 108–109); and
(e) There is a British Islands connection (s 107 IPA2016, with 'British Islands connection' being defined at s 107(4)).

The relevant law enforcement chiefs are identified in Parts 1 and 2 or Schedule 6 to the IPA2016 and include:

- The Chief Constable of a police force maintained under s 2 Police Act 1996;
- The Commissioner or Assistant Commissioner of the metropolitan Police Service;
- The Commissioner of the City of London Police;
- The Chief Constable of the Police Service of Scotland;
- The Chief Constable or Deputy Chief Constable of the Police Service of Northern Ireland;
- The Director General of the National Crime Agency;
- The Chief Constable of the British Transport Police;
- The Chief Constable of the Ministry of Defence Police;
- The Provost Marshalls of the Royal Navy Police, the Royal Military Police and the Royal Air Force Police;
- A senior immigration official designated for this purpose by the Secretary of State;
- A senior HMRC official who is designated for this purpose by the Secretary of State or the Commissioner of HMRC;
- The Chair of the Competition and Markets Authority;
- The Police and Investigations Review Commissioner.

On application by the Director General of the Security Service, the Chief of the Secret Intelligence Service, the Director of GCHQ, or the Chief of Defence Intelligence, the Secretary of State may issue a targeted EI warrant if the Secretary of State considers the warrant necessary in the interests of national security; for the purpose of preventing or detecting serious crime; or in the interests of the economic well-being of the UK so far as those interests are relevant to the interests of national security (s 102 IPA2016: similar powers in relation to MI5, MI6, and GCHQ apply to the Scottish Ministers, s 103 IPA2016).

Section 14 of IPA2016 restricts the effect of s 93 PA97. An interference with property authorization under s 93 PA97 must not be used for the obtaining of communications, private information, or equipment data if the conduct would constitute an offence against the Computer Misuse Act 1990. In such circumstances an equipment interference warrant must be sought unless another statutory search power applies (EI Code, para 3.27).

9.1.2 What does a targeted equipment interference warrant allow?

An equipment interference warrant allows a range of methods or conduct to be used to obtain communications, equipment data, or other information. EI Code, para 3.3 provides examples to illustrate the range of methods that may be used, and these include the covert downloading of data from unattended devices, use of a user's login without their knowledge, and the utilization of software applications or vulnerabilities.

To the extent that surveillance is necessary and is used to obtain communications, equipment data, or other information, an equipment interference warrant may include authorization of such surveillance for these purposes without the need for separate authorization under RIPA2000 (EI Code, para 3.17).

EI product may be used in evidence. It is therefore especially important to ensure interference is accurately authorized to ensure that the evidence is not challenged as being unfairly prejudicial, thus rendering it liable to being deemed inadmissible and being excluded under s 78 PACE.

Persons, equipment, and locations that can lawfully be the subject of a targeted EI warrant are listed in s 101 IPA2016 (see also EI Code, paras 5.7–5.18):

(a) equipment belonging to, used by, or in the possession of a particular person or organization;

(b) equipment belonging to, used by, or in the possession of a group of persons who share a common purpose or who carry on, or may carry on, a particular activity;

(c) equipment belonging to, used by, or in the possession of more than one person or organization, where the interference is for the purpose of a single investigation or operation;

(d) equipment in a particular location;

(e) equipment in more than one location, where the interference is for the purpose of a single investigation or operation;

(f) equipment which is being, or may be, used for the purposes of a particular activity or activities of a particular description;

(g) equipment which is being, or may be, used to test, maintain, or develop capabilities relating to interference with equipment for the purpose of obtaining communications, equipment data, or other information;

(h) equipment which is being, or may be, used for the training of persons who carry out, or are likely to carry out, such interference with equipment.

The requirements that a warrant must satisfy in relation to these subjects are set out in tabulated form in s 115(3) and (4) IPA2016. If an EI warrant is thematic in nature, instead of being specially directed towards a particular person, organization, or location, being directed towards a group of people sharing a common aim, then the warrant should describe or name as many of the persons comprising that group as possible and should identify the purpose of the group that gives rise to the need for a thematic warrant (EI Code, para 5.14).

9.1.3 The duration, renewal, modification, and cancellation of EI warrants

A targeted EI warrant may be issued for a period of up to six months beginning on the day that the warrant was issued having received prior approval (s 116 IPA2016). It may be renewed or cancelled before the six-month period expires and will cease to have effect at the end of six months if not renewed. An urgent EI warrant is one that has been issued without prior approval from the IPC or a Judicial Commissioner, and for which the issuing official considers there is an urgent need. The IPC must be informed and within three working days from the issuing of the urgent warrant must decide whether to approve the issuing of the warrant and notify the issuer of the decision. If retrospective approval is not granted, the urgent warrant ceases to have effect immediately and may not be renewed (s 109 IPA2016; see also EI Code paras 5.55–5.72). An urgent warrant otherwise ceases to have effect on the fifth day after it was issued.

If the renewal conditions (s 117(2) IPA2016) are met, the appropriate person may renew a warrant at any time during the period of an urgent warrant or during the period of thirty days prior to which a non-urgent EI warrant would cease to have effect (the renewal period, s 117(5) IPA2016).

Warrants issued to intelligence agencies under ss 102, 103, or 104 IPA2016 may be modified by either the Secretary of State (or Scottish Minister) or a senior official acting on behalf of the Secretary of State (or Scottish Minister) (ss 118–122).

Law enforcement EI warrants issued under s 106 IPA2016 may be modified by the law enforcement chief or if issued by an appropriate delegate, that person (s 123 IPA2016). The only permissible modifications are (s 123(2) IPA2016):

(a) adding to the matters to which the warrant relates (see section 101(1) and (2)), by including the details required in relation to that matter by section 115(3) or (5);
(b) removing a matter to which the warrant relates;
(c) adding (in relation to a matter to which the warrant relates) a name or description to the names or descriptions included in the warrant in accordance with section 115(3) or (5);
(d) varying or removing (in relation to a matter to which the warrant relates) a name or description included in the warrant in accordance with section 115(3) or (5);
(e) adding to the descriptions of types of equipment included in the warrant in accordance with section 115(4)(a);
(f) varying or removing a description of a type of equipment included in the warrant in accordance with section 115(4)(a).

Any of the appropriate persons may cancel an EI warrant at any time, and must do so if any of the relevant grounds for it being issued are no longer necessary, or if the conduct authorized in the warrant is no longer proportionate. For law enforcement EI warrants this means that if the law enforcement chief no longer considers the warrant to be necessary:

• for the purpose of preventing or detecting serious crime; or
• for the purpose of preventing death or for preventing/mitigating injury to a person's physical or mental health, then the warrant must be cancelled immediately (s 125 IPA2016).

The effect of s 125 IPA2016 on the cancellation of equipment interference warrants is to impose on the law enforcement chief officer issuing the warrant under Part 5 IPA2016 a duty to maintain a continuous review of proportionality issues in each instance a warrant is issued, from the moment the warrant is issued until the warrant is cancelled or otherwise ceases to have effect.

9.1.4 **What does a targeted examination warrant allow?**

A targeted examination warrant allows the person to whom it is addressed to select protected material obtained under a bulk EI warrant issued to an intelligence agency so that equipment data and any information that is not private information may be examined (s 99(9) IPA2016).

9.1.5 **Protections in relation to equipment interference warrants**

Consistent with one of the primary purposes of the IPA2016, Part 5 provides safeguards in relation to unauthorized disclosure of the existence or contents of a warrant; EI warrants issued against MPs or members of other legislatures; items subject to legal privilege; confidential journalistic material; and sources of journalistic information (ss 111–114 and 129–134 IPA2016; see also EI Code, Chapter 9).

It is an offence for which imprisonment may be sentenced (s 134 IPA2016) to make any unauthorized disclosure (s 132(1) IPA2016) concerning:

(a) the existence or contents of the warrant;
(b) the details of the issue of the warrant or of any renewal or modification of the warrant;
(c) the existence or contents of any requirement to provide assistance in giving effect to the warrant;
(d) the steps taken in pursuance of the warrant or of any such requirement;
(e) any of the material obtained under the warrant in a form which identifies it as having been obtained under a warrant under this Part (s 132(4) IPA2016).

Section 133 of IPA2016 makes provision for four types of excepted disclosures in relation to matters specifically authorized by the warrant; disclosures made to the IPC; disclosures made in compliance with legal proceedings; and disclosures of a general nature to EI warrants in general rather than any particular warrant.

Confidential personal information and constituency business communications between an MP (or member of another relevant legislature) and another person (s 111 IPA2016); items subject to legal privilege (variously defined in the different UK jurisdictions: see EI Code, para 9.39 for the applicable legislative instruments) (s 112 IPA2016); and material relating to confidential journalistic material and journalistic sources (ss 113–114 IPA2016) are covered by additional protections, special application procedures, and reporting requirements which are set out in detail in paras 9.31–9.78 of the EI Code.

9.1.6 The new regime

The Investigatory Powers Act 2016 is 305 pages long, comprising 272 sections and ten multi-part Schedules. It will be understood that such length precludes any opportunity in a book of this nature to present anything more than an introduction to the key elements of the new regime. (This, in part, is the rationale for concentrating on law enforcement agency powers under IPA2016 rather than intelligence community powers.) The Act seeks to clarify and update authorization of intrusive investigation conduct in relation to data on and about computers and any other equipment producing or capable of producing 'electromagnetic, acoustic or other emissions'. In doing so it expands relevant terminology, in ways it is to be hoped will not confuse, with law enforcement chief officers now empowered to 'issue warrants' for conduct under this Act (warrants hitherto being a term reserved for types of court order), whilst being empowered to 'authorize' conduct under RIPA2000. The new regime for covert investigation of computers does not significantly alter the authorization regimes in relation to other aspects of covert investigation and computers, to which issues we now turn.

9.2 What Action Requires a Directed Surveillance Authority in Relation to the Investigation of Computers?

In circumstances where a kidnapper or blackmailer is communicating with the victim via email, as with the monitoring of phone calls in such circumstances, with the written consent of one of the parties to the communication, the communication may be lawfully monitored under a directed surveillance authority (ss 3(2), 26(2), and 28 RIPA2000).

Directed surveillance *may* also be appropriate where the surveillance is to be carried out in an internet café, but the exact tactics to be employed and the desired product would dictate the exact authority regime required. For instance, if the investigator's intention was to intercept emails being sent from a terminal in the café, then an interception warrant would be required. A directed surveillance authority would be appropriate in circumstances where the intention was to monitor a suspect's use of the computer by camera or by the deployment of surveillance officers in the café, *but* where the use of a camera meant that both sides of chatroom conversation could be seen and this was the purpose of the surveillance, then an interception warrant would be required.

9.3 What Action Requires an Intrusive Surveillance Authority in Relation to the Investigation of Computers?

Where surveillance is to be conducted on use made of a computer in private residential dwellings, hotel rooms, office premises, or in a private vehicle, an intrusive surveillance authority with IPC *prior approval* will be required. If the surveillance also requires entry into and trespass onto property, and or inter- ference with the computer that is to be monitored, then a property interfer- ence authority will also be required (see Chapters 7 and 8).

For example, the deployment of devices onto a home computer, either by physical attachment or remotely via software, will necessitate interference with property prior to the surveillance being carried out. Because the surveillance is being carried out in a dwelling, it will be intrusive. Similarly, remote activation of a home computer will constitute both an interference with property (the remote activation of the computer) and intrusive surveillance (the conduct of surveillance in a private dwelling).

9.4 What Action Requires an Interception Authority in Relation to the Investigation of Computers?

The interception of communications whilst in the course of their transmission made via computers constitutes interception for which a Secretary of State's warrant is required (see Chapter 11).

Important case law exists in relation to emails. It was held that s 1(5) RIPA2000 must be read as providing implicit lawful authority within the context of s 9 PACE, even where the net effect amounts to an interception of email outside the warranted regime provided for under s 5 RIPA2000 (*NTL Group Ltd v Ipswich Crown Court* [2002] EWHC Admin 1585). In this case a service provider had to divert (thus intercept) emails to an alternative server pending judicial consider- ation of an application for a production order. The production order was granted and investigators were allowed to access the emails that had been stored in this manner. The product from such interception could be used in evidence (s 18(4) and (5) RIPA2000). This approach would seem to be preserved under the IPA2016.

9.5 What Action Requires a CHIS Authority in Relation to the Investigation of Computers or Using Computers?

Where it is proposed to deploy investigators or victims acting on behalf of in- vestigators, to interact with suspects via a computer either by email, webcam, or in chatrooms, a CHIS authority will be required if it is proposed to use, for the purpose of the investigation, any information obtained by the investigator as a result of the online relationship in circumstances in which the other party will not be aware of the investigator's true purpose in acquiring such information.

Covert online investigation to identify internet offenders creates the potential for 'blue-on-blue' situations to arise: circumstances in which two undercover, online investigators interact online and begin to investigate each other. Proper procedures administered by the NCA are in place to avoid this.

It is good practice to video the interaction of undercover investigators online for evidential integrity purposes. The use of webcams should be avoided unless the investigator is an undercover investigator also trained to engage in, and for the purpose of the investigation intending to conduct, face-to-face meetings. (Investigators should be aware that in-built webcams and microphones in the computers that they are using might be remotely accessed as a counter-surveillance measure.)

Deployment of a conventional CHIS (formerly known as an informer) to obtain information via an online interactive relationship also requires a CHIS authority. Where a CHIS coincidentally is requested to obtain information from a database to which he or she has lawful access, if this does *not* involve the CHIS maintaining a relationship that facilitates the accessing or obtaining of the information, it would not appear to require an authorization.

9.6 Accessing Protected Electronic Information under RIPA2000

Within the context of a covert investigation under the RIPA2000 governance regime, accessing protected electronic information presents particular challenges. It may not always be possible to maintain secrecy in these circumstances and investigations which, to avoid compromise, must necessarily remain secret from those under investigation will have to be managed accordingly.

The exercise of covert investigation powers under RIPA2000 may result in investigators acquiring *possession* of protected electronic information (PEI). PEI is defined in para 3.12 of the Investigation of Protected Electronic Information Code of Practice (hereafter the IPEI Code) and includes *encrypted or password-protected digital data*. (PEI can also come into the possession of investigators through the exercise of overt investigation powers or through voluntary surrender of such material: see IPEI Code, para 3.13.)

Further Information and reading

The IPEI Code relates to PEI acquired through RIPA2000 powers. It will be recalled from section 9.1 that the EI Code deals with protection of material acquired using IPA2016 powers.

> The RIPA Codes of Practice are available at <https://www.gov.uk/government/collections/ripa-codes> (accessed 12 January 2018).
>
> The IPA2016 Codes of Practice are available at https://www.gov.uk/government/ consultations/investigatory-powers-act-2016-codes-of-practice> (accessed 12 January 2018).

Having acquired *possession* of PEI, investigators then need to obtain *access* to the protected information in an intelligible form.

Investigator access to PEI is legislated for under Part III RIPA2000, specifically s 49. Public authorities can only seek access to PEI using the RIPA2000 Part III statutory provisions if the authority has received prior written approval to seek such statutory access from the National Technical Advisory Centre (NTAC) (IPEI Code, para 3.10; also para 9.3). Such prior written approval can be provided on a case-by-case basis. Alternatively NTAC can provide a general written approval for any public authority deemed competent by NTAC to make applications for permission to issue a requirement notice under s 49.

Obtaining *access* to PEI is an overt action because necessarily it will involve assistance from third parties: an individual or individuals who hold the passwords needed to access, or encryption key(s) needed to decrypt—and so render intelligible—the protected information. The third party may, of course, be the suspect under investigation or an associate.

The statutory provisions (see also IPEI Code, Chapter 3) enable investigators:

- to require *disclosure of PEI* in an intelligible form (s 49 RIPA2000); or
- to require disclosure of the *means to access* PEI (s 50(3)(c) and s 51 RIPA2000); or
- to require disclosure of the *means of putting* PEI in an intelligible form (s 50(3)(c) and s 51 RIPA2000).

Information security is paramount and the statutory framework is designed to minimize possible collateral disclosure of or access to additional information beyond that which is specifically sought. It is, after all, the specific protected information that is of relevance to the investigation, not (necessarily) the means by which the information is protected. Of the three possible courses of action identified, it is the first which is to be used at all times unless investigators reasonably believe that the required assistance to render the PEI intelligible or compliance with such a requirement are unlikely to be forthcoming or effective. The second and third powers listed are 'more likely to be exercised in relation to individuals who are the subject of investigation and are responsible for protecting information which is believed to be evidence of unlawful conduct or relevant material to the investigation' (IPEI Code, para 3.8; see also Chapter 6 of the Code).

A s 49 notice under RIPA2000 requiring disclosure of PEI in an intelligible form, or disclosure of the means to access PEI, or of the means of putting PEI in an intelligible form, can only be served by an investigator who has received prior permission. (Note that Part III RIPA2000 prefers the arguably weaker 'permission' rather than the more forceful 'authorization').

9.6.1 Who may give permission for the issuing of a s 49 notice?

Appropriate written permission for the giving of a s 49 notice may be granted by persons identified in Schedule 2 RIPA2000 (see also IPEI Code, Chapter 9). In summary:

- a person holding a specified judicial office—this is the default option to which the options below are exceptions available only in specified circumstances;
- the Secretary of State;
- in relation to PEI (likely to be) obtained as a consequence of action under Part III PA97, an authorizing officer as defined in that Act; or
- a person exercising a statutory function, subject to specified general requirements.

Appropriate additional permission is required where disclosure of a key is required rather than merely disclosure of the PEI in intelligible form (IPEI Code, para 9.26). The duration of the permission will be set out in the written permission and PEI cannot be obtained once the written permission expires (s 7, Schedule 2, RIPA2000).

Applications for permission must contain such information as is specified in IPEI Code, para 4.13, and must be in a format prescribed in IPEI Code, paras 4.17–4.21.

The protected information to which investigators desire access must be described 'as precisely as possible' in the application so that the recipient of the s 49 notice is able to identify and render legible only the specific information subject of the notice (IPEI Code, paras 4.27–4.30).

General information to be provided to those receiving such a notice at the time it is served is set out in IPEI Code, para 4.35.

A s 49 notice may be issued where the following criteria are met:

- once the applicant has appropriate permission; *and*
- the applicant reasonably believes that:
  a. a key to PEI is in the possession of a person (s 49(2) RIPA2000); *and*
  b. a disclosure requirement is necessary:
     i. in the interests of national security (s 49(3) RIPA2000); or
     ii. for the purpose of preventing or detecting crime (need not be serious crime) (s 49(3) RIPA2000); or
     iii. in the interests of the economic well-being of the United Kingdom (s 49(3) RIPA2000); or
     iv. for the purpose of securing the effective exercise or proper performance by any public authority of any statutory power or statutory duty (s 49(2) (b)(ii) RIPA2000); and

c. the imposition of the requirement is proportionate to what is sought to be achieved by its imposition (s 49(2)(c) RIPA2000); and

d. it is not reasonable to obtain access to the PEI in an intelligible form other than by service of a notice (s 49(2)(d) RIPA2000; see also IPEI Code, para 3.15).

The obligations imposed on the person on whom a s 49 notice is served are set out in s 50 RIPA2000 and elaborated in IPEI Code, Chapter 5. The recipient of such a notice:

- may use any key or keys in his or her possession to access the PEI and then put it in an intelligible form; *and*
- is required to disclose the PEI in an intelligible form; *and*
- is required to make the disclosure in accordance with the s 49 notice (IPEI Code, para 5.1).

The recipient of a s 49 notice, or their legal advisor, may contact NTAC to verify the authenticity of the notice (IPEI Code, para 4.22).

Nothing prevents the recipient of a s 49 notice voluntarily disclosing the key or password so that investigators can access the protected information, and in doing so the recipient will satisfy the obligation under the notice. A s 49 notice should usually only be served on a corporate body following prior consultation with that body as to the feasibility and cost of executing the request (IPEI Code, para 4.7). A notice can only be served on a corporate body without prior consultation where the investigator has 'reasonable grounds for believing' that prior consultation would 'prejudice an investigation or operation and this includes where the corporate body or firm is suspected of complicity in unlawful conduct' (IPEI Code, para 4.6). At issue here is the likely disruption to legitimate business activity arising from the service of a s 49 notice.

To preserve the integrity of an ongoing covert investigation, in specified circumstances *certain public authorities may impose a requirement for secrecy* upon those who are required to provide the PEI in an intelligible form (s 54 RIPA2000).

The purpose of the secrecy requirement is to prohibit those providing access to the PEI from 'tipping off' persons subject to the investigation. Tipping off is made a criminal offence under s 54 RIPA2000 (note that the section also establishes numerous statutory defences to this offence).

9.6.2 Which public authorities can require secrecy under s 54?

- Those police forces listed in s 56 RIPA2000 (as amended)
- The National Crime Agency
- The Scottish Police Service
- Any of the intelligence services.

9.6.3 **In what circumstances may secrecy be required?**

The secrecy requirement 'is designed to preserve—but only where necessary—the covert nature of an investigation and to deter deliberate and intentional behaviour designed to frustrate statutory procedures and assist others to evade detection' (IPEI Code, para 10.9). Secrecy may be required of the person on whom a s 49 notice is served and every other person who becomes aware of the notice and its contents (s 54(1) RIPA2000).

Three preconditions must be met before secrecy can be imposed as part of a s 49 requirement to disclose:

1. the person giving permission for the s 49 notice to be issued must consent to the inclusion of a secrecy requirement (s 54(2) RIPA2000); *and*
2. PEI must have come into the possession of, or be likely to come into the possession of, one of the public authorities listed at 9.9.2 (s 54(3) RIPA2000); *and*
3. secrecy is needed 'to maintain the effectiveness of any investigation or operation or of investigatory techniques generally, or in the interests of the safety or wellbeing of any person' (s 54(3) RIPA2000; see also IPEI Code, para 10.10).

The requirement for secrecy must be clearly stated on the notice, and those upon whom it is imposed must be made explicitly aware of the requirement (IPEI Code, para 10.13).

Investigators must be aware that some software systems have the function of automatically alerting persons to the fact that PEI has been accessed. Such 'automatic tipping off' can 'conflict with a secrecy requirement' (IPEI Code, para 10.16). It will be for investigators to establish, if possible, whether the intended recipient of the notice uses such software and if so what, if any, steps can be taken to preserve the integrity of the covert investigation.

Little in the way of case law has been decided so far concerning PEI. In *R v S and A* [2008] EWCA Crim 2177, the court considered whether requiring a suspect to comply with a s 49 notice infringed the principle against self-incrimination. The Court of Appeal held that any engagement of the privilege against self-incrimination was 'very limited'.

Further information and reading

Although the appellants' knowledge of the means of access to the data may engage the privilege against self-incrimination, it would only do so if the data itself—which undoubtedly exists independently of the will of the appellants and to which the privilege against self-incrimination does not apply—contains incriminating material. If that data was neutral or innocent, the knowledge of the means of access to it would similarly be either neutral or innocent. On the other hand, if the material were, as we have assumed, incriminatory, it would

---

> be open to the trial judge to exclude evidence of the means by which the prosecution gained access to it. Accordingly the extent to which the privilege against self-incrimination may be engaged is indeed very limited.
>
> *R v S and A* [2008] EWCA Crim 2177, para 24

9.7 Good Practice for the Covert Investigation of Computers

It will always be good practice to consult expert advice (both legal and technical) in relation to computers. Prior to the establishment of computer or hi-tech crime units within the police service, it was not unheard of for colleagues 'who knew a bit about computers' to volunteer to investigate computers and the digital evidence such devices contained. This is no longer advisable or acceptable. Under the ACPO hi-tech crime strategy all ACPO police forces acquired both network and digital forensic investigation capability. There is similar expert provision for police in Scotland. Other organizations also have hi-tech investigation units. These experts should be approached for advice and guidance and will probably be the only persons trained to conduct covert computer investigation tactics.

Only trained staff should undertake computer investigation. This applies not only to the deployment of surveillance devices or software, but also to interaction with suspects via computers.

9.8 Issues for Consideration Regarding the Investigation of Computers and Social Media

As has been seen, there is much from the armoury of investigation techniques and tactics that can be employed in relation to computers. Nevertheless, there are a number of issues that complicate such investigation and, in some cases, await clarification.

Jurisdiction is an issue for the serving of Data Protection Act notices on internet service providers (ISPs). Usually the municipal law of the location of the ISP's servers applies. Web addresses or an email account ending '.com' may indicate that the address-owner or ISP is US-based, and so application for data will have to be made either via formal mutual legal assistance mechanisms or via other recognized routes such as requests to the FBI legal attaché at the US Embassy, who will be able to issue a notice under US federal law as part of police-to-police informal mutual assistance. A US-based ISP which also runs '—.co.uk' email accounts may, depending on the company, recognize UK Data Protection Act notices in respect of such accounts because they purport to be UK-based, regardless of where the server actually is. At least one US-based ISP with offices in the UK will accept UK Data Protection Act notices served at its UK offices for any of the email accounts it services. Practice will vary from ISP to ISP and computer investigation units will be best placed to advise on such issues.

The same principles apply to covert investigation in the virtual world as in the real world. Will the proposed activity engage Article 8 rights? Is it being conducted covertly, without the knowledge of the person being investigated? Will private information about any person be acquired or accumulated over time?

The fact that, through their use of social media, individuals may render themselves more susceptible to being surveilled does not negate the need for covertly conducted investigation of such individuals to be appropriately authorized (see, for example, comments on monitoring social media in the OSC *Annual Report 2016-17*, para 15.2). The internet and social media, to varying degrees, are the virtual equivalent of real-world public spaces. What complicates such matters for investigators is not knowing whether information posted is genuine and accurate, or whether it has been posted by the individual to whom it relates or by another person, perhaps acting maliciously.

Where investigators propose to communicate with others and intend to use assumed or disguised identities to do so, then a CHIS authority may be required if a relationship is to be established or maintained, in a manner calculated to ensure that one party is unaware of the real purpose to which the relationship is being put, and the relationship is being used to obtain, facilitate access to, or disclose information without the knowledge of one of the parties in the relationship (CSPI Code, para 2.29; CHIS Code, para 4.32).

In his 2011–12 Annual Report, the Chief Surveillance Commissioner observed (para 5.18) that: 'The internet is a surveillance device as defined by RIPA section 48(1) ... The ease with which an [investigation] activity meets the legislative threshold demands improved supervision.'

In his 2013–14 Annual Report, the Chief Surveillance Commissioner cautioned (para 5.30) that 'repeat viewing of individual "open source" sites for the purpose of intelligence gathering and data collection should be considered within the context of the protection that RIPA affords to such activity'. He went on (para 5.33) to 'strongly advise all public authorities empowered to use RIPA to have in place a corporate policy on the use of social media in investigations'. In connection with the management of CHISs, it is the role of the Senior Responsible Officer in each relevant public authority to have in place a strategic approach to such issues: it seems relatively little extra effort (for the potential benefit to be gained) for the same individual to drive policy in the directed surveillance arena also.

Computer covert investigation scenario

A concerned parent has reported that her thirteen-year-old daughter has struck up a relationship with an individual in a chatroom on the internet using a home-based computer. The individual purports to be a fourteen-year-old male and has suggested to the daughter that they meet. The parent is suspicious because the fourteen-year-old male insists that the daughter keeps the meeting a secret from her parents. After further investigation, information suggests that this is not a fourteen-year-old but a thirty-two-year-old male. Investigators wish to continue communicating in the chatroom with the male using a decoy officer, in order to set up a meeting where the intention is to arrest the male.

Trained specialist *covert computer investigators* or *undercover operatives* must be deployed in order to continue the communication, and therefore a CHIS authority is required. A directed surveillance authority will also be required for the one-sided consensual interception of the communications data.

Checklist of key issues when considering whether or not to deploy covert investigation techniques

- What evidence or intelligence is being sought?

- How is it relevant to the operation under consideration?

- What is the least intrusive means of securing such evidence or information?

- Has the least intrusive means of securing the evidence or information been attempted? If not, why not?

- What is the likelihood of collateral intrusion against the privacy of persons not being investigated? How will collateral intrusion be prevented (or if not, minimized) and how will the product of collateral intrusion be managed?

- What are the risks to the organization of such tactics? (Chapter 4)

- What are the risks to the organization's staff of such tactics? (Chapter 4)

- What are the risks to the public or specific third parties when such tactics are deployed? (Chapter 4)

- What are the risks to the subject of the investigation? (Chapter 4)

- Will the proposed methods breach Article 8(1)? (Chapter 2.2.1)

- Is there justification for doing so provided by Article 8(2)? (Chapter 2.2.4)

- How is the legality test met? (Chapter 2.2.3)

- How is the legitimacy test met? (Chapter 2.2.4)

- How is the necessity test met? (Chapter 2.2.5)

- How is the proportionality test met? (Chapter 2.2.5)

- Are the arguments justifying the application to use covert investigation based on reliable information/intelligence, or has the applicant adopted a 'tick-the-box' approach to completing the application without giving full consideration to the facts of the case and the issues arising?

- Have the arguments justifying the granting of authorization to use covert investigation been fully articulated, or has the authorizing officer merely paid lip service to the pro forma authorization template via which authority is granted?

- When should this authority be reviewed? What circumstances will or may arise that will necessitate review before then?

- How are the methods by which the evidence/intelligence will be obtained to be protected at trial? (Chapter 5)

- How will the product of the surveillance be managed? (Chapter 5)

Planning covert investigation actions

Remember to include the PLAN for covert investigation tactics in all investigation policy-book entries relating to covert investigation considerations and decisions.

P Proportionality

Why is it proportionate to obtain the intended product of this surveillance in the manner proposed? (Chapter 2.2.5)

L Legitimacy

What is the legitimate purpose of the proposed action: the prevention of disorder or crime; the interests of national security; the interests of public safety; the interests of the economic well-being of the country; the protection of health or morals; the protection of the rights and freedoms of others? (Chapter 2.2.4)

A Authority to Undertake Proposed Action

What is the lawful foundation and authority for the proposed action? From whom must authorization be sought? (Chapter 2.2.3)

N Necessity of Proposed Action

Why is the proposed action necessary? (Chapter 2.2.5)

Obtaining
Communications Data

10.1 **Introduction**

Obtaining communications data is not, strictly speaking, a *covert* investigation technique. Whilst it may be a line of enquiry undertaken before the person under investigation becomes aware of the investigation, the obtaining of communications data does not involve the active monitoring of a suspect's self-incriminating conduct as it happens. Communications data establishes the fact that a communication has taken place but does not reveal the content or meaning of the communication.

To the extent that communications data analysis exposes patterns of communications and a network of associations as well as demonstrating the fact of any given communication, it provides enhanced corroborated and inferential information not only about the investigation subject, but also enhanced corroborated and inferential information about third parties with whom the investigation subject has communicated. These third parties may not be committing any wrong-doing that would otherwise justify (both legally and morally) the intrusion of investigation.

The potential for significant intrusion against the privacy of both investigation subjects and third parties from communications data analysis necessitates an authorization regime for obtaining communications data (albeit a less stringent regime than that required for communication interception). The authorization regime for obtaining communications data is set out in the same legislation that governs the authorization and undertaking of interception of communications (which is a covert investigation technique). Hence both the potential for significant intrusion and the legal architecture provide a rationale for including the obtaining of communications data in this volume.

Communications data are distinguished from *communications content* and from *secondary data* ('a broader category of data than communications data', Interception of Communications Code of Practice, para. 2.12). Both communications data and secondary data comprise different constituent data types. Investigators will find it useful to be aware of the differences, and the implications arising therefrom.

Having previously been regulated by Part I RIPA2000 (which Part has been repealed), the obtaining of communications data is now governed by Part III of IPA2016. (The power of the Secretary of State to order the retention of communications data by communication service providers under Part IV of IPA2016 is not discussed here.)

10.2 **Data Definitions**

IPA2016 identifies different types of data and the definitions are summarized in Table 10.1.

Table 10.1 Summary of IPA2016 data definitions

IPA2016	Type of data	Definition	Acquisition regime
s 261(5)	Communications data	Comprises both 'entity data' and 'events data' held by or on behalf of a telecommunications operator; relating to an entity to which a telecommunications service is provided; attached to logically associated with a communication transmitted by such a service; available directly from a telecommunications system; about the architecture of a telecommunications system; which is not about a specific person; and which is not communications content.	s 61 Designated Senior Officer
s 261(3)	Entity data	Any data about an entity (a person or thing: s 261 (7)); or about an association between a telecommunications service (or part thereof) and an entity; which identifies or describes the entity; and which is not 'events data'.	s 61 Designated Senior Officer
s 261(4)	Events data	Any data which identifies or describes an event on, in of by a telecommunications system in which one or more entities are engaged in a specific activity and a specific time.	s 61 Designated Senior Officer
s 261(6)	Communications content	Any element of a telecommunication, or any data attached or logically associated with the communication that reveals anything of what might reasonably be considered to be the meaning of the communication but does not include any meaning derived merely from the fact of the communication or any data relating to the transmission of the communication. Systems data is not communication content.	ss 15 and 19 Secretary of State
s 16	Secondary data	Comprises 'identifying data' and 'systems data'.	ss 16 and 19 Secretary of State
s 263(2) and (3)	Identifying data	Data which may be used to identify any person, event, apparatus, system or service; or the location of any person, event or thing; including data relating to the fact, type, method, and pattern of the event; or the time or duration of the event.	ss 16 and 19 Secretary of State
s 263(4)	Systems data	Any data that enables or facilitates, identifies, or describes anything connected with the function of a postal service, a telecommunications service, or a telecommunications system (including relevant apparatus). Systems data is not communication content.	ss 16 and 19 Secretary of State

10.3 **For What Purpose May Communications Data be Obtained?**

Communications data may be obtained only for ten specified purposes (s 61(7) IPA2016)—which are *agency-specific*. No public authority is empowered to rely on all of them, as will be explained in the following sections. An authorization for the obtaining of communications data may be granted only when it is *necessary*:

(a) in the interests of national security;

(b) for the purpose of preventing or detecting crime or of preventing disorder;

(c) in the interests of the economic well-being of the United Kingdom so far as those interests are also relevant to the interests of national security;

(d) in the interests of public safety;

(e) for the purpose of protecting public health;

(f) for the purpose of assessing or collecting any tax, duty, levy or other imposition, contribution, or charge payable to a government department;

(g) for the purpose of preventing death or injury or any damage to a person's physical or mental health, or of mitigating any injury or damage to a person's physical or mental health;

(h) to assist investigations into alleged miscarriages of justice;

(i) where a person (P) has died or is unable to identify themselves because of a physical or mental condition:
  (i) to assist in identifying P; or
  (ii) to obtain information about P's next of kin or other persons connected with P or about the reason for P's death or condition; or

(j) for the purpose of exercising functions relating to:
  (i) the regulation of financial services and markets; or
  (ii) financial stability.

10.4 **Which Agencies May Obtain Communications Data?**

A far wider range of public authorities are empowered to obtain communications data than are empowered to intercept communications. Those public authorities empowered to obtain communications data are listed in Schedule 4 to the IPA2016 (s 70(1)–(2) IPA2016).

In summary, they include:

- Police Act 1996 s 2 police forces in England and Wales
- The Metropolitan Police Service and the City of London Police Force
- The Police Services of Scotland and of Northern Ireland
- The National Crime Authority

- British Transport Police
- The Ministry of Defence Police
- The Armed Forces Police
- The Security and Intelligence Services
- Specified units within the Ministries of Defence, and Justice, and the Home Office
- Specified units with the Departments of Health; for Transport; and for Work and Pensions
- HM Revenue and Customs
- Serious Fraud Office
- Independent Police Complaints Commissioner
- Police Ombudsman for Northern Ireland
- Police Investigations and Review Commissioner (Scotland)
- Specified health services and ambulance authorities in England, Wales, Scotland, and Northern Ireland
- Fire and rescue authorities in England, Wales, Scotland, and Northern Ireland
- Health and Safety Executive
- Competition and Markets Authority
- Criminal Cases Review Commission
- Scottish Criminal Cases Review Commission
- Department for Communities in Northern Ireland
- Department of Justice in Northern Ireland
- Financial Conduct Authority
- Food Standards Agency and Food Standards Scotland
- Gambling Commission
- Gangmasters and Labour Abuse Authority
- Information Commissioner
- Office of Communications

This Schedule may be amended by regulations issued by the Secretary of State.

Section 73 of IPA2016 provides, in addition to those public authorities listed in Schedule 4, that local authorities are also relevant public authorities which may obtain communications data under Part III IPA2016.

Schedule 4 also specifies which of the ten lawful purposes for which communications data may be obtained apply to each of the public authorities listed. No agency may rely on all ten purposes to obtain communications data. For example, the civilian police services can obtain communications date for purposes (a), (b), (c), (d), (e), (g), and (i) listed at 10.3. The security and intelligence services can only obtain communications data for purposes (a), (b), and (c). Only the Criminal Cases Review Commission and the Scottish Criminal Cases Review Commission can obtain communications data for purpose (h).

A local authority Designated Senior Officer (DSO) may grant an authorization for obtaining communications data *only* (s 73(3) IPA2016) if it is necessary (s 61(1 (a) IPA2016) for the purpose of preventing or detecting crime or of preventing disorder (s 61(7)(b) IPA2016).

Investigators and DSOs from each of the empowered public authorities will need to be fully aware, through reference to Schedule 4, which of the lawful purposes apply to their agency.

10.5 **Who May Authorize the Obtaining of Communications Data?**

A DSO may authorize any officer of the public authority to engage in any conduct which is for the purpose of obtaining communications data derived from or about a telecommunications system from any person (s 61(2) IPA2016) if the DSO considers:

- it is necessary for one of the lawful purposes set out in s 61(7) IPA2016; and
- it is necessary to obtain the data for a specific operation or investigation (or for developing, testing, and maintaining systems and capabilities for obtaining communications data); and
- the conduct authorized is proportionate to what is sought to be achieved (s 61(1) IPA2016).

Schedule 4 to the IPA2016 details the minimum office, rank, or position to be held by a DSO in each public authority (s 70(3)–(7) IPA2016).

A local authority DSO is someone who holds within the local authority the position of director, head of service, or service manager (or equivalent), or a higher position (s 73(2) IPA2016).

Within certain public authorities, different ranks of DSO can authorize the obtaining of different types of communications data. For example, in the civilian police services a superintendent can authorize the obtaining of both entity and events data, but an inspector may only authorize the obtaining of entity data. Likewise, in HMRC a senior officer can authorize the obtaining of both entity and events data, but a higher officer may only authorize the obtaining of entity data.

To ensure independent, dispassionate, and objective consideration of the necessity and proportionality tests for any given authorization, no DSO may authorize the obtaining of communications data in relation to any operation or investigation with which the DSO is involved or working on (s 63(1) IPA2016).

Further restrictions apply if the communications data is, or can only be obtained by processing, an internet connection record. In such circumstances no local authority DSO may grant an authorization, and DSOs from agencies other than local authorities may only grant such an authorization if any of three conditions are met: see Table 10.2.

Local authority DSOs are subject to the further restriction that they can grant an authorization *only* if the local authority is party to a *collaboration agreement*

Table 10.2 The conditions for obtaining internet connection record communications data

Condition A (s 62(3) IPA2016)	The DSO considers that it is necessary, for a purpose falling within section 61(7), to obtain the data to identify which person or apparatus is using an internet service where: (a) the service and time of use are already known, but (b) the identity of the person or apparatus using the service is not known.

Condition B
 	
(s 62(4) IPA2016)
	(a) the purpose for which the data is to be obtained falls within section 61(7) but is not the purpose falling within section 61(7)(b) of preventing or detecting crime, and
	(b) the designated senior officer considers that it is necessary to obtain the data to identify—
	
	  (i) which internet communications service is being used, and when and how it is being used, by a person or apparatus whose identity is already known,
	  (ii) where or when a person or apparatus whose identity is already known is obtaining access to, or running, a computer file or computer program which wholly or mainly involves making available, or acquiring, material whose possession is a crime, or
	  (iii) which internet service is being used, and when and how it is being used, by a person or apparatus whose identity is already known.

Condition C
 	
(s 62(5) IPA2016)
	(a) the purpose for which the data is to be obtained is the purpose falling within section 61(7)(b) of preventing or detecting crime,
	(b) the crime to be prevented or detected is serious crime or other relevant crime, and
	(c) the designated senior officer considers that it is necessary to obtain the data to identify—
	
	  (i) which internet communications service is being used, and when and how it is being used, by a person or apparatus whose identity is already known,
	  (ii) where or when a person or apparatus whose identity is already known is obtaining access to, or running, a computer file or computer program which wholly or mainly involves making available, or acquiring, material whose possession is a crime, or
	  (iii) which internet service is being used, and when and how it is being used, by a person or apparatus whose identity is already known.

that is certified by the Secretary of State (s 74 IPA2016). Collaboration agreements (ss 78–80 IPA2016) allow public authorities to share DSOs and Single Points of Contact (on Single Points of Contact, see 10.6). This provision enables the pooling of resources and ensures that authorities which infrequently need to obtain communications data may avail themselves, as and when required, of the expertise and facilities available in those agencies that regularly obtain communications data.

Local authority authorizations are subject either to judicial approval (s 75 IPA2016: in England and Wales a JP; in Scotland a Sheriff; and in Northern Ireland a magistrates' court District Judge) or to Judicial Commissioner approval (s 77 IPA2016) and cannot be acted upon until the appropriate approval has been received.

The authorization process must be documented in writing or in some form that produces a record of authorization being applied for and granted (s 64(4) IPA2016).

The authorization must specify (s 64(1) IPA2016):

(a) the office, rank, or position held by the designated senior officer granting it;
(b) the matters falling within section 61(7) by reference to which it is granted;
(c) the conduct that is authorized (all conduct in accordance with or in pursuance of the authorization will be lawful for the purposes of obtaining communication data, s 81 IPA2016);
(d) the data or description of data to be obtained; and
(e) the persons or descriptions of persons to whom the data is to be, or may be, disclosed or how to identify such persons.

And if requirements by notice are to be imposed on the telecommunications service operator, then the authorization must also state (s 64(2) IPA2016):

(a) the operator concerned; and
(b) the nature of the requirements to be imposed.

A notice imposing requirements on an operator:

(a) must specify:
  (i) the office, rank, or position held by the person giving it;
  (ii) the requirements that are being imposed; and
  (iii) the telecommunications operator on whom the requirements are being imposed, and
(b) must be given in writing or (if not in writing) in a manner that produces a record of its having been given.

An authorization lasts for one month from the day it was granted, but may be renewed before the expiry of that period (s 65 IPA2016). A DSO who granted an authorization may cancel it at any time and *must* cancel it if it is considered that the requirements for authorization are no longer satisfied (s 65(4) IPA2016).

Section 81(1) of IPA2016 makes conduct lawful in accordance with or in pursuance of the written authorization for all purposes in connection with obtaining communications data. To avail investigators of this protection, the DSO must detail in writing all the proposed conduct in the authorization.

Conduct undertaken to obtain communications data that is not described—and so specifically authorized—in the authorization may by subject to legal challenge, with courts able to exercise the discretion under s 78 Police and Criminal Evidence Act 1984, for example, to exclude from evidence any communications data obtained other than by authorized conduct. The drafting of the written authorization matters. Compliance with the written authorization matters.

10.6 **Single Points of Contact**

Practicalities and feasibility dictate that requests for communications data made by a public authority to telecommunications service providers should be channelled through a central mechanism serving the whole organization. Individual investigators must not approach telecommunications service providers directly. This is a well-established practice of long standing and is reinforced with a statutory obligation. Section 76 of IPA2016 requires the use of properly trained and accredited individuals—called Single Points of Contact (SPOC) (defined at s 76(4) IPA2016)—to facilitate the acquisition of communications data and to act as single channels of communication between public authorities and communications service providers.

DSOs must consult their relevant SPOC before issuing an authorization to obtain communications data (s 76(1) IPA2016) unless the exceptional circumstances of an imminent threat to life or another emergency, or the interests of national security, dictate that the requirement for prior consultation should not apply (s76(2) and (3)).

The SPOC may advise an investigator and/or the DSO (s 76(5)–(7) IPA2016) on:

- appropriate methods for obtaining the data being sought;
- whether it is reasonably practical to obtain the data being sought;
- the cost and resource implications for both the public authority and the telecommunications service provider;
- likely unintended consequences of the proposed authorization;
- any issues concerning the lawfulness of the proposed authorization;
- whether requirements imposed by virtue of an authorization have been met;
- how the use of obtained data has supported the relevant operation or investigation;
- any other effects of an authorization.

Such prior advice will be particularly relevant in circumstances where a public authority that infrequently obtains communication data is party to a collaboration agreement allowing access to the DSOs and SPOC in an agency that has experience and expertise in such matters.

10.7 **What Significant Case Law Has Been Decided in Relation to Communications Data?**

At the time of writing, other than in relation to general principles regarding legality, necessity, and proportionality (see Chapter 2), there has been relatively little case law decided specifically in relation to communications data, and none in relation to the provisions of the IPA2016. Some of the key cases discussed in relation to interception touch upon communications data (see Chapter 11).

Proportionality is of particular relevance in the acquisition of communications data because so much data is generated and so much data potentially can be acquired. A blanket request for all available communications data over a given period at the outset of an investigation will fail the proportionality test because it will result in a significant amount of data about an individual's communications, much of which will be irrelevant and therefore an unjustifiable intrusion into both that individual's privacy and that of those persons with whom communication has been made. Requests made later in the course of an investigation, which are more targeted and focused as a result of more precise lines of enquiry emerging during the developing investigation, will be more likely to satisfy the proportionality requirements.

Checklist of key issues when considering whether or not to deploy covert investigation techniques

- What evidence or intelligence is being sought?

- How is it relevant to the operation under consideration?

- What is the least intrusive means of securing such evidence or information?

- Has the least intrusive means of securing the evidence or information been attempted? If not, why not?

- What is the likelihood of collateral intrusion against the privacy of persons not being investigated? How will collateral intrusion be prevented (or if not, minimized) and how will the product of collateral intrusion be managed?

- What are the risks to the organization of such tactics? (Chapter 4)

- What are the risks to the organization's staff of such tactics? (Chapter 4)

- What are the risks to the public or specific third parties when such tactics are deployed? (Chapter 4)

- What are the risks to the subject of the investigation? (Chapter 4)

- Will the proposed methods breach Article 8(1)? (Chapter 2.2.1)

- Is there justification for doing so provided by Article 8(2)? (Chapter 2.2.4)

- How is the legality test met? (Chapter 2.2.3)

- How is the legitimacy test met? (Chapter 2.2.4)

- How is the necessity test met? (Chapter 2.2.5)

- How is the proportionality test met? (Chapter 2.2.5)

- Are the arguments justifying the application to use covert investigation based on reliable information/intelligence, or has the applicant adopted a 'tick-the-box' approach to completing the application without giving full consideration to the facts of the case and the issues arising?

- Have the arguments justifying the granting of authorization to use covert investigation been fully articulated, or has the authorizing officer merely paid lip service to the pro forma authorization template via which authority is granted?

- When should this authority be reviewed? What circumstances will or may arise that will necessitate review before then?

- How are the methods by which the evidence/intelligence will be obtained to be protected at trial? (Chapter 5)

- How will the product of the surveillance be managed? (Chapter 5)

Planning covert investigation actions

Remember to include the PLAN for covert investigation tactics in all investigation policy-book entries relating to covert investigation considerations and decisions.

P Proportionality

Why is it proportionate to obtain the intended product of this surveillance in the manner proposed? (Chapter 2.2.5)

L Legitimacy

What is the legitimate purpose of the proposed action: the prevention of disorder or crime; the interests of national security; the interests of public safety; the interests of the economic well-being of the country; the protection of health or morals; the protection of the rights and freedoms of others? Chapter 2.2.4)

A Authority to Undertake Proposed Action

What is the lawful foundation and authority for the proposed action? From whom must authorization be sought? (Chapter 2.2.3)

N Necessity for Proposed Action

Why is the proposed action necessary? (Chapter 2.2.5)

11

Interception of Communications

11.1 **Introduction**

The IPA2016 is the second overhaul of communication interception law since interception of telecommunications was first put on a statutory basis in the Interception
of Communications Act 1985. The IPA2016 consolidates and elaborates the framework established in the first major overhaul, the RIPA2000, whilst retaining key
policy principles that have always underpinned UK interception law. The new legislation has been prompted in part by technological developments—the logistics
of communication, of communications data, and of interception have changed—
and partly to incorporate within the legislative framework agency conduct brought
to public attention by the disclosures of former CIA contractor Edward Snowden,
the lawfulness of which agency conduct was, at best, ambiguous.

Part 1 of RIPA2000 is repealed; the intentionally short-lived Data Retention
and Investigatory Powers Act 2014 is repealed; and agency conduct in relation
to facilitating interception communication through property interference and
wireless telegraphy has now been brought within the compass of the IPA2016,
with relevant sections of the PA97 and the Wireless Telegraphy Act 2006 accordingly amended. Data retention measures enacted in the Counter-Terrorism and
Security Act 2015 are now replaced by IPA2016.

Further information and reading

The policy and legislative background to the IPA2016 is detailed in the
Explanatory Notes which have been published to accompany the Act. The
notes are accessible in PDF format at <http://www.legislation.gov.uk/ukpga/
2016/25/notes/contents> (accessed 26 July 2017).

The Act is divided into several Parts.

1. General privacy protections (discussed in this chapter)
2. Lawful interception of communications (discussed in this chapter)
3. Obtaining communications data (discussed in chapter 10)
4. Retaining communications data (applies to telecommunications operators,
   outside the remit of this book)
5. Equipment interference (discussed in this chapter)
6. Bulk warrants (intelligence agencies only, outside the remit of this book)
7. Bulk personal dataset warrants (intelligence agencies only, outside the
   remit of this book)
8. Oversight arrangements (discussed as applicable throughout this book)
9. Miscellaneous and general provisions
10. Schedules.

So, the new legislation consolidates in one Act all the necessary statutory tools
to undertake lawful communications interception. It distinguishes those tools
available to both law enforcement agencies and the intelligence community
from those tools available only to the intelligence community. In a significant

change, the decision of the Secretary of State to issue an interception warrant is now subject to prior approval by a Judicial Commissioner.

As with RIPA2000, IPA2016 is supported by multiple Codes of Practice. At time of writing, only the *draft* versions of these Codes have been made available. This chapter therefore proceeds with references based on the draft versions, pending publication of final versions. If nothing else, the draft versions can be taken to signal intent.

Further information and reading

The Codes of Practice are accessible online in PDF format at <https://www.gov.uk/government/consultations/investigatory-powers-act-2016-codes-of-practice> (accessed 27 July 2017).

The following Codes of Practice have been drafted:

1. Interception of Communications (hereafter Interception Code)
2. Equipment Interference (hereafter Equipment Code)
3. Bulk Acquisition of Communications Data (hereafter Bulk Acquisition Code)
4. Security and Intelligence Agencies' Retention and Use of Bulk Personal Datasets
5. National Security Notices.

The Codes of Practice are lengthy and detailed and contain numerous scenario examples in presenting guidance about the interception procedures to be followed by public authorities. The Codes are admissible as evidence in both criminal and civil proceedings and if deemed relevant, any provision within the Codes may be taken into account by a court or tribunal or the IPC.

The role of the independent Commissioner, who must hold or have held a senior judicial appointment, is created by s 227 IPA2016 and supersedes the Chief Surveillance Commissioner, s 233 (see also ss 75–94). The Investigatory Powers Commissioner oversees compliance with the provisions of the Act and considers concerns reported about any utilization of these provisions (s 229). Agencies are required to report relevant errors in their use of these powers to the Commissioner (s 231).

Communications interception is regarded as a particularly serious and significant intrusion into private life and it engages Article 8 of the ECHR, given domestic effect in England and Wales by s 6 Human Rights Act 1998. Accordingly, the use of interception under warrant is reserved for the prevention or detection of *serious* crime.

Definition of serious crime, s 263 IPA2016

For the purposes of this legislation serious crime means

(a) the offence, or one of the offences, which is or would be constituted by the conduct concerned is an offence for which a person who has reached the age of 18 (or, in relation to Scotland or Northern Ireland, 21) and has no previous convictions could reasonably be expected to be sentenced to imprisonment for a term of 3 years or more, or

(b) the conduct involves the use of violence, results in substantial financial gain or is conduct by a large number of persons in pursuit of a common purpose.

Interception of communications can only be carried out in circumstances for which a lawful authority is available (s 6 IPA2016). Lawful authority for interception exists in two forms: specific statutory provision without a warrant; and with a warrant.

It is a criminal offence intentionally to intercept in the United Kingdom any communication without lawful authority (s 3(1) IPA2016). The penalty for this offence is two years' imprisonment or an unlimited fine. Additionally the Investigatory Powers Commissioner can impose fines in certain circumstances (s 7 IPA2016) and provision is also made for civil redress for the sender or intended recipient of an unlawfully intercepted communication (s 8 IPA2016; see also Interception Code, Chapter 3).

Definition of interception

Interception is defined in s 4 IPA2016. A communication is intercepted when:

- during the course of the transmission of a communication by a telecommunications system,
  - o a person modifies or interferes with a telecommunications system or its operation; and/or
  - o monitors transmissions made by means of the system; and/or
  - o monitors transmissions made by wireless telegraphy to or from apparatus that is part of the system;
- in order to make any of the communication content available to a person who is not the sender or receiver of the communication, either

  - o while it is being transmitted or
  - o at any time when the communication is stored in or by the system.

Definition of communication

A communication in this context is defined (s 261(2) IPA2016) as:

(a) anything comprising speech, music, sounds, visual images or data of any description, and

(b) signals serving either for the impartation of anything between persons, between a person and a thing or between things or for the actuation or control of any apparatus.

See also the definition of 'content' (s 261(6) IPA2016) discussed at 11.3.2.

This chapter concentrates on the regime governing law enforcement access to and use of interception. For reasons of space, necessarily what follows is a summary of key elements which should be supplemented with close reading of the original statute and supporting codes when planning an operation.

11.2 Lawful Interception Without a Warrant

There are four general circumstances in which lawful authority exists for interception without a warrant:

- with the consent of the sender or the recipient (s 44 IPA2016);
- for administrative or certain specified enforcement purposes (ss 45–48 IPA2016);
- in connection with the management of specified institutions (prisons, psychiatric hospitals, and immigration detention facilities) (s 49–51 IPA2016); and
- in accordance with overseas mutual legal assistance requests (s 52 IPA2016).

In relation to accessing stored communication content, see also 11.6 of this chapter.

11.2.1 Interception with the consent of the sender or recipient

Where *both* the sender and the receiver of the communication consent to a communication being intercepted, no further authority is required (s 44(1) IPA2016). Historically this has been termed two-party consent.

Where only one party to the communication consents to the interception, being either the sender or the recipient, then the interception will be lawful only if it is part of an authorized directed surveillance operation under Part 2 of RIPA2000 (or under RIP(S)A 2000). The written directed surveillance authority must specify that the interception of a communication with one party's consent is part of the authorized conduct (s 44 IPA2016; Interception Code, para 12.4–2.5).

The product from this category of interception may be used in evidence.

11.2.2 Interception for administrative and specified enforcement purposes

A postal or telecommunications service provider may intercept communications transmitted by such services for the purposes of providing and operating any postal or telecommunications service, and for ensuring that enactments in relation to provision and operation are complied with (s 45 IPA2016; Interception Code, para 12.6).

Subject to such regulations as may be made by the Secretary of State, businesses may intercept communications for the purposes of monitoring or record-keeping in relation to transactions or other business activities undertaken by the business, using only equipment provided by the relevant business for the purpose of undertaking its business activities (s 46 IPA2016; Interception Code, para 12.7–12.8).

HM Revenue and Customs may intercept a communication by means of a public postal service under s 159 Customs and Excise Management Act 1979 as applied by virtue of s 105 Postal Services Act 2000 or that section and another enactment (s 47 IPA2016; Interception Code, para 12.7–12.8).

Section 47 IPA2016 also authorizes the interception of a communication being transmitted by a public postal services pursuant to paragraph 9 of Schedule 7 to the Terrorism Act 2000 (Interception Code, para 12.7–12.8).

OFCOM, the Office of Communications established by s 1 Office of Communications Act 2002, may intercept communications in connection with the granting of wireless telegraphy licences, the prevention or detection of interference with wireless telegraphy and the enforcement of provisions under Parts 2 and 3 Wireless Telegraphy Act 2006 (s 48 IPA2016).

The product from these categories of interception may be used in evidence.

11.2.3 Interception in connection with specified institutions

Subject to 'Prison Rules' made under s 47 Prison Act 1952, s 39 Prisons (Scotland) Act 1989, or s 13 Prison Act (Northern Ireland) 1953, communication interception may take place in prisons if it is conduct exercised under a power conferred by the prison rules (s 49 IPA2016).

In hospitals providing high security psychiatric services (as defined in s 4 National Health Service Act 2006), interception of communications is authorized under s 50 IPA2016 if such interception is conduct pursuant to or in accordance with a relevant direction (as defined at s 50 (2)) given to the body providing such services at those premises. Section 50 IPA2016 makes equivalent provisions for hospitals in Scotland.

Communication interception in immigration detention facilities is authorized by s 52 IPA2016 if such conduct exercises any power conferred by or under relevant rules established in accordance with the Immigration and Asylum Act 1999.

The Interception Code offers no guidance in relation to ss 49–51 IPA2016. Reference should be made, instead, to the relevant institutional rules.

The product from these categories of interception may be used in evidence.

11.2.4 **Interception in accordance with overseas mutual legal assistance requests**

Four conditions must be met for interception in accordance with a mutual legal assistance (MLA) request to be lawful (s 51 IPA2016; Interception Code, para 12.9–12.11).

1. The interception must be carried out by or on behalf of a telecommunications operator in relation to the use of a telecommunications service provided by the operator.
2. The interception must be carried out in response to a formal request made by a competent foreign authority pursuant to a relevant international agreement between the foreign authority and the United Kingdom (relevant international agreements being designated by the Secretary of State for the purpose of s 51 IPA2016).
3. The individual whose communications are to be intercepted must be outside the United Kingdom. Or, *both* the authority making the request *and* the telecommunications service provider must have grounds for believing that the individual whose communications are to be intercepted is outside the United Kingdom.
4. Any further conditions stipulated by the Secretary of State for the purposes of this section must be met.

The effect of s 50 IPA2016 is that the United Kingdom's obligations under Article 17 of the EU Convention on Mutual Assistance in Criminal Matters are met (Interception Code, para 12.11). At time of writing, the consequences for such arrangements following 'Brexit' are unknown.

The product from this category of interception may be used in evidence.

Outside these provisions, communication interception will only be lawful if authorized by a warrant.

11.3 **Lawful Interception with a Warrant**

Under s 15 IPA2016 warrants may be issued to law enforcement agencies or intelligence agencies to undertake *targeted interception* (s 15(2)), *targeted examination* (s 15(3)), and *mutual assistance interception* (s 15(4)).

Under s 136 IPA2016 warrants may be issued to *intelligence agencies* for *bulk interception of overseas communications*, the obtaining of secondary data from such communications, and selected examination of such communication content and secondary data, subject to the restrictions and conditions set out in s 136.

This chapter concentrates on s 15 warrants.

The product of warranted interception may *not* be used in evidence in criminal trials (s 56 IPA2016; Interception Code, para 9.3)).

In practice, such product is used to generate opportunities to gather evidence by more conventional means. For example, interception product may identify an opportunity to conduct visual and/or audio surveillance and so gather and adduce evidence through the direct witness testimony of investigators conducting the surveillance.

11.3.1 **Which persons may apply for a s 15 warrant?**

Only a limited number of agencies can apply for an interception warrant (s 18 IPA2016), far fewer than can undertake directed surveillance (see Chapter 6):

- The Director General of the National Crime Agency (on behalf of the NCA and on behalf of law enforcement agencies in England and Wales)
- The Metropolitan Police Commissioner
- The Chief Constable of the Police Service of Northern Ireland
- The Chief Constable of the Police Service of Scotland
- The Commissioners for HM Revenue & Customs
- A foreign competent authority for the purposes of an MLA request
- The Director General of the Security Service (MI5)
- The Chief of the Secret Intelligence Service (MI6)
- The Chief of the Government Communications Headquarters (GCHQ)
- The Chief of Defence Intelligence.

11.3.2 **Types of warrant available under s 15**

The conduct that may be authorized by different types of warrant obtained under s 15 IPA2016 is set out in Table 11.1.

Where authorization has been granted only for the obtaining of secondary data, but the conduct pursuant to that authorization also captures communication content, only the secondary data may be examined by the persons to whom the warrant is issued.

Definitions

The definition of the key terms listed below may be summarized as follows:

Communication content means any element of a communication, or data logically attached to or associated with a communication, that might reasonably be considered to be the meaning of the communication, other than meaning derived from the fact of the communication (s 261 (6) IPA2016). (See also the definition of 'communication' (s 261(2) IPA2016) discussed at 11.1)

Secondary data comprises systems data and identifying data (s 15(4) IPA2016).

Systems data means data that is comprised in, part of, attached to, or logically associated with the communication that facilitates the operation and functioning of the communication transmission (s 15(5) and s 263(4) IPA2016). Systems data is not content (s 261(6)(b) IPA2016).

Identifying data means data that is comprised in, part of, attached to, or logically associated with the communication; is capable of being logically separated from the remainder of the communication; and if so separated would not convey any meaning of the communication; and which for the purposes of transmission identifies any person, apparatus, system, service, event, or location (s 15(6) and s 263(2) IPA2016).

Warrants issued to law enforcement agencies for targeted interception for convenience may be combined with authorization for other covert investigation interventions depending on the operational management needs of any given investigation.

The Director General of the National Crime Agency (on behalf of the NCA and on behalf of law enforcement agencies in England and Wales); the Metropolitan Police Commissioner; the Chief Constable of the Police Service of Northern Ireland; the Chief Constable of the Police Service of Scotland; and the Commissioners for HM Revenue & Customs may apply to the Secretary of

Table 11.1 Conduct that may be authorized by a s 15 warrant

ss 15(2) and 15(5) Targeted interception	(a) Interception of the content of communications transmitted via postal or telecommunications services;
	(b) Obtaining secondary data from communications transmitted via postal or telecommunications services;
	(c) Disclosure of anything obtained in relation to (a) and (b) to the person to whom the warrant is addressed or anyone acting on that person's behalf;
	(d) Conduct necessary to achieve the above authorized conduct;
	(e) Conduct for obtaining related systems data.
s 15(3) Targeted examination	Selection of relevant communications content obtained under the authority of a Bulk Interception Warrant (Part 1, Chapter 6, IPA2016) for examination; selection of the relevant content being made on the basis of identifiable criteria.
s 15(4) Mutual assistance	(a) Making a MLA request to a foreign competent authority for interception to be undertaken outside the UK;
	(b) Providing assistance in response to a MLA request made by a foreign competent authority for interception to be undertaken inside the UK;
	(c) Disclosure of anything obtained in relation to (a) and (b) to the person to whom the warrant is addressed or anyone acting on that person's behalf.

State for warrants that combine authorization for targeted interception with authorization for one or more of the following (Schedule 8, para 3, IPA2016; Interception Code, paras 5.84–5.102):

- authorization for targeted equipment interference (s 106 IPA2016);
- authorization for property interference (s 93 PA97);
- authorization for directed surveillance (s28 RIPA2000);
- authorization for intrusive surveillance (s 32 RIPA2000).

11.3.3 Subject matter of warrants

Section 17 IPA2016 establishes that a warrant may relate to:

(a) a particular person or organization;
(b) a single set of premises;
(c) a group of persons who share a common purpose or who carry on a particular activity;
(d) more than one person or organization, or more than one set of premises where the conduct authorized or required by the warrant is for the purpose of a single investigation or operation; or
(e) testing or training activities (in relation to the conducting of interception).

In the Interception Code items (a) and (b) are referred to as 'targeted warrants' (paras 5.6–5.10), and items (c) and (d) as 'targeted thematic warrants' (paras 5.11–5.17). Thematic warrants incur the vulnerability of being used for 'fishing trips' and so an enhanced level of descriptive authorization detail is required in the warrant itself, which will require corresponding levels of detail in an application for such a warrant (s 31(4)–(5) IPA2016; Interception Code, paras 5.13–5.17).

Further information and reading

s 15(3) IPA2016 allows for targeted examination warrants to be issued to access communications content that has been obtained under a Bulk Interception Warrant.

A Bulk Interception Warrant (s 136 IPA2016) relates to overseas-related communications and/or secondary data from such communications and may only be applied for by or on behalf of the head of an intelligence agency (s 138 IPA2016).

A law enforcement investigator cannot therefore apply for a Bulk Interception Warrant but may apply for a warrant to access specific content within the overseas communications or secondary data relating to such communications, acquired pursuant to a Bulk Interception Warrant. Such authorization is made through a targeted examination warrant. In order to apply for a targeted examination warrant, the investigator will need to provide clearly identifiable criteria with which to filter the content or secondary data being sought from the bulk communications/secondary data that has been acquired (paras 5.32–5.33 Interception Code).

Part 6, IPA2016; Chapter 6 Interception Code

11.4 **What Authority Regime is Required for Warranted Interception of Communications?**

On application by one of the persons identified at 11.3.1, the Secretary of State may issue a targeted warrant, subject to the prior approval of a Judicial Commissioner. (In Scotland, a targeted interception warrant may be issued by a Scottish Minister under ss 21 and 22 IPA2016; Interception Code, paras 5.43–5.45.) If the Secretary of State (or Scottish Minister) is not immediately available to sign the warrant, his or her authorization may be provided verbally and a delegated Senior Official may sign the warrant on behalf of the Secretary of State (Interception Code, para 5.45).

The format of targeted interception warrant applications, targeted examination warrant applications, and mutual assistance warrants is prescribed in the Interception Code at paras 5.30, 5.33, and 5.34 respectively. The applications must be detailed so that the Secretary of State can be satisfied as to the necessity and proportionality of the interception and can be satisfied as to the implementation of the required safeguards and protections (see 11.5). Note that applications for warrants intended to acquire legally privileged communications and applications for warrants where the acquisition of legally privileged material is not intended but likely each have additional criteria to be met (Interception Code, para 9.47).

The format of the warrants themselves is set out at Interception Code, paras 5.35, 5.38, and 5.39 respectively.

The Secretary of State, or as it may be the Scottish Minister, may only issue a targeted warrant when one or more of the statutory tests for necessity are met (ss 19 and 20 IPA2016), the statutory tests of necessity being:

- in the interests of national security;
- for the purposes of preventing or detection serious crime;
- in the interests of the economic well-being of the UK so far as those interests are also interests of national security and the information relates to the acts/intentions of persons outside the UK;
- for the purpose of giving effect to the provisions of an EU mutual assistance instrument or an international mutual assistance agreement.

In relation to thematic warrants the detail documented in the application must be sufficient to enable the Secretary of State and the Judicial Commissioner to arrive at a sound judgement about the likely interference with privacy and so make a proper decision about the necessity and proportionality of the conduct authorized (Interception Code, paras 5.18–5.19).

A warrant may not be considered necessary on these grounds if it is considered necessary only for the purpose of gathering evidence for use in any legal proceedings (s 20(5) IPA2016).

In addition to there being grounds for necessity (as already outlined), the Secretary of State must also consider that:

- the conduct authorized by the warrant is proportionate to what is sought to be achieved by that warrant (s 19(1)(b) IPA2016);
- satisfactory arrangements exist for the retention and disclosure of material in the UK and the disclosure of material overseas (s 19(1)(c) IPA2016); and
- the decision to issue the warrant has been approved by a Judicial Commissioner (s 19(1)(d) IPA2016).

The Secretary of State may not issue a warrant without Judicial Commissioner approval unless the matter is urgent (Interception Code, paras 5.41 and 5.46). A matter will be considered urgent only if:

- there is an imminent threat to life or serious harm; or
- there is a limited time to act on an intelligence-gathering opportunity or an investigative opportunity; and
- in each of these circumstances, it is not reasonably practicable to obtain Judicial Commissioner approval before issuing the warrant.

The issuing of an urgent warrant must be reviewed by a Judicial Commissioner within three working days (Interception Code, paras 5.51–5.55).

A warrant issued under the non-urgent procedure is valid for six months and may be renewed no earlier than 30 days before the warrant expires An urgent warrant is valid for five days. A warrant may only be renewed if the renewal has been approved by a Judicial Commissioner. Provisions for the modification of warrants are set out in the Interception Code, paras 5.69–5.79.

The Secretary of State (or as it may be the Scottish Ministers or Senior Officials) may cancel a warrant at any time and must do so as soon as the grounds for necessity no longer exist or the interception ceases to be proportionate. This obligation in turn creates an obligation on the investigative and intelligence agencies to keep each interception and the operation to which it pertains under regular review so as to be able to notify the Secretary of State as soon as possible when the warrant is no longer justified (Interception Code, paras 9.12–9.14). Interception should stop immediately it ceases to be justified and agencies should not wait for the cancellation of the warrant before terminating the interception.

11.5 Safeguards and Protections

Controversies and consultation during the drafting of the Investigatory Powers Bill highlighted the importance of safeguards and protections in the interception process if the public are going to accept interception as a justifiable investigative intervention and confer upon the tactic the seal of perceived legitimacy. The concerns raised are reflected in the architecture of the Act and announced in the first two sections. By way of introduction, s 1 IPA2016 asserts:

- 'This Act sets out the extent to which certain investigatory powers may be used to interfere with privacy.' (s 1(1))
- 'This Part imposes certain duties in relation to privacy and contains other protections for privacy.' (s 1(2))

Section 2 imposes overarching duties in relation to privacy. In implementing any of the provisions established under the IPA2016, a public authority *must* have regard to:

- whether what is sought to be achieved by the warrant, authorization, or notice could reasonably be *achieved by other less intrusive means* (s 2(2)(a));
- whether the level of protection to be applied in relation to any obtaining of information by virtue of the warrant, authorization, or notice is higher because of the particular *sensitivity of that information* (s 2(2)(b));
- the *public interest in the integrity and security* of telecommunication systems and postal services (s 2(2)(c)); and
- any other aspects of the *public interest in the protection of privacy* (s 2(2)(d)).

IPA2016 thus identifies which aspects of the public interest are to be prioritized when considering the use of interception and interception product. To counter this statutory direction with the argument that the public have an interest in bringing criminals to justice is to misconstrue the issues. Recall the reasoning set out in Chapter 1 at 1.1. In relation to criminal justice, the public interest is vested in the integrity and proper operation of the criminal justice system and all its constituent elements (such as the use of specific statutory powers) as a fundamental pillar of a liberal democratic society. This principle is echoed in s 2(2)(c) IPA2016. The antithesis generates the controversies and concerns identified in the pre-legislative consultation for this statute.

The strategic philosophy thus articulated, the IPA2016 then prescribes the policies and practices that will preserve and promote the fundamental principles:

- Limited public authority access to interception as a tool (s 18)
- Limitations on the use to which intercept product may be put (s 56 and Schedule 3)
- Considerations of necessity (ss 19 and 20)
- Considerations of proportionality (ss 19 and 20)
- Safeguards for the retention and disclosure of material (ss 53 and 54)
- Special procedures in relation to Members of Parliament (s 26)
- Special procedures in relation to legally privileged material (s 27)
- Special procedures in relation to confidential journalistic material (s 28)
- Special procedures in relation to the identification of journalistic sources (s 29).

All of which provisions are intended to assist and guide public authorities in acting in ways that are compatible with ECHR protected rights (s 6(1) HRA).

11.5.1 Safeguards for the retention and disclosure of interception product

Investigations relying upon interception product must be managed so as to minimize:

- the *number of persons* to whom the product is disclosed or made available;
- the *extent* to which any of the product is *disclosed or made available*;
- the *extent* to which any of the product is *copied*;
- the *number of copies* made (s 53(2) IPA2016) [emphasis added].

In practice, this is likely to mean that not all investigators in any given investigation team should have access to interception product. An investigation manager can assign tasks relating to lines of enquiry generated by interception without needing to disclose the product that gave rise to the enquiry tasks.

Investigators to whom interception product is disclosed must need access to the actual product in order to undertake their duties; and the duties must directly relate to one of the specified purposes itemised immediately below. Investigators to whom disclosure of interception product is intended must hold an appropriate security vetting clearance (Interception Code, para 9.15).

Interception product may only be retained and/or disclosed for specified purposes (s 53(3) IPA2016):

- Retention and/or disclosure is, or is likely to become necessary:
  - in the interests of national security;
  - for the purpose of preventing or detecting serious crime;
  - in the interests of the economic well-being of the UK to the extent that such interests engage national security;
- Retention and/or disclosure is necessary to enable the Secretary of State (or as it may be the Scottish Ministers) to undertake statutory functions under the IPA2016;
- Retention and/or disclosure is necessary to enable the Judicial Commissioners or the Investigatory Powers Tribunal to undertake any of their functions;
- Retention and/or disclosure is necessary to ensure that prosecutors can discharge their obligations in relation to ensuring the fairness of criminal proceedings;
- Retention and/or disclosure is for the performance of any duty under the Public Records Act 1967 or the Public Records (Northern Ireland) Act 1923.

There are no other reasons for which interception product may be retained or disclosed.

The same restrictions apply to interception product disclosed to overseas authorities (s 54). Disclosure to overseas authorities cannot be made unless the

Secretary of State (or a Scottish Minister) is satisfied that safeguards equivalent to those required by s 53 are in place in the requesting jurisdiction.

There is a statutory duty not to make unauthorized disclosures of:

- interception product;
- secondary data;
- details concerning the issue, renewal, or modification of a warrant; or
- the existence of any requirement to assist in giving effect to the warrant (s 57 IPA2016).

Any such unauthorized disclosure is an offence for which the sanction is imprisonment, or a fine, or both (s 59 IPA2016).

Section 58 provides very limited exemptions from the general prohibition on disclosure. These 'excepted disclosures' allow relevant information to be provided to persons whose assistance is needed in executing a warrant; to specified bodies for carrying out their respective statutory functions; to legal advisers for the purpose of receiving advice; and for the purpose of satisfying statistical reporting regulations made by the Secretary of State (Interception Code, paras 9.5–9.10).

Interception product, including all copies, extracts, or summaries identifiable as being the product of an intercepted communication, should be destroyed as soon as practicable once grounds for its retention cease (Interception Code, para 9.22).

11.5.2 Provisions in relation to Members of Parliament

Where the purpose of a targeted interception warrant or a targeted examination warrant is to access the content of communications sent by or to a member of a relevant UK legislature or a UK MEP, the Secretary of State may not issue the warrant without the prior approval of the Prime Minister (s 26 IPA2016).

The relevant legislatures are the House of Commons, the House of Lords, the Scottish Parliament, the National Assembly of Wales, and the Northern Ireland Assembly. This protection also applies to communications to and from MEPs elected to represent a UK constituency at the European Parliament.

The accompanying Code of Practice provides guidance on additional safeguards to be implemented when a legislator's communications being contemplated for interception contain, or are likely to contain, confidential personal information and/or constituency business information. Intentional acquisition of such information requires specific justification of the necessity and proportionality for doing so. Unintended but likely collateral acquisition requires special consideration of possible mitigation and product management measures (Interception Code, para 9.39). Such justifications and considerations must be documented in the application for a warrant in these circumstances.

11.5.3 Provisions relating to legally privileged material

The protection from interception afforded to legally privileged material is not absolute, but is qualified and restricted by stringent criteria.

> **Further information and reading**
>
> 'Legally privileged material' is defined in:
> - s 10 Police and Criminal Evidence Act 1984 (for England and Wales);
> - s 263 IPA2016 (for Scotland); and
> - Art 12 Police and Criminal Evidence (Northern Ireland) Order 1989 (for Northern Ireland).

Applications for targeted interception warrants and targeted examination warrants made with the intention of acquiring communications comprising legally privileged material must include a statement declaring this purpose, in addition to the other information required to be documented in an application (s 27(2) IPA2016; Interception Code, para 9.47).

Section 27(4) stipulates that a warrant to intercept communications, or undertake targeted examination of communications, that comprise legally privileged material may only be issued in *exceptional and compelling circumstances*.

Exceptional and compelling circumstances will not exist unless (s 27(6)):

- the public interest in preserving the confidentiality of legal privilege is, in the specific circumstances, outweighed by the public interest in obtaining the information;
- there are no other reasonable means of obtaining the information; and
- the information sought is necessary for preventing death or serious injury.

It is for the Secretary of State and the Judicial Commissioner independently to determine that such exceptional and compelling circumstances exist. Such exceptional and compelling circumstances will arise 'only in a very restricted range of cases' (Interception Code, para 9.48). The interests of the economic well-being of the UK are specifically excluded from these provisions (s 27(5) IPA2016).

Exceptional and compelling circumstances do not in and of themselves justify the issuing of a warrant to intercept legally privileged communications. If such circumstances are held to exist, then the Secretary of State must satisfy him- or herself that suitable arrangements for the handling, retention, and destruction of privileged material are in place before the warrant may be issued (s 27(9) IPA2016).

When legally privileged material has been obtained by interception and is retained for purposes other than its destruction, a report must be made to the Investigatory Powers Commissioner (IPC) (Interception Code, paras 9.62–9.64). Except in urgent cases, investigators cannot act upon or otherwise disseminate legally privileged material obtained by interception until the IPC has been informed.

To serve the public interest in the fair and proper operation of the criminal justice system, investigators must take all reasonable steps to ensure that prosecutors and other officials concerned in the conduct of legal proceedings to which the legally privileged material pertains do not see the material (Interception Code, para 9.67).

11.5.4 Provisions relating to confidential journalistic material and sources

---

Definitions

'Journalistic material' means material created or acquired for the purpose of journalism (s 264 (2) IPA2016).

The content of a communication sent to a journalist, which the sender intends the journalist to use for the purposes of journalism, is to be regarded as journalistic material.

'Confidential journalistic material' means:

(a) in the case of material contained in a communication, journalistic material which the sender of the communication:
    (i) holds in confidence, or
    (ii) intends the recipient, or intended recipient of the communication to hold in confidence;
(b) in any other case, journalistic material which a person holds in confidence (s 264(6) IPA2016).

A person holds journalistic material 'in confidence' if:

(a) the person holds it subject to an express or implied undertaking to hold it in confidence, or
(b) the person holds it subject to a restriction on disclosure or an obligation of secrecy contained in an enactment. (s 264(7) IPA2016).

See also Interception Code, paras 9.69–9.71.

A 'source of journalistic information' is:

- an individual who provides material intended to be used for journalism, or knowing that the material would likely be used in this way; and
- any person acting as an intermediary between the sender of journalistic material and its intended recipient (s 263(1) IPA2016).

See also Interception Code, para 9.73.

See Interception Code, para 9.75 for criteria to consider in determining whether an individual is a journalist. Use of social media in and of itself does not define the user as a journalist.

If the purpose of an interception warrant is to authorize the interception of communications that contain or comprise confidential journalistic material, then the applicant for such a warrant must declare this purpose in the application.

The person considering the authorization of a warrant in these circumstances (or as may be, the application for examination of selected content acquired pursuant to a bulk interception warrant) must be satisfied that 'appropriate safeguards relating to the handling, retention, use and disclosure of such material are in place' (Interception Code, paras 9.72, 9.74, and 9.79).

Similar requirements are imposed when the purpose of the warrant application is to identify or confirm the source of journalistic material.

In each circumstance, the relevant safeguards required to be in place are set out in s 53 IPA2016:

(a) the number of persons to whom any of the material is disclosed or otherwise made available;
(b) the extent to which any of the material is disclosed or otherwise made available;
(c) the extent to which any of the material is copied;
(d) the number of copies that are made (s 53(2) IPA2016),

must all be kept to the minimum necessary to achieve one of the following authorized purposes (s 53(3) IPA2016), such authorized purposes being if, and only if:

(a) it is, or is likely to become, necessary:
    (i) in the interests of national security;
    (ii) for the purpose of preventing or detecting serious crime, or
    (iii) in the interests of the economic well-being of the United Kingdom so far as those interests are also relevant to the interests of national security, if it relates to the acts or intentions of persons outside the United Kingdom,
(b) it is necessary for facilitating the carrying out of any functions under this Act of the Secretary of State, the Scottish Ministers or the person to whom the warrant is or was addressed;
(c) it is necessary for facilitating the carrying out of any functions of the Judicial Commissioners or the Investigatory Powers Tribunal under or in relation to this Act;
(d) it is necessary to ensure that a person (P) who is conducting a criminal prosecution has the information P needs to determine what is required of P by P's duty to secure the fairness of the prosecution; or
(e) it is necessary for the performance of any duty imposed on any person by the Public Records Act 1958 or the Public Records Act (Northern Ireland) 1923.

A report must be made to the Investigatory Powers Commissioner as soon as is reasonably practicable when confidential journalistic material or material that identifies a journalistic source is retained for purposes other than destruction (Interception Code, para 9.83).

11.6 **Accessing Stored Communications**

Accessing the content of communications stored in or by a telecommunications system before or after transmission, such as text messages or voicemail, constitutes interception (s 4(4)(b) IPA2016). However, before making an application for an interception warrant to access such content, investigators should consider whether any other applicable and relevant statutory provisions that might authorize access to stored communication content.

Various powers of search, acquisition, seizure, production, or inspection are available under:

- The Police and Criminal Evidence Act 1984
- The Terrorism Act 2007 (Schedule 7)
- The Proceeds of Crime Act 2002
- The Firearms Act 1968
- The Protection of Children Act 1978
- The Theft Act 1968
- The Misuse of Drugs Act 1971
- The Customs and Excise Management Act 1979.

Section 6(1)(c)(ii) IPA2016 provides that accessing *stored* telecommunications content using a relevant statutory power other than a power provided by IPA2016 will be lawful interception. (See also Interception Code, paras 12.12–12.16.)

Stored communications can also be obtained using an equipment interference warrant.

In any given investigation, investigators and investigation managers will need to determine which, if any, alternative statutory powers may be used to access stored content such as voicemails, emails, or text messages depending on the circumstances of the case. The various statutory powers will be context-specific and care should be exercised to ensure the correct power is employed.

11.7 **Equipment Interference for the Purposes of Interception**

To the extent that interception of communications content or the acquisition of communications data requires equipment to be interfered with, such interference must be authorized. Any interference likely to constitute an offence under the Computer Misuse Act 1990 and/or engage protected human rights must be authorized under Part 5 IPA2016 (s 14 IPA2016). Equipment interference for intercepting communications content or acquiring communications data cannot any longer be authorized under Part III PA97. However, if the proposed interference with property is not for the purposes of obtaining communications, equipment data, or other information, then a property interference authorization under Part II PA97 will be required.

Equipment interference warrants authorize interference with any equipment for the purpose of:

- intercepting communications;
- acquiring equipment data; and
- acquiring stored communications.

They may also authorize:

- any incidental conduct necessary for undertaking that which is expressly authorized by the warrant.

Material lawfully obtained under an equipment interference warrant may be used evidentially (Equipment Code, para 3.13).

If the equipment interference is conducted in conjunction with directed or intrusive surveillance, such surveillance may lawfully be included in and authorized by the equipment interference warrant without needing a separate authority under RIPA2000 (Equipment Code, paras 3.17–3.19). However, where the purpose of the equipment interference warrant is to enable interception of communication content, then an interception warrant is required in conjunction with the equipment interference warrant or a combined warrant must be applied for (Equipment Code, para 3.22). An equipment interference warrant cannot authorize interception of content as coincidental to the equipment interference.

Definitions

For the purpose of Part V IPA2016 (Equipment interference)

'Communication' means (s 135 IPA2016):

(a) anything comprising speech, music, sounds, visual images, or data of any description; and
(b) signals serving either for the impartation of anything between persons, between a person and a thing or between things or for the actuation or control of any apparatus.

'equipment' means: 'equipment producing electromagnetic, acoustic or other emissions or any device capable of being used in connection with such equipment'.

'equipment data' means (s 100 IPA2016):

> 'systems data' (s 263(4) IPA2016): any data that enables or facilitates, identifies or describes anything connected with the function of a postal service, a telecommunications service, or a telecommunications system (including relevant apparatus). (Systems data is not communication content.)
>
> or
>
> 'identifying data' (s 263(2) and (3) IPA2016): data which may be used to identify any person, event, apparatus, system, or service; or the location of any person, event or thing; including data relating to the fact, type, method, and pattern of the event; or the time or duration of the event.

Conduct that constitutes equipment interference includes (but is not limited to):

- Using another person's login details to access data stored on a computer
- Covertly downloading data directly from an unattended device
- Covertly and remotely downloading data from a device
- Exploiting software vulnerabilities
- Deploying key logging software.

Equipment interference may be authorized in a targeted equipment interference warrant or in a targeted examination warrant (s 101 IPA2016), or in a bulk equipment interference warrant (s 176 IPA2016), although the latter two warrants are available only to the intelligence services. Law enforcement officers may apply for targeted equipment interference warrants only (s 106 IPA2016).

11.7.1 **Who may issue targeted equipment interference warrants?**

A 'law enforcement chief' listed in Schedule 6 Table Part 1 and Table Part 2 IPA2016 may issue a targeted equipment interference warrant on application by an appropriate law enforcement officer in relation to the chief, or in other words, a member of the chief officer's own organization, unless formal collaboration arrangements stipulate otherwise.

In summary, these persons are:

Part 1

- The Chief Constable of a police force maintained under s 2 Police Act 1996
- The Commissioner or Assistant Commissioner of the Metropolitan Police Service
- The Commissioner of the City of London Police
- The Chief Constable of the Police Service of Scotland
- The Chief Constable or Deputy Chief Constable of the Police Service of Northern Ireland
- The Director General of the National Crime Agency
- The Chief Constable of the British Transport Police
- The Chief Constable of the Ministry of Defence Police
- The Provost Marshal of the Royal Navy Police
- The Provost Marshal of the Royal Military Police
- The Provost Marshal of the Royal Air Force Police.

Part 2

- Designated senior immigration officials
- Designated senior HM Revenue and Customs officials
- The Chair of the Competition and Markets Authority
- The Chair and Deputy Chair of the Independent Police Complaints Commission

- The Police Investigations and Review Commissioner.

The intelligence and security agencies, GCHQ, and Defence Intelligence may also apply for such authorizations.

A law enforcement chief as defined in Schedule 6 may issue warrants that combine authorities for targeted equipment interference with authorizations under s 93 PA97, s 28 RIPA2000, and s 32 RIPA2000 (Schedule 8, para 11 IPA2016).

11.7.2 Considerations in issuing a targeted equipment interference warrant

The distinction in Schedule 6 between those law enforcement chiefs listed in Part 1 and those listed in Part 2 is relevant to the purposes for which targeted equipment interference warrants may be issued in a law enforcement context (see Table 11.2).

Table 11.2 Purposes for which a targeted equipment interference warrant may be issued by persons listed in Schedule 6 IPA2016

Persons listed in Parts 1 and 2, Schedule 6	Persons listed in Part 1 only, Schedule 6
s 106(1) IPA2016	**s 106(3) IPA2016**
(a) the law enforcement chief considers that the warrant is necessary for the purpose of preventing or detecting serious crime [and in Northern Ireland only, national security as well s 106 (6) IPA2016];	(a) the law enforcement chief considers that the warrant is necessary for the purpose of preventing death or any injury or damage to a person's physical or mental health or of mitigating any injury or damage to a person's physical or mental health;
(b) the law enforcement chief considers that the conduct authorized by the warrant is proportionate to what is sought to be achieved by that conduct;	(b) the law enforcement chief considers that the conduct authorized by the warrant is proportionate to what is sought to be achieved by that conduct;
(c) the law enforcement chief considers that satisfactory arrangements made for the purposes of sections 129 and 130 (safeguards relating to disclosure etc.) are in force in relation to the warrant; and	(c) the law enforcement chief considers that satisfactory arrangements made for the purposes of sections 129 and 130 (safeguards relating to disclosure etc.) are in force in relation to the warrant; and
(d) except where the law enforcement chief considers that there is an urgent need to issue the warrant, the decision to issue the warrant has been approved by a Judicial Commissioner.	(d) except where the law enforcement chief considers that there is an urgent need to issue the warrant, the decision to issue the warrant has been approved by a Judicial Commissioner.

All of the criteria set out in s 106(1) and in s 106(3) must be satisfied for the persons listed in Part 1 and Part 2 to be empowered to issue a targeted equipment interference warrant. Note the need for prior approval from a Judicial Commissioner before the warrant can be executed. (Those matters that the Judicial Commissioners must consider are set out in s 108, with ss 109 and 110 making provision for the issuing of warrants in urgent cases without Judicial Commissioner prior approval. Failure to plan sufficient time to obtain Judicial Commissioner approval of a warrant before it is executed does not constitute urgency. See also Equipment Code, paras 5.55–5.63.)

Important additional restrictions are placed on the officials listed in Part 2 Schedule 6 IPA2016 by s 106 subsections (7) and (13) (immigration); (8) and (9) (HM Revenue and Customs); (10) (Competition and Markets Authority); (11) (IPCC); and (12) Police Investigations and Review Commission. For these officials, s 106(1)(a) is further qualified by the stipulation that the serious crime must relate only to matters within their agency jurisdiction.

Section 107 prescribes that the following people may only issue a targeted equipment interference warrant when they consider there to exist a British Islands connection in the matter (s 107 IPA2016):

- The Chief Constable of a police force maintained under s 2 Police Act 1996
- The Commissioner or Assistant Commissioner of the Metropolitan Police Service
- The Commissioner of the City of London Police
- The Chief Constable of the Police Service of Scotland
- The Chief Constable or Deputy Chief Constable of the Police Service of Northern Ireland
- The Chief Constable of the British Transport Police
- The Chief Constable of the Ministry of Defence Police
- The Chair and Deputy Chair of the Independent Police Complaints Commission
- The Police Investigations and Review Commissioner.

The Director General of the National Crime Agency may not issue a targeted equipment interference warrant to a member of a collaborative police force unless the Director General considers that there is a British Islands connection (s 107 (3) IPA2016).

Further Information and Reading

'British Islands' means collectively the United Kingdom of Great Britain and Northern Ireland, the Channel Islands, and the Isle of Man (Schedule 1, Interpretation Act 1978).

For the purposes of s 107 IPA2016, a British Islands connection exists if:

(a) any of the conduct authorized by the warrant would take place in the British Islands (regardless of the location of the equipment that would, or may, be interfered with);

(b) any of the equipment which would, or may, be interfered with would, or may, be in the British Islands at some time while the interference is taking place; or

(c) a purpose of the interference is to obtain:

(i) communications sent by, or to, a person who is, or whom the law enforcement officer believes to be, for the time being in the British Islands,

(ii) information relating to an individual who is, or whom the law enforcement officer believes to be, for the time being in the British Islands, or

(iii) equipment data which forms part of, or is connected with, communications or information falling within sub-paragraph (i) or (ii).

The requirement for a British Islands connection does not apply to the intelligence and security services when issuing a warrant under s 106 IPA2016.

Targeted equipment interference warrants may be issued for up to six months duration, renewable for a further six months (ss 116–117 IPA2016; Equipment Code paras 5.64–5.72), and may if necessary, be modified by the person issuing or an issuing delegate (s 123 IPA2016; Equipment Code, paras 5.81–5.85: modifications to warrants issued by law enforcement chiefs require notification to and prior approval by the Judicial Commissioner). Urgent warrants expire after five days, the Judicial Commissioner having been informed of the warrant's issuance within three working days of it being issued. If the tests of necessity and proportionality cease to be met, the person issuing such a warrant must cancel it, s 125 IPA2016 providing that the person issuing such a warrant may cancel it at any time.

11.7.3 Safeguards and protections

Sections 111–114 IPA2016 provide similar safeguards and protections in relation to equipment interference warrants that are provided for in relation to interception (see Chapter 9, 9.1.5 and 11.5).

11.8 Protecting Privacy

Requiring the authority of a Secretary of State (or as it may be a Scottish Minister)—and in certain circumstances the authority of the Prime Minister— signals the government perspective that there is no greater intrusion into private and family life than the interception of communications. (Although a case could be argued that interactive surveillance—the use of informers and under-cover operatives—engages Article 8 rights with even greater significance because the moral and material harms arising from such intrusion are compounded by the moral and material harms of the active deception that is necessary in such deployments, but the current statutory framework does not reflect such a perspective.)

Accordingly, the protection of privacy is a *leitmotif* throughout the IPA2016 and its accompanying Codes of Practice. Some provisions have already been introduced in this chapter—special protections in relation to Parliamentarians' communications or legally privileged and confidential journalistic material, for example. The privacy *leitmotif* first appears in the overture to the Act, in which general duties on relation privacy are set out before any provision is made to empower interception.

In considering the issuing, modification, renewal, or as it may be the prior approval of such an authority—and the cancellation of any authority provided for by IPA2016—a public authority must have regard to:

(a) whether what is sought to be achieved by the warrant, authorization, or notice could reasonably be achieved by other less intrusive means;
(b) whether the level of protection to be applied in relation to any obtaining of information by virtue of the warrant, authorization, or notice is higher be-cause of the particular sensitivity of that information (for example: legally privileged material; information likely to identify or confirm a journalistic source; confidential information);
(c) the public interest in the integrity and security of telecommunication sys-tems and postal services; and
(d) any other aspects of the public interest in the protection of privacy (s 2(2) IPA2016).

Such considerations must be made having regard to others including (a provi-sion which indicates the following list is not to be considered exclusive):

(a) the interests of national security or of the economic well-being of the United Kingdom;
(b) the public interest in preventing or detecting serious crime;
(c) other considerations which are relevant to:
    (i) whether the conduct authorized or required by the warrant, authoriza-tion, or notice is proportionate; or
    (ii) whether it is necessary to act for a purpose provided for by this Act;

(d) the requirements of the Human Rights Act 1998; and
(e) other requirements of public law (s 2(4) IPA2016).

The various applicable tests for 'necessity' are defined throughout the Act and have been considered above (for example, see 11.4).

The benchmark for the consideration of proportionality is not the seriousness of the crime under investigation, but whether the product which is sought is proportionate to the means being employed to obtain it. Any assessment of proportionality—in relation to the provisions of the IPA2016 (note: the Codes of Practice accompanying RIPA2000 set out slightly different considerations for proportionality and these are discussed at Chapter 2, 2.2.5) 'involves balancing the seriousness of the intrusion into the privacy against the need for the activity in investigative, operational and capability terms. The conduct authorised should offer a realistic prospect of bringing the expected benefit and should not be disproportionate or arbitrary' (Interception Code, para 4.11).

No interference with privacy will ever be proportionate if the desired information can reasonably be obtained by less intrusive means (Interception Code, para 4.14).

The Interception Code requires the following to be considered (para.4.15):

- the extent of the proposed interference with privacy against what is sought to be achieved;
- how and why the methods to be utilized will cause the least possible interference to both the subject of the investigation and any third parties;
- whether the proposed interception is an appropriate and reasonable use of the legislation, all other reasonable alternatives having been considered; and
- what other methods to obtain the desired information or outcome have either been implemented unsuccessfully or disregarded.

Such considerations must be made—and the reasoning documented—at each stage of the authorization process: by the applicant investigator; by the person authorizing; and, as applicable, by the judicial officer considering approval of the proposed authority.

The consideration of proportionality is a matter that investigators and investigation managers must maintain under constant review within the investigation risk management regime. Whilst the proportionality test for a single intervention might be satisfied, the overall proportionality of the investigation as a whole must also be considered regularly as an investigation progresses: a long series of numerous serious intrusions against privacy may be viewed as cumulatively disproportionate.

Checklist of key issues when considering whether or not to deploy covert investigation techniques

- What evidence or intelligence is being sought?
- How is it relevant to the operation under consideration?
- What is the least intrusive means of securing such evidence or information?

- Has the least intrusive means of securing the evidence or information been attempted? If not, why not?

- What is the likelihood of collateral intrusion against the privacy of persons not being investigated? How will collateral intrusion be prevented (or if not, minimized) and how will the product of collateral intrusion be managed?

- What are the risks to the organization of such tactics? (Chapter 4)

- What are the risks to the organization's staff of such tactics? (Chapter 4)

- What are the risks to the public or specific third parties when such tactics are deployed? (Chapter 4)

- What are the risks to the subject of the investigation? (Chapter 4)

- Will the proposed methods breach Article 8(1)? (Chapter 2.2.1)

- Is there justification for doing so provided by Article 8(2)? (Chapter 2.2.4)

- How is the legality test met? (Chapter 2.2.3)

- How is the legitimacy test met? (Chapter 2.2.4)

- How is the necessity test met? (Chapter 2.2.5)

- How is the proportionality test met? (Chapter 2.2.5)

- Are the arguments justifying the application to use covert investigation based on reliable information/intelligence, or has the applicant adopted a 'tick-the-box' approach to completing the application without giving full consideration to the facts of the case and the issues arising?

- Have the arguments justifying the granting of authorization to use covert investigation been fully articulated, or has the authorizing officer merely paid lip service to the pro forma authorization template via which authority is granted?

- When should this authority be reviewed? What circumstances will or may arise that will necessitate review before then?

- How are the methods by which the evidence/intelligence will be obtained to be protected at trial? (Chapter 5)

- How will the product of the surveillance be managed? (Chapter 5)

Planning covert investigation actions

Remember to include the PLAN for covert investigation tactics in all investigation policy-book entries relating to covert investigation considerations and decisions.

P Proportionality

Why is it proportionate to obtain the intended product of this surveillance in the manner proposed? (Chapter 2.2.5)

L Legitimacy

What is the legitimate purpose of the proposed action: the prevention of disorder or crime; the interests of national security; the interests of public safety; the interests of the economic well-being of the country; the protection of health or morals; the protection of the rights and freedoms of others? (Chapter 2.2.4)

A Authority to Undertake Proposed Action

What is the lawful foundation and authority for the proposed action? From whom must authorization be sought? (Chapter 2.2.3)

N Necessity of Proposed Action

Why is the proposed action necessary? (Chapter 2.2.5)

Covert Human Intelligence Sources

12.1 **Introduction**

As the law was originally enacted, the deployment of a covert human intelligence source (a CHIS) was equated with directed surveillance in the hierarchy of covert investigation methods and the statutory regulation thereof. Such a deployment therefore appeared to be considered a lesser intrusion into an individual's private life than deploying an audio or a video-recording device inside that person's dwelling; and lesser still than eavesdropping on a telephone conversation that person might have. Secondary legislation introducing an enhanced authorization regime was enacted in 2013 because by then unhappy experience disclosed at court and corroborated through subsequent inquiry and revelation had exposed the widely rippling adverse consequences of mismanagement in this arena. CHIS is a term of art for a variety of conduct that engages multiple moral as well as legal harms. In ascending degree of deception, manipulation, and betrayal, a CHIS can be a test purchase operative (TPO); a CHIS can be an undercover officer (UCO); a CHIS can be an informer: one small acronym encompasses a bewilderingly broad range of realities, roles, and responsibilities.

Whereas the other forms of directed, intrusive, or interception surveillance each constitutes what is essentially just a different form of secret (and often remote) monitoring, the deployment of a CHIS involves direct engagement and interaction both with the subject of an investigation and with any third parties who happen to be present in the deployment arena. An individual under investigation who comes to realize that he or she has been covertly watched or listened to may well feel coercively exposed, their privacy infringed, but an individual under investigation (or a person innocently associating with one such) who subsequently learns that they have been interacting with a CHIS is likely to feel betrayed rather than merely exposed; their autonomy violated rather than merely their privacy infringed.

For the deployment of a CHIS to succeed, the CHIS may not merely monitor but must actively practise some degree of deception: whether it be a TPO pretending to be a bona fide customer to secure evidence of an illicit retail; whether it be a UCO using a false identity and playing a role to inveigle him- or herself into another's misplaced confidence for the longer-term corroboration of evidence or intelligence; or whether it be an informer betraying a trust, perhaps long-held, in exchange for some form of perceived personal benefit, inflicting public harm on another for private gain (as it may be: cash reward; lenient consideration; revenge; self-satisfaction; or some other private motivation).

The state and its agents cause significant moral harms to others when a CHIS in whichever role is deployed, the degree of moral harm so caused increasing along the spectrum from TPO, through UCO, to informer.

The moral harms do not just befall those being investigated and their associates. CHISs, too, suffer adverse moral and material consequences. The private lives of informers and UCOs are intruded upon, as well as the private lives of those being investigated. Living a lie takes an emotional and psychological toll (see Evans and Lewis, 2013, for numerous examples of this). There is the constant fear of being discovered; the fear of retribution; and retribution itself, sometimes murderous (see Johnson, 2005). The deceptively simple appeal of living a life less ordinary is often delusional and so, often, morally harmful in and of itself. The moral compass can be severely diverted by creative illusion, especially when an individual's well-being depends upon successful concealment and camouflage. Nor will the CHIS necessarily be respected for his or her sacrifice (notwithstanding any duty of care): when Judas sought to return the thirty pieces of silver, his attempted refund was rejected on the grounds that the reward was tainted by betrayal and butchery (Gospel according to Matthew c27:vv3–8; an attitude derived from ancient law and custom, see Deuteronomy c27:v25).

Institutions, as well as individuals, suffer. The use of covert investigation (including the deployment of any given CHIS) in practical terms may be necessary; in given circumstances may be legally justifiable; in given circumstances may be morally justifiable. Nevertheless, having to resort to lies and deception inevitably corrodes the integrity of any institution the purpose of which is to serve the common good. It does so because lies and deception undermine all relationships, be it a relationship between individuals, a relationship between an individual and an institution, or a relationship between an institution and the community it serves. And ultimately the criminal justice system serves to regulate and restore social order when relationships have corroded, corrupted, or collapsed, or were not civilly cast and composed in the first place. So actions by criminal justice actors that employ deceit and dishonesty particularly imperil integrity: the integrity of self; the integrity of institution; and the integrity of the criminal justice system.

A utilitarian might argue that the ends justify the means; but that line of argument invites the associated argument that it will be acceptable on occasions for law enforcers and regulators to break laws they are charged with enforcing in order to catch law-breakers (at face value, an evident contradiction). That approach requires very weighty justification.

Such is the context within which investigators use CHISs (in the sense that tradespersons use tools). It is an unsavoury world, but one with which investigation agencies on occasion may have to engage. Whether or not the relative lack of significance that seems to be attached to the utilization of CHISs within the statutory regime contributed to the lack of respect and consideration for all parties evident in the (mis-)management of the operations chronicled by Rob Evans and Paul Lewis is a speculation that lies outside the remit of this book. Nevertheless, the episodes these authors document highlight the complexities of the issues engaged when agencies contemplate using CHISs.

We do not suggest that CHISs should never be deployed. We do suggest that this area of investigation methodology engages far greater moral and legal complexity than the current statutory regime recognizes. (Some support for this interpretation seems evident in the expanded revised Code of Practice, which seeks to elaborate with policy and procedure the relative lack of statutory guidance.) The extraordinary revelations arising from the conduct of some officers within the Metropolitan Police Service's Special Demonstration Squad (SDS), which resulted in UCOs whilst on deployment fathering children with the persons against whom they were deployed, present the extreme end of the moral and material dangers that ensue from CHIS deployment. Such sensationalism risks skewing sober, sensible, and strategic debate. The conduct of some SDS officers that triggered significant public outrage illustrates how badly CHIS deployments can go wrong if not properly managed. The law has little to say on the moral issues arising from CHIS deployment. Investigators, applicants, authorizing officers, and approving officers must nevertheless have at the forefront of their minds the moral issues within the context of which the current statutory architecture has been constructed.

Further reading and information

On the mis-management of UCOs, see Rob Evans and Paul Lewis, *Undercover: The True Story of Britain's Secret Police* (Faber & Faber, London, 2013).

On the realities faced by informers, see Graham Johnson, *Powder Wars: The Supergrass Who Brought Down Britain's Biggest Drug Dealers* (Mainstream Publishing, Edinburgh, 2005).

On the ethics of police use of informers, see Clive Harfield, 'Police informers and professional ethics', *Criminal Justice Ethics* 31(2) (2012), 73–95.

On secrecy in police work, see Sissela Bok, *Secrets: On the Ethics of Concealment and Revelation* (Vintage Books, New York, 1989).

For a robust critique of (American) police reliance upon informers and the adverse consequences for society and the criminal justice system, see Alexandra Natapoff, *Snitching: Criminal Informants and the Erosion of American Justice* (New York University Press, New York, 2009).

12.2 What Is a CHIS?

So what is a CHIS? How is this entity defined in law? The following are sequential tests derived from the statutory definition at s 26(8) RIPA2000.

Definition of a CHIS

(1) Does the potential source *establish* or *maintain* a relationship (personal or otherwise)?

(2) Is the relationship conducted in a manner *calculated to ensure that one party is unaware of its real purpose*? (See s 28(9) RIPA2000 for a definition of covert purpose.)

If the answer to these preliminary tests is *yes*, three further tests are applied:

(3) Is the purpose of the relationship to facilitate the obtaining of information?
(4) Is the purpose of the relationship to facilitate access to information?
(5) Is the purpose of the relationship to facilitate the disclosure of information obtained during (or as a consequence of) the relationship without the knowledge of one of the parties?

If the answer to any one of these three tests is *yes*, then taken in conjunction with tests 1 and 2, the source is a CHIS whose conduct must be properly authorized and managed. CHIS authorization is necessary in all circumstances where the CHIS uses and exploits a personal relationship to acquire information from another person that the other person would regard as being private information. The issue is not who the CHIS is nor what he or she produces, but the new relationships that are established or the existing relationships that are maintained and the covert use that is made of these relationships (see also CHIS Code, para 2.12).

In the context of this statutory definition, the word *'establishes'* means to 'set up'; to create a relationship which did not previously exist (CHIS Code, para 2.13).

In the context of this statutory definition, the word *'maintains'* means to sustain an already established relationship over a period of time (CHIS Code, para 2.13).

The mere fact of repeated contact does not necessarily mean that a relationship is established thereby or maintained. The CHIS Code provides two similar but subtly different examples of a TPO deployment (at para 2.13), in which the difference is the degree of trust established by the TPO with the person suspected of making illegal sales. If a TPO merely makes a number of purchases over a period of time, spending no more time in the company of the suspected seller than is necessary to complete each individual transaction, then no relationship is established or maintained. In these circumstances a directed surveillance authorization is required because the TPO is gathering information which cumulatively demonstrates a pattern of conduct and behaviour and so comprises personal information. Where the TPO needs first to engage with the suspected seller in order to engender trust because the seller will only sell to known and trusted customers, then a relationship has been established as per the statutory definition, and a CHIS authorization will be required.

12.3 **What Is a Relevant Source?**

The Regulation of Investigatory Powers (Covert Human Intelligence Sources: Relevant Sources) Order 2013 (SI 2013/2788) came into force on 1 January 2014 and created the new characterization of certain CHISs as 'relevant sources': a direct response to the management issues arising from the debacle of the Metropolitan Police SDS long-term, undercover deployments.

Individuals are considered to be relevant sources when:

- they meet the criteria to be defined as a CHIS (see 12.2); and
- they hold an office, rank, or position with a prescribed agency.

The agencies prescribed in the Order (SI 2013/2788) as currently enacted (and also listed in Annexe B of the CHIS Code) are:

- A police force maintained under s 2 PA97
- The City of London Police
- The Metropolitan Police
- The Police Service of Northern Ireland
- The Police Service of Scotland
- The Ministry of Defence Police
- The Royal Navy Police
- The Royal Military Police
- The Royal Air Force Police
- The British Transport Police
- The National Crime Agency
- Her Majesty's Revenue and Customs
- The Home Office.

A CHIS employed by an agency other than those listed above will not be a relevant source. In essence, a relevant source is an undercover officer who works for the police, customs, or Home Office.

12.4 What Are 'Confidential Sources', 'Confidential Contacts', and 'Tasked Witnesses'?

There has been considerable confusion in a number of organizations over what have been termed variously 'confidential sources', 'confidential contacts', 'confidential source (or contact) register', and 'tasked witnesses'. With the exception of the more recent 'tasked witness', these terms appear to have come into use well before the enacting of RIPA2000 as a means of managing informants (rather than, and distinct from, informers) from a variety of backgrounds whose true identity had to be protected. They are not terms that have any statutory basis under RIPA2000 or its supporting secondary legislation. Indeed, in his Annual Report for 2006–07, the Chief Surveillance Commissioner observed that he was:

> disturbed by the introduction, in some forces, of the term 'tasked witness' as an apparent alternative to the correct, legally-recognised, term 'covert human intelligence source'. These individuals have been engaged in a manner that

establishes or maintains a covert relationship and I have not been satisfied that the arrangements for their welfare, security and management have been of the standard required by law. The reasons for the introduction of this term are not clear, but it appears to me that the explanation may be a lack of trained handlers or the ignorance of senior investigating officers. I will continue to criticise the term and, when appropriate, the impropriety of the activity which it may embrace.

(para 8.9)

Any person providing information to investigating authorities under circumstances outlined in the definition box at 12.2 will be a CHIS and must be managed according to the statutory provisions of RIPA2000, the secondary legislation, and the relevant Code.

Where organizations have categories of confidential sources or contacts, tasked witnesses, and a register of such, these should be reviewed to ascertain whether or not they should be registered as CHISs.

The key determinants are the relationship and the purpose to which it is put. Thus not all those who provide information to investigators fit the definition of a CHIS. The CHIS Code, paras 2.16–2.25, elaborates upon conduct that falls outside the definition of a CHIS. For example, an individual who simply volunteers information within his or her personal knowledge will not be a CHIS. Individuals bound by professional or statutory duty to make specified disclosures in given circumstances will not be CHISs. An individual tasked with recording the registration numbers of all vehicles arriving at a given location (to use the example illustrated at para 2.22 of the CHIS Code) will not be a CHIS because no relationship is established or maintained for this particular purpose: but if the information so gathered amounts to personal information, then a directed surveillance authority will be necessary if the information is being gathered on behalf a public authority so regulated.

12.5 **What Is a Senior Responsible Officer?**

The CHIS Code, para 9.1, *requires* (not merely recommends) that every relevant public authority must have a senior responsible officer who shall be responsible for:

- the integrity of the process in place within the public authority for the management of CHIS;
- compliance with Part II of the Act and with this Code;
- oversight of the reporting of errors to the relevant oversight Commissioner and the identification of both the cause(s) of errors and the implementation of processes to minimize repetition of errors;
- engagement with the IPCO inspectors when they conduct their inspections, where applicable; and

- where necessary, oversight of the implementation of post-inspection action plans approved by the relevant oversight Commissioner.

In order to be able to fulfil these responsibilities, the senior responsible officer is likely to be a member of the executive leadership group.

12.6 **Which Public Authorities May Deploy CHISs?**

Public authorities empowered to utilize CHISs are defined in Schedule 1 RIPA2000 as amended. This is accessible online via <http://www.legislation. gov.uk/ukpga/2000/23/contents> (accessed January 2018). Readers should be aware that although the online statutory database will have the latest available updated version of the Schedule (which has changed numerous times since original enactment), the online version may not have been amended to take account of all recent changes. The website will provide information about which amendments have yet to be updated in the published version of the Schedule.

Some public authorities are empowered to use directed surveillance under s 28 RIPA2000 but not to deploy CHIS under s 29 RIPA2000. Other public authorities are empowered to do both. Authorizing officers will need to understand clearly what it is that their organization is empowered to do, and what conduct and relationships fall within and outside the definition of a CHIS.

12.7 **What Powers Does the Law Provide in Relation to CHISs?**

RIPA2000 distinguishes between the *use* of a CHIS and the *conduct* of a CHIS and so distinguishes authorization accordingly. The requirement for authorization is derived from the fact that a human relationship is to be manipulated covertly (which fact will always engage Article 8 ECHR rights) rather than because private information will be gained thereby (CHIS Code, para 2.11).

Further information and reading

CHIS Code paras 2.6 and 2.7 provide the following definitions:

> An authorization for the use of a CHIS will be necessary to authorize steps taken by a public authority in relation to a CHIS.

Investigators must be authorized to use a CHIS at the operational level.

> An authorization for conduct will authorize steps taken by the CHIS on behalf, or at the request of a public authority.

Any conduct undertaken by the CHIS on behalf of the organization must be authorized at the tactical level.

Although it will be common practice to authorize both use of and conduct by simultaneously, authorizing officers must ensure that each is properly distinguished and appropriately authorized.

Three general types of conduct may be authorized for a CHIS (s 29(4) RIPA2000):

- Any such activities involving conduct by a CHIS or the use of a CHIS as are specified in the authorization. This gives considerable latitude to authorizing officers and is very flexible. By the same token, if a particular conduct is not mentioned on the authority, it will not be authorized. This reaffirms the importance of precision when drafting applications and authorizations.
- Conduct by or in relation to a specified subject to whose actions the CHIS authorization relates.
- Conduct carried out for the purposes of or in connection with a specific investigation or operation, as described in the authorization.

12.7.1 Can a CHIS participate in crime as part of their authorized conduct?

On criminal participation, either by an informer or by an undercover operative, RIPA2000 is essentially silent, leaving much room for interpretation.

One interpretation holds that, since RIPA2000 does not specifically permit infiltration and participation (in other words there is no specific statutory provision for participation), no CHIS may be authorized to engage in such conduct because this might fail the lawfulness test under Article 8 ECHR. Such an interpretation would severely inhibit the use of CHISs, particularly when investigating serious organized crime, and such an interpretation is inconsistent with a case law tradition that unambiguously authorizes participation in furtherance of criminal activity within very strict parameters.

An alternative interpretation of s 27 RIPA2000 has been hypothesized that accommodates the view that any conduct properly authorized under Part II of RIPA2000 will be lawful if it is specifically authorized and the conduct is in accordance with the authorization. The lawfulness of a CHIS's conduct in this interpretation would be contingent upon the extent to which the CHIS complies with the authorization (s 27(1) RIPA2000). On this account it follows that the authority itself must be precise and detailed, with reasons given for each decision and direction. Conduct not specified in the authorization will not be lawful. The briefing of CHISs should be fully documented so as to demonstrate not only that the individual has been properly briefed but that the terms of reference are fully understood, particularly where infiltration or some degree of participation are being authorized. 'If an authorization covers participation in a criminal offence, and the authorization itself is valid (that is to say, it meets the statutory tests), then it would appear that the behaviour of the CHIS is not criminal' (Fitzpatrick, 2005, 29). An example developed by Fitzpatrick is that of a CHIS infiltrating a terrorist organization, as a consequence of which the operative has to wear insignia associated with the organization. Such conduct would be a criminal offence under the Terrorism Act 2000 but would nevertheless be necessary to maintain cover.

Further information and reading

B Fitzpatrick, 'Covert human intelligence sources as offenders', *Covert Policing Review* (2005), 15–32.

Note: the level of offending envisaged as being authorized in Fitzpatrick's example is minor in terms of its harmful consequence. This is surely important in such considerations. The conduct is criminalized, but when balanced against the safety and welfare of the CHIS on deployment in the first place, and the anticipated benefit of the information that will be gathered through the deployment in the second place, the offending (the wearing of a prohibited symbol) is a matter upon which the Crown Prosecution Service (CPS) might reasonably take the view that the public interest is not best served in these circumstances by prosecuting the CHIS for wearing the symbol. In such circumstances the authorization should document such considerations, and any authority granted should specify that authority is granted to display this symbol as necessary and proportionate conduct to preserve the safety of the CHIS, thus minimizing the risk of reprisals such as criminal assault being inflicted upon the CHIS.

On its face, however, the wording of s 27(1) RIPA2000 does not explicitly empower authorizing officers to authorize criminal conduct on the part of a CHIS (and there seems to be no attempt to draw a line between criminal conduct that might justifiably be authorized and criminal conduct that could never be justifiably authorized, such as murder). That CHISs should enjoy no guaranteed exemption from criminal liability seems to be supported by the construction of s 27(2), which provides that an investigator will not be liable to *civil liability* in respect of conduct that is incidental to properly authorized conduct or which is not authorized but is capable of being so and for which authorization might reasonably have been sought. Exemption from an incidental tort or trespass is very different from criminal liability exemption.

Parliament's intentions about how far infiltration should go were outlined in a debate about one of the many statutory instruments, although the declaration is hardly definitive:

> It was always the intention that the Act would not provide immunity from prosecution. The intention was that it would provide ECHR cover for the use of a CHIS. However, we have since reconsidered, taken further advice and concluded that, in a very limited range of circumstances, it may be possible that participation in a criminal offence might be rendered lawful by virtue of

a *correctly authorised CHIS authorisation*. Ultimately, it still remains a matter for the prosecution authorities and the courts to decide whether an authorisation would render conduct that would usually be considered unlawful as lawful.

(Bob Ainsworth MP, *Hansard* Fifth Standing Committee
on Delegated Legislation, col 004 (3 July 2002); emphasis added.)

The revised CHIS Code provides little in the way of elucidation, merely stating (para 1.9) that neither RIPA2000 Part II nor the CHIS Code 'is intended to affect the existing practices and procedures surrounding criminal participation of CHIS'. For existing practices, see the case law discussed at 12.19.

It is suggested here that the 'very limited range of circumstances' referred to in Parliament, in which a qualified and circumscribed authorization to participate in some minor way that contributes to the furtherance of a criminal offence might be granted, have been defined through case law. This interpretation is consistent with para 1.9 of the CHIS Code.

12.8 What Authority Regime Is Required for a CHIS?

Persons who can act as authorizing officers for the authorization of CHIS use and CHIS conduct are prescribed in the Regulation of Investigatory Powers (Directed Surveillance and Covert Human Intelligence Sources) Order 2010 (SI 2010/521), as amended by the Regulation of Investigatory Powers (Covert Human Intelligence Sources: Relevant Sources) Order 2013 (SI 2013/2788). These Orders are accessible online at <http://www.legislation.gov.uk/uksi/2010/521/contents/made> and <http://www.legislation.gov.uk/uksi/2013/2788/contents/made> respectively (accessed 12 January 2018).

Before authorizing the deployment of a CHIS, the authorizing officer must believe (s 29(2) and (3)) three things: that

(1) it is *necessary* to so deploy for one of the following reasons:
   • in the interests of national security;
   • for the purpose of preventing or detecting any crime or preventing disorder;
   • in the interests of the economic well-being of the UK;
   • in the interests of public safety;
   • for the purpose of protecting public health;
   • for the purpose of assessing or collecting any tax, duty, levy, or other imposition, contribution, or charge payable to a government department; or
   • for other purposes which may be specified by order of the Secretary of State;
(2) the authorized conduct is *proportionate* to what is sought to be achieved by the conduct or use (see also CHIS Code, paras 3.2–3.5); and
(3) that arrangements are in place for the management of the CHIS that meet the criteria prescribed in s 29(5) RIPA2000 (see also CHIS Code, Chapter 6).

The majority of organizations empowered under RIPA2000 are only able to deploy CHISs for the purpose of *preventing or detecting any crime* or *preventing disorder* (Regulation of Investigatory Powers (Directed Surveillance and Covert Human Intelligence Sources) Order 2003 (SI 2003/3171)).

Appropriate authorization of a CHIS is discussed in the CHIS Code, paras 2.10–2.12. Rather belying the understated statutory treatment of CHISs, the Code describes the deployment of a CHIS as 'particularly intrusive and high-risk' (para 2.10), and the moral significance of such deployment has been briefly alluded to in the introduction to this chapter. For the authorization of directed surveillance, the nub of the proportionality issue lies in whether the proposed surveillance method is proportionate to the information that will be gained by use of this method. When authorizing CHIS deployment, at the heart of the proportionality considerations is whether the manipulation of a human relationship (a prima facie intrusion into private life) is proportionate to the information that will be gained thereby.

First the *use* of a CHIS must meet the necessity and proportionality tests; then the proposed *conduct* of the CHIS must meet the necessity and proportionality tests. If the desired information can be obtained by other less intrusive means, then the deployment of a CHIS will not be proportionate (CHIS Code, para 3.4). (The CHIS Code says 'reasonably obtained' (para 3.4), but that wording is taken from s 32 RIPA2000 in relation to intrusive surveillance and not from s 29 RIPA2000 which relates to CHIS authorization. It is not obviously apparent from the face of the Act that this less stringent test applies to considerations of proportionality in relation to CHIS authorization.)

The authorizing officer is required to take into account a number of factors before granting the authorization.

Paragraphs 3.8–3.11 CHIS Code require the authorizing officer to take into account the risk of collateral intrusion and to ensure that measures have been taken to minimize such intrusion. Authorizing officers must document the anticipated collateral intrusion and detail the action taken to minimize it and the consequences thereof.

Paragraphs 3.17–3.18 CHIS Code require both the applicant and the authorizing officer to be aware of any local community sensitivities and any adverse impact on community confidence and safety that might arise from the deployment.

Further information and reading

The CHIS Code provides explanation for what is required where a CHIS authorization is combined with another type of covert investigation authorization; and where more than one CHIS might be authorized within a single authorization.

> 3.19 A single authorisation may combine two or more different authorisations under Part II of the 2000 Act. For example, a single authorisation may

---

> combine authorisations for intrusive surveillance and the conduct of a CHIS. In such cases the provisions applicable to each of the authorisations must be considered separately by the appropriate authorising officer. Thus, a superintendent or an assistant chief constable (for relevant sources), can authorise the conduct of a CHIS but an authorisation for intrusive surveillance by the police needs the separate authorisation of a chief constable (and the prior approval of a Surveillance Commissioner, except in cases of urgency).
>
> [...]
>
> 3.22 A single authorisation under Part II of the 2000 Act may be used to authorise more than one CHIS. However, this is only likely to be appropriate for operations involving the conduct of several undercover operatives acting as CHISs in situations where the activities to be authorised, the subjects of the operation, the interference with private and family life, the likely collateral intrusion and the environmental or operational risk assessments are the same for each officer. If an authorisation includes more than one relevant source, each relevant source must be clearly identifiable within the documentation sent to the OSC. In these circumstances adequate records must be kept of the length of deployment of a relevant source to ensure the enhanced authorisation process set out in the 2013 Order and Annex B of this code can be adhered to.
>
> Where a combined authorization is sought for the deployment of a CHIS and from the Secretary of State for the carrying out of intrusive surveillance, the Secretary of State is the authorizing officer.
>
> CHIS Code, paras 3.19–3.22

Written authorities last for twelve months (CHIS Code, para 5.14) and must be regularly reviewed (CHIS Code, paras 5.16–5.17). Authorizations must be cancelled by the authorizing officer as soon as there is no further need for the registered individual to act as a CHIS (CHIS Code, para 5.28). There is no need to wait until the end of the twelve-month period to cancel an authorization.

12.9 When Is Judicial Approval Required for a CHIS Authorization?

Section 38 Protection of Freedoms Act 2012 amended RIPA2000 by adding new ss 32A and 32B, the effect of which has been to introduce an additional element into the process for the authorization of CHISs who are to be used by or on behalf of local authorities.

Once the prescribed authorizing officer for a local authority (SI 2010/521) has granted an authorization under s 29 RIPA2000, the authorization does not take effect—and so the CHIS's deployment cannot commence—until such time (if any) as a relevant judicial authority (a Justice of the Peace in England and Wales; a Sheriff in Scotland; or a magistrates' court district judge in Northern Ireland) makes an order approving the granting of the authorization.

The relevant judicial authority may approve the granting of the authority or renewal if, and only if:

- at the time the local authority authorizing officer granted the authorization, he or she had reasonable grounds for believing the authorization to be *necessary* for the purpose of preventing or detecting crime or of preventing disorder; *and*
- at the time the local authority authorizing officer granted the authorization, he or she had reasonable grounds for believing the authorized CHIS conduct to be *proportionate* to what is sought to be achieved by carrying it out (that the methods to be used are proportionate to the product that will be derived); *and*
- at the time that approval for the granting of the authorization is sought, there remain reasonable grounds for believing that the authorization is *necessary* for the purpose of preventing or detecting crime or of preventing disorder and for believing that the authorized CHIS conduct is *proportionate* to what is sought to be achieved by carrying it out; *and*
- the local authority authorizing officer is so designated under s 29 RIPA 2000; *and*
- the grant of the authorization does not breach any prohibition imposed by s 29(7)(a) or any restriction imposed by s 30(3) RIPA 2000; *and*
- any other conditions that may have been imposed by an Order made by a Secretary of State have been complied with.

If the magistrate (or other relevant judicial authority) refuses to approve the granting of the authorization, then he or she may make an order quashing the authorization.

12.10 What Powers Does the Law Provide in Relation to a Relevant Source?

A relevant source is, first and foremost, a CHIS. The relevant source distinction is derived from the employment circumstances of certain CHISs.

Therefore, the statutory requirements for the use and conduct of a relevant source are the same as those described in 12.7 for a CHIS.

Relevant sources differ from other CHISs in that an enhanced authorization regime is required for relevant sources.

12.11 What Authority Regime Is Required for a Relevant Source?

The authorization regime for relevant sources is an enhancement of the regime for other CHISs and comes in two parts: deployments of less than twelve months (by inference); and deployments of longer than twelve months (by virtue of secondary legislation). The prescribed offices, ranks, and positions for author-izing relevant sources are set out in the Regulation of Investigatory Powers (Directed Surveillance and Covert Human Intelligence Sources) Order 2010 (SI 2010/521) as amended by the Regulation of Investigatory Powers (Covert Human Intelligence Sources: Relevant Sources) Order 2013 (SI 2013/2788).

The first enhancement is the increased seniority required to authorize the use and conduct of a relevant source. For example, in police agencies the au-thorizing officer for the use and conduct of a CHIS may be a Superintendent or above, but for the authorization of a CHIS who is a relevant source, the author-izing officer must be an Assistant Chief Constable or above.

The authorizing officer who grants a s 29 authorization for the use and con-duct of a relevant source (for a deployment of less than twelve months) must notify a Judicial Commissioner in writing or by electronic means, within seven days of granting the authority.

The written, or electronically transmitted, notice must include:

1. why the authorization is necessary (the grounds for necessity are set out in Article 5 (6) of the 2013/2788 Order);
2. an explanation of why the authorized use and the authorized con-duct are each proportionate to what is sought to be achieved (s 29(2)(b) RIPA2000); and
3. personal confirmation that the required arrangements are in place for the management of the relevant source (s 29(2)(c) RIPA2000).

It is open to the IPC or the Judicial Commissioners to respond to such notifica-tion with comments. In the event that IPCO comments are made, the author-izing officer 'will wish to consider' such comments (CHIS Code, para 5.10).

The second enhancement of the authorization regime is engaged when deploy-ment is in relation to a single investigation or operation for a period that exceeds twelve months or a series of periods that cumulatively exceed twelve months. Such an authorization is labelled a *'long term authorization'* in the 2013/2788 Order. The precise method of calculating the accumulated twelve months that will constitute a long-term deployment is set out in the CHIS Code (paras 5.24–5.25).

Long-term authorizations require authorizing officers yet more senior: in the police service, for instance, whereas an Assistant Chief Constable or above can authorize a relevant source, only a Chief Constable can grant a *long-term author-ization* for a relevant source. Even then, a Chief Constable cannot grant such an authorization without prior approval.

12.12 When Is Prior Approval Required for a Relevant Source Authorization?

Where a designated public authority is empowered to grant *long-term authoriza-tions* for the use and conduct of a relevant source, the authorization may not be granted without prior approval from the IPC and Judicial Commissioners (CHIS Code, para 5.23).

Note: this is a more rigorous 'prior approval' scheme than that imposed for intrusive surveillance. Whereas for intrusive surveillance, the authorizing officer grants the authorization but then surveillance may not commence until a Surveillance Commissioner's written approval of the authorization so granted has been received (approval comes prior to conduct), in relation to proposed long-term deployments of a relevant source, Surveillance Commissioner written prior approval is required *before the authorization can be granted* (approval comes prior to authorization).

If it is anticipated that an existing deployment may exceed twelve months, thus necessitating an application for renewal, then the IPC and Judicial Commissioners must be notified in writing at the point that the existing authorization has been in effect for nine months (CHIS Code, para 5.26). There should be available a risk assessment indicating how the relevant source may be safely extracted in the event that the Surveillance Commissioners refuse to approve a renewal of an authorization.

12.13 Legal Privilege, Other Confidential Material, and Enhanced Authorization

Confidential information exists in four categories:

- Communications subject to legal privilege.
- Communication about constituency business between a Member of Parliament and another person.
- Personal information, expressly or by implication held in confidence, relating to the physical or mental health of an individual or to the spiritual counselling of an individual where that individual can be identified from the information concerned.
- Material held in confidence having been acquired or created for the purposes of journalism, including communications conveying information to be used for the purposes of journalism.

If it is likely that knowledge of any confidential information, particularly legally privileged material, will be acquired by a CHIS, deployment is subject to a higher level of authority.

Those who, by virtue of their seniority in office, rank, or position, are empowered to authorize the use and conduct of a CHIS in circumstances when legally privileged material or other confidential information will or is likely to be acquired, are prescribed in the Regulation of Investigatory Powers (Directed Surveillance and Covert Human Intelligence Sources) Order 2010 (SI 2010/521). They are also listed in Annex A to the CHIS Code.

Where a relevant source has access to, or is likely to have access to, legally privileged material or other confidential information, the authorization procedures must comply with both SI 2010/521 and SI 2013/2788 (CHIS Code, para 4.3).

Where the intention is to *deploy a CHIS in order to obtain, provide access to, or disclose knowledge of legally privileged material*, then *prior approval* is required from a designated approving officer (in the case of police investigations, the Surveillance Commissioners) *before an authorization can be granted or renewed.*

Further information and reading

Approving officers may only approve, and authorizing officers may only authorize, the use or conduct of CHISs to acquire knowledge of matters subject to legal privilege if they are satisfied that there are *exceptional and compelling* circumstances that make the authorization *necessary*.

Such circumstances will arise only in a very restricted range of cases (eg where there is a threat to life or to national security).

The approving and authorizing officers must be satisfied it will be reasonably likely that the specific knowledge of matters subject to legal privilege that will be acquired by the CHIS will counter the specific and exceptional threat being confronted.

Once obtained, such knowledge may only be used to counter the specific threat, and not for any other purpose.

CHIS Code, paras 4.7, 4.14

Confidential information that is acquired unintentionally by a CHIS and which is retained on record by the investigators must be reported to and made available to the IPCO inspection team during the next inspection immediately following acquisition (CHIS Code, para 4.12). For example, a person under investigation might sufficiently trust an undercover officer to make unsolicited disclosure of material that would otherwise be subject to legal privilege. As the circumstances in *Turner v R* [2013] EWCA Crim 642 illustrate, suspects do confide in those they trust and discuss matters subject to legal privilege with such confidantes.

Further discussion of issues concerning CHISs and access to legally privileged and confidential information is presented in Chapter 4 of the CHIS Code.

12.14 What Information Is Required in an Application for a CHIS?

Written applications for a CHIS authority should describe *both* the purpose of the operation/investigation (ie the *use* to which the agency will be putting the CHIS) *and* the *conduct* for which authorization is sought. CHIS Code, para 5.11

details further information that should be included in applications. The following matters should be recorded:

- the reasons why the authorization is necessary in the particular case and on the grounds listed in s 29(3) of the 2000 Act (eg for the purpose of preventing or detecting crime);
- the purpose for which the CHIS will be tasked or deployed (eg in relation to drug supply, stolen property, a series of racially motivated crimes etc);
- where a specific investigation or operation is involved, the nature of that investigation or operation;
- the nature of what the CHIS conduct will be;
- the details of any potential collateral intrusion and why the intrusion is justified;
- the details of any confidential information that is likely to be obtained as a consequence of the authorization;
- the reasons why the authorization is considered proportionate to what it seeks to achieve;
- the level of authorization required (or recommended, where that is different); and
- a subsequent record of whether authorization was given or refused, by whom, and the time and date.

In urgent cases authorized orally in the first instance, the following should be recorded in writing as soon as practicable:

- the reasons why the authorizing officer considered the case so urgent that an oral instead of a written authorization was given; or
- the reasons why the officer entitled to act in urgent cases considered the case so urgent and why it was not reasonably practicable for the application to be considered by the authorizing officer.

12.15 Review, Renewal, and Cancellation of Authorities

Written authorities last for twelve months (CHIS Code, para 5.14) and must be regularly reviewed (CHIS Code, paras 5.16–5.17). The reviews are to be documented and these records held for three years (CHIS Code, Chapter 7).

An authorization may be renewed, but before any authorization is renewed it must be reviewed (CHIS Code, para 5.18). The authorizing officer renewing an authorization must be able to demonstrate that the results of the prior review have been taken into consideration.

An authorization issued under the urgency provisions (CHIS Code, paras 5.5–5.7) lasts for seventy-two hours.

All applications for renewal should document the following matters (CHIS Code para 5.27):

- whether this is the first renewal;
- if not the first renewal, then every occasion on which the authorization has been renewed previously;
- any significant changes to the information in the initial application or previous renewal;
- the reasons why it is necessary for the authorization to continue;
- the use made of the CHIS in the period since the grant, or, as applicable, the latest renewal, of the authority;
- the tasks given to the CHIS during the period and the information obtained from the use or conduct of the CHIS; and
- the results of the regular reviews of the use of the CHIS.

The authorizing officer who granted or renewed the authorization (or the person now undertaking that role if the original authorizing officer has been redeployed) must cancel the authorization (CHIS Code, para 5.28):

(a) if he or she is satisfied that the *use* or the *conduct* of the CHIS no longer satisfies the criteria for authorization; or
(b) if the arrangements for the CHIS's management no longer satisfy the requirements prescribed in s 29 RIPA2000.

Cancellation of the authorization does not negate an agency's responsibility, where necessary, for the safety and welfare of the CHIS. The duty of care may remain after the use and conduct have ended.

Further information and reading

CHIS Code, paras 3.12–3.16 and 5.16–5.27 discuss the reviewing and renewal of CHIS authorities; paras 5.28–5.29 discuss cancellations.

12.16 **Juveniles and Vulnerable Persons as CHISs**

Special safeguards apply when investigators contemplate the deployment of a CHIS who is under the age of eighteen years. A more senior authorizing officer is required than for an adult CHIS: in the case of the police service, the authorizing officer must be at least an assistant chief constable. The relevant customs officer will be band 11 or above, and in other organizations the designated individual is often the chief executive or director. The relevant ranks and positions are defined in Annex A of the CHIS Code. Special provisions pertaining to the use and conduct of such CHISs are outlined in the Regulation of

Investigatory Powers (Juveniles) Order 2000, SI 2000/2793. (See 'Further information and reading' below.)

The authorization of a juvenile CHIS lasts for one month instead of the twelve-month authorization for adult CHISs. No CHIS under sixteen can be authorized to provide information about any person with parental responsibility for the juvenile (CHIS Code, para 4.24).

Amending the previous definition, the revised CHIS Code, para 4.23, describes a vulnerable individual as a 'person who by reason of mental or other disability, age or illness, is or may be unable to take care of themselves, or unable to protect themselves against significant harm or exploitation'. Such individuals should only be deployed as CHISs in the most exceptional circumstances and, as with juveniles, a higher level of authorizing officer is specified in Annex A of the Code (CHIS Code, para 4.23).

Further information and reading

The Regulation of Investigatory Powers (Juveniles) Order 2000, SI 2000/2793, made 10 October 2000, in force 6 November 2000, provides additional regulation regarding juvenile CHISs. The following paragraphs are extracts from that Order. ('Guardian', in relation to a source, has the same meaning as is given to 'guardian of a child' by s 105 Children Act 1989.)

Sources under 16: prohibition

3.—No authorisation may be granted for the conduct or use of a source if—
    (a) the source is under the age of sixteen; and
    (b) the relationship to which the conduct or use would relate is between the source and his parent or any person who has parental responsibility for him.

Sources under 16: arrangements for meetings

4.—
    (1) Where a source is under the age of sixteen, the arrangements referred to in section 29(2)(c) of the 2000 Act must be such that there is at all times a person holding an office, rank or position with a relevant investigating authority who has responsibility for ensuring that an appropriate adult is present at meetings to which this article applies.
    (2) This article applies to all meetings between the source and a person representing any relevant investigating authority that take place while the source remains under the age of sixteen.
    (3) In paragraph (1), 'appropriate adult' means—
        (a) the parent or guardian of the source;
        (b) any other person who has for the time being assumed responsibility for his welfare; or
        (c) where no person falling within paragraph (a) or (b) is available, any responsible person aged eighteen or over who is neither

---

a member of nor employed by any relevant investigating authority.

Sources under 18: risk assessments etc.

5.—An authorisation for the conduct or use of a source may not be granted or renewed in any case where the source is under the age of eighteen at the time of the grant or renewal, unless—

- (a) a person holding an office, rank or position with a relevant investigating authority has made and, in the case of a renewal, updated a risk assessment sufficient to demonstrate that:
  - (i) the nature and magnitude of any risk of physical injury to the source arising in the course of, or as a result of, carrying out the conduct described in the authorisation have been identified and evaluated; and
  - (ii) the nature and magnitude of any risk of psychological distress to the source arising in the course of, or as a result of, carrying out the conduct described in the authorisation have been identified and evaluated;
- (b) the person granting or renewing the authorisation has considered the risk assessment and has satisfied himself that any risks identified in it are justified and, if they are, that they have been properly explained to and understood by the source; and
- (c) the person granting or renewing the authorisation knows whether the relationship to which the conduct or use would relate is between the source and a relative, guardian or person who has for the time being assumed responsibility for the source's welfare, and, if it is, has given particular consideration to whether the authorisation is justified in the light of that fact.

Sources under 18: duration of authorisations

6.—In relation to an authorisation for the conduct or the use of a source who is under the age of eighteen at the time the authorisation is granted or renewed, section 43(3) of the 2000 Act shall have effect as if the period specified in paragraph (b) of that subsection were one month instead of twelve months.

12.17 **CHISs, the Internet, and Social Media**

Using the internet and social media to acquire private information in circumstances where Article 8 rights are engaged will require directed surveillance authorization. Where a CHIS is using the internet or social media to establish or maintain the relationship that will define the investigator as a CHIS, then such use and conduct must be authorized (CHIS Code, para 4.32).

Where an individual who performs the role of a CHIS using social media also has a personal social media presence in their own true identity, this may represent a significant vulnerability in their operating environment as a CHIS (particularly if identifiable images of the person acting as a CHIS have been posted by themselves or anyone else). Such vulnerabilities must be managed and will have to be removed, avoided, reduced, or accepted as circumstances demand.

12.18 What Management Regime Is Required for a CHIS?

The management regime is defined in s 29(5) RIPA2000. It is essentially a statutory requirement for CHIS vulnerability and risk management.

It includes specific arrangements to ensure that the source is independently managed and supervised via a three-tier hierarchy of supervision, that records are kept of the use made of the source, and that the source's identity is protected from those who do not need to know it. (The Secretary of State can amend these arrangements by order.) The responsibility for the management and supervision of a source falls to specified individuals within the organization benefiting from the use of the source. As there may be cases where a source carries out activities for more than one organization, it is provided that only one organization will be identified as having responsibility for each requirement in relation to such arrangements and recordkeeping.

There must be a person within the organization using the CHIS who is responsible for day-to-day dealings with the CHIS (usually called the handler). Handlers will be supervised by controllers who must have general oversight of the use of the source.

The highest tier comprises an individual of suitable rank whose function it is to maintain records of how CHISs are used. These records are scrutinized annually by the IPCO.

At the level of strategic management, the CHIS Code, para 9.1, requires that every relevant public authority must have a Senior Responsible Officer whose responsibilities have been presented at 12.5.

Understanding the operating environment and the vulnerabilities and risks inherent therein (see Chapter 4) is essential for successful CHIS management, whether the CHIS be an informer or an undercover investigator. It is an ongoing dynamic process which should be documented as thoroughly as possible and kept under daily review.

Thorough documentation in the form of precisely worded authorizations and terms of reference, comprehensive contact sheets, and comprehensively documented instructions to CHISs is also good practice that will assist in subsequent public interest immunity (PII) applications as well as recording the integrity of the CHIS deployment for external scrutiny.

Further information and reading

The Regulation of Investigatory Powers (Source Records) Regulations 2000, SI 2000/2725, specify the particulars to be documented in the records for each CHIS, pursuant to s 29(5)(d) RIPA2000 (made 4 October 2000, in force 1 November 2000):

(a) the identity of the source;

(b) the identity, where known, used by the source;

(c) any relevant investigating authority other than the authority maintaining the records;

(d) the means by which the source is referred to within each relevant investigating authority;

(e) any other significant information connected with the security and welfare of the source;

(f) any confirmation made by a person granting or renewing an authorisation for the conduct or use of a source that the information in paragraph (d) has been considered and that any identified risks to the security and welfare of the source have where appropriate been properly explained to and understood by the source;

(g) the date when, and the circumstances in which, the source was recruited;

(h) the identities of the persons who, in relation to the source, are discharging or have discharged the functions mentioned in section 29(5) (a) to (c) of the 2000 Act or in any order made by the Secretary of State under section 29(2)(c);

(i) the periods during which those persons have discharged those responsibilities;

(j) the tasks given to the source and the demands made of him in relation to his activities as a source;

(k) all contacts or communications between the source and a person acting on behalf of any relevant investigating authority;

(l) the information obtained by each relevant investigating authority by the conduct or use of the source;

(m) any dissemination by that authority of information obtained in that way; and

(n) in the case of a source who is not an undercover operative, every payment, benefit or reward and every offer of a payment, benefit or reward that is made or provided by or on behalf of any relevant investigating authority in respect of the source's activities for the benefit of that or any other relevant investigating authority.

12.19 What Significant Case Law Applies to CHISs?

In the absence of precise statute prior to RIPA2000, the lawful parameters around informers, infiltration, and the use of test purchase as an evidence-gathering mechanism were determined by case law. RIPA2000 is largely silent on CHISs other than to provide the framework for authorization and the risk management regime.

General endorsement for the deployment of informers and undercover investigators was approved in *R v Birtles:* 'whilst the police are entitled to make use of information concerning an offence already laid on and while ... it may be proper for the police to encourage the informer to take part in the offence, the police must never use an informer to encourage another to commit an offence which he would not otherwise commit' ([1969] 1 WLR 1047; and confirmed in *R v Horseferry Road Magistrates Court ex p Bennett (No. 1)* [1994] 1 AC 42).

The value of informers to the authorities recognized in *Birtles* has continued to be acknowledged. In *R v King* (1998) 7 Cr App R (S) 227, Lane LCJ opined:

> One of the most effective weapons in the hands of the detective is the informer. Once the identity of a suspect can be established, even if he does not confess, it will often be possible to obtain scientific or other evidence to connect the suspect with a crime and so corroborate the informer. It is to the advantage of law abiding citizens that criminals should be encouraged to inform upon their criminal colleagues.

The wider benefit to society of this form of covert investigation was also remarked upon by Woolf LCJ in *R v J* [2001] 1 Cr App R (S) 79:

> In the battle against drugs it is absolutely essential that the prosecuting authorities are given information which can help to lead to the detection of others who are engaged in this trade. The courts must do what they can to assist those who are involved in trying to combat the ever growing trade in drugs by giving incentives to those who are convicted and come to be sentenced to provide information.

In *R v Clarke* (1985) 80 Cr App R 344, the court accepted that motive was irrelevant to the liability of an accessory to the fact, but held that it was 'quite another thing to conclude ... that conduct which is overall calculated and intended not to further but to frustrate the ultimate result of the crime is always immaterial and irrelevant'. In essence, this provides a mechanism outside RIPA2000 for rendering lawful behaviour that would otherwise be unlawful, which should be viewed within the context of para 2.10 of the Code.

Further information and reading

The issues raised by *R v Clarke* are considered in a wider context in B Fitzpatrick, 'Covert human intelligence sources as offenders: the scope of immunity from the criminal law', *Covert Policing Review* (2005), 15–32.

It is helpful to consider the numerous key cases thematically. They draw some very fine lines between what is acceptable and what is not.

12.19.1 **Agent provocateur**

It is a fundamental principle that CHISs, be they (participating) informers or undercover investigators, should never incite the commission of a crime. Participating informers, as seen in the general authority of *R v Birtles*, may only participate in offences which are already laid on, ie are already planned. Their role should only be minor.

An *agent provocateur* is defined in *R v Mealey and Sheridan* [1974] 60 Cr App R 59 at 61, quoting the 1928 Royal Commission on Police Powers (Cmd 3297): 'a person who entices another to commit an express breach of the law which he would not otherwise have committed and then proceeds or informs against him in respect of such offence.' This sets the boundary of unacceptable behaviour.

But in also defining what was acceptable, the same judgment held that a person infiltrating a criminal organization, either as an undercover investigator or as a participating informer, must show a 'certain amount of interest and enthusiasm' for the proposed criminality in order to maintain their cover and render the infiltration tactic effective.

Teixeira de Castro v Portugal (1999) 28 EHRR 101 provides a clear example of investigators who went too far. Two undercover investigators posed as drug addicts and asked Teixeira to supply them with heroin. He had no heroin in his house, being a dealer in cannabis, but the investigators took him to another house and persuaded him to buy heroin there in order to sell it to the investigators. The Strasbourg court held that the investigators had incited the commission of an offence that would not otherwise have been committed.

Likewise in *R v Moon* [2004] EWCA Crim 2872, investigators were held to have encouraged Moon, a mere drug user, to become a supplier and so commit more serious offences that she would not otherwise have committed. Her conviction was quashed on appeal. *Moon* took a contradictory view to an earlier judgment, *R v Coutts-Jarman* [2001] EWCA Crim 2376, in which the Court of Appeal upheld the conviction for supplying drugs in circumstances where investigators had made six increasingly pressurized demands for Coutts-Jarman to sell them drugs, the last demand 'reinforced' with the claim that the partner of the intending purchaser was in serious withdrawal.

The investigators in *R v Edwards* [1991] Crim LR 45 adopted a more passive role, making a test purchase which, far from being the isolated instigation argued by the defence, was demonstrably within the context of a wider pattern of drug dealing by the suspect.

Behaviour that similarly fell short of constituting incitement was confirmed in *R v Pattemore* [1994] Crim LR 836, in which the defendant had acquiesced with the requests of an informer. The court held there had been no pressure applied to the defendant and that fairness to the defence had to be balanced in this case by fairness to the public.

Specifically in relation to test purchase operations, *DPP v Marshall and Downes* [1988] 3 All ER 683 established that the tactic itself was not deception in law just because investigators did not reveal their true identities. The tactic itself was re-affirmed as legitimate in *Borough of Ealing v Woolworths Plc* [1995] Crim LR 58, which also held that deploying an eleven-year-old boy to try to purchase products restricted to persons over eighteen years old was legitimate where the test purchaser had passively sought a purchase rather than actively tried to persuade the retailer.

Courts have taken notice of test purchase operative behaviour in determining whether investigators have incited an offence. Acting like an ordinary customer was taken to include the use of aggressive language in *R v Chandler* [2001] EWCA Crim 3167. In *R v Byrne* [2003] EWCA Crim 1073, the court noted that investigators had done nothing to tempt Byrne 'to move outside her usual way of life' (at para 12). Similarly in *R v Jones* [2010] EWCA Crim 925, the court held that an undercover officer had not overstepped the boundary of incitement when engaged in asking questions of a cannabis paraphernalia retailer (who provided advice about growing tomatoes in a context when no reasonable person could have concluded that the conversation was not really about growing cannabis).

Whether the deployment of a test purchase operative requires authorization as a CHIS will depend on the full facts of the investigation. The CHIS Code, para 9.12, offers contrasting examples of circumstances in which CHIS authorization may or may not be considered for test purchase operations. Use of recording equipment by test purchase operatives will amount to directed surveillance.

Case law criteria establishing whether an informer has acted as an agent provocateur

(1) Was a crime of the same kind as that charged already afoot at the time of the intervention of the CHIS?
(2) Had the defendant committed an offence of a class which he would not have committed but for the encouragement of the CHIS?
(3) Had the defendants a propensity to engage in the crime charged?
(4) Did the CHIS play a major part in the criminal activity?
(5) Is the court certain, in retrospect, of the CHIS's reliability?
(6) Was the CHIS's participation approved in accordance with the statutory regime?
(7) Is the offence so grave that the public interest could justify the use of such tactics?

Based on *R v Ameer and Lucas* [1977] Crim LR 104. The judgment in *R v Ameer and Lucas* was disapproved by *R v Sang* [1980] AC 402, at 430, but this seven-part test applied in the case still has relevance.

12.19.2 **Entrapment**

Closely connected to the problem of an investigator acting as *agent provocateur* is the issue of entrapment: an investigator creating situations in which suspects commit offences that they would not otherwise have committed. 'It is simply not acceptable that the state through its agents should lure its citizens into committing acts forbidden by the law and then seek to prosecute them for doing so': thus Lord Nicholls in *R v Loosley* [2001] UKHL 53, para 1. This defining principle having been set, there are investigative actions that fall short of entrapment and the boundaries are defined in case law.

It is well established in English law that entrapment is no defence (*R v Sang* [1980] AC 402; *R v Smurthwaite and Gill* [1994] 1 All ER 898), but that does not release investigators from the obligation to act lawfully. If offenders take advantage of an opportunity to commit a crime and in doing so play a trick on themselves, then this is considered a lawful means of securing evidence. Hence *R v Christou and another* [1992] 4 All ER 559, in which the defendants sold stolen property to undercover police officers masquerading as second-hand property dealers in a shop. Police had established the shop for the very purpose of recovering stolen property from those willing to sell it. Another example is *Williams and another v DPP* [1993] 3 All ER 365, in which an insecure lorry containing dummy packets of cigarettes was parked unattended in a street, thus constituting a tethered-goat-type lure. Once again, those who took the opportunity to steal from the lorry were held to have played a trick on themselves.

In *Nottingham City Council v Amin* [2000] 1 WLR 1071, a taxi driver had agreed to take two special constables on duty in plain clothes to a specified area in the city for which they paid a fare. The taxi driver had no licence to ply for hire in that area. It was held that the police had a duty to enforce the law and that it was not offensive to provide an individual with an opportunity to commit a crime which had then been taken up. The defendant did not have to take advantage of the opportunity.

These should be viewed within the context of *R v Loosley* [2001] UKHL 53, which reaffirmed that where the involvement of an accused was a direct result of incitement by an investigator, then the evidence should rightfully be excluded under s 78 PACE. But where the investigator had done no more than provide an opportunity for the accused to commit a crime, in exactly the same circumstances as another person might have provided such an opportunity (ie a test purchase investigator purporting to be a drug addict when trying to secure evidence of the accused's dealing), there was no reason why the evidence should be excluded, particularly if it was part of a properly authorized operation in which every effort had been made to secure corroboration through tape-recording.

Ormerod, in essence, summarizes a test for entrapment in his paper in *Covert Policing Review* (2006) and this test was applied by the court in *R v Moore and Burrows* [2017] EWCA Crim 85.

KEY POINTS IN DETERMINING WHETHER INVESTIGATORS HAVE ENGAGED IN ENTRAPMENT

- What was the trigger for the operation? Was there reasonable suspicion that the person subject to the operation was already engaged in the suspected criminality?
- Was the operation properly authorized and supervised?
- Was the operation a proportionate response to the offence?
- Was the investigator's conduct no more than to offer the suspect an opportunity to commit the crime—was the investigator acting in an unexceptional way given the type of crime in question? Did the investigator cause the crime?
- Was the conduct with the suspect contemporaneously recorded?

Based on Ormerod, 2006, 72 and 75

Further information and reading

For wider discussion of the issue of entrapment, see:

- D Ormerod, 'Recent developments in entrapment', *Covert Policing Review* (2006), 65–86;
- S McKay, 'Entrapment: competing views on the effect of the Human Rights Act 1998 on the English criminal law', *European Human Rights Law Review* (2002), 764; and
- A Ashworth, 'Redrawing the boundaries of entrapment', *Criminal Law Review* (2002), 161–179.

12.19.3 Securing evidence

The extent to which undercover investigators can secure evidence by questioning those with whom they interact is constrained by the PACE Codes of Practice in relation to interviews. The Codes have been held to apply to interviews outside a police station or other custody centre (*R v Christou and another* [1992] 4 All ER 559).

In *R v Bryce* [1992] 4 All ER 567, investigators asked questions that were essentially evidential in nature and so constituted an unlawful interview because the PACE regime had not been complied with. In *R v Christou and another* [1992] 4 All ER 559, the undercover officers had asked only such questions as were necessary to maintain their cover as second-hand property dealers.

In *Bryce*, the conversations had not been tape-recorded, whereas in *Christou* they had been. Tape-recording such interactions ensures that there is an accurate and unassailable record of conversations between CHISs and suspects or investigators. Tape-recordings will demonstrate, for instance, that a conversation is an offence in the commission rather than a conversation about past events that constitutes an admission. The value of this was established in *R v*

Smurthwaite and Gill [1994] 1 All ER 898, which also identified good-practice criteria for such recordings, reaffirmed in *R v Mann and Dixon* [1995] Crim LR 647, and in *R v Horseferry Road Magistrates Court exp Bennett (No. 1)* [1994] 1 AC 42. More recently, *R v Kennedy, Palmer and Warburton* (unreported, 2001) reaffirmed the value of tape-recording and the expectation of courts that this represented 'best evidence': proceedings were stayed due to inadequate police recording and documentation of the alleged offending and interaction with investigators. In *R v Hardy and Hardy* [2002] EWCA Crim 3012, the Court of Appeal held that the tape-recording by undercover officers of telephone conversations which they had with the suspects (subsequently defendants) did not amount to interception because these were conversations about which the officers could testify as witnesses and for which the recordings merely provided corroboration.

....

Case law criteria for assessing fairness at trial where it is sought to exclude evidence from undercover operations

The court will consider:

(1) whether the CHIS acted as an *agent provocateur*;
(2) the nature of any entrapment;
(3) whether the recorded evidence constitutes an offence in progress or an admission of an historical offence;
(4) whether the investigator's role in securing the evidence was active or passive;
(5) whether there is an unassailable record or robust corroboration of what occurred;
(6) whether the CHIS abused his role to ask questions that should have been put only under the PACE Codes.

Based on *R v Smurthwaite and Gill* [1994] 1 All ER 898.

....

12.19.4 Protecting informers

Case law going back as far as 1794 has established the principle that it is in the public interest to protect the identities of CHISs, unless to do so would deny a defendant the chance to establish innocence and thus lead to a miscarriage. As was seen in Chapter 6.12.2, the same principle was extended to the protection of observation points.

Further information and reading

The protection of informers: the historical precedent for the protection of the identity of police informers is to be found in: *Hardy's case* (1794) 24 St Tr 199; *AG v Briant* (1846) 15 M&W 169; *Marks v Beyfus* [1890] 25 QBD 494; *D v NSPCC* [1978] AC 171; *R v Hennessy* (1979) 68 Cr App R 419; *R v Hallett and others* [1986] Crim LR 462; *R v Turner (Paul)* [1995] 1 WLR 264; *R v Pattemore* [1994] Crim LR 836.

> Through the statutory CHIS management regime and the relevant Code of Practice, RIPA2000 establishes that public authorities have a duty of care towards informers (R Billingsley, 'Duty of care for informers', *The Police Journal*, 78 (2005), 210–211).

Case law criteria—test for duty of care

Caparo Industries Plc v Dickman & others [1990] 2 AC 605 establishes a three-point test to identify whether a duty of care exists.

(1) Damage/harm must have been done.
(2) There must be proximity in the relationship between the person alleging damage/harm and the party alleged to be negligent.
(3) It must be reasonable, in the circumstances, for a duty of care to exist.

In *Donnelly v CC of Lincolnshire & Others* [2001] Po LR 313; [2001] All ER (D)) the *Caparo* test was applied in circumstances where a CHIS claimed his anonymity had been assured by police who subsequently revealed his identity during suspect interviews. The CHIS suffered damage/harm (his life was imperilled); his relationship to Lincolnshire Police was proximate (he was an informer providing information covertly to the police); and it was reasonable in these particular circumstances for the informer to expect a duty of care from police.

These and other cases are considered at length in Billingsley (2005), 209–221.

Swinney and another v Chief Constable of Northumbria [1996] 3 All ER 449 affirmed that there was a general duty of care to take reasonable steps to avoid public disclosure of information provided by a CHIS. Documented information provided by an informer was stolen from an unattended police car. The person about whom the information had been provided subsequently subjected the informer and her family to threats and arson attacks, having been told who had provided information to the police.

There have been case law exceptions: *R v Agar* [1990] 2 All ER 442 established that where there were *specific, detailed* allegations of a set-up, the defence could ask investigators about their sources. This did not establish a disclosure precedent nor did it provide a vehicle for defence fishing trips. *Savage v Chief Constable of Hampshire* [1997] 2 All ER 631 held that an informer who chose to disclose his role could not be prevented from doing so on public policy grounds.

In relation to protecting CHISs through a PII application, *R v H and C* [2004] 2 AC 134 confirms that neutral material or material damaging to the defendant need not be disclosed and should not, therefore, be brought to the attention of the court. Where a CHIS testifies at court, it is legitimate for the defence to seek to ascertain the circumstances in which the CHIS was recruited, details of the assistance provided and the rewards made, and the motivation of the CHIS.

12.19.5 Disclosure of CHIS authorities

In light of the issues exposed in relation to the long-term deployments of undercover officers from the Metropolitan Police SDS, it might reasonably be anticipated that defence counsel will have particular interest in future in the authorization of undercover officers: specifically, what conduct has been explicitly authorized or expressly prohibited. Whereas an informer will usually not be exposed to testifying at trial, an undercover officer may well be a professional witness upon whom the prosecution depends. Thus issues concerning undercover officers should be revealed to the prosecutor, who will then be obliged to consider what should be disclosed to the defence.

The statutory presumption of disclosure is founded in the CPIA. Because surveillance authorities may contain sensitive detail, exposure of which would be against the public interest, such authorities may be scheduled as sensitive unused material. Unless the requirements of the disclosure regime are directly engaged, for example, the authorization documentation contains material that tends to undermine the prosecution case or will assist the defence case, authorization documentation will not normally be disclosed (*R v GS* [2005] EWCA Crim 887; see also *R v Jones* [2010] EWCA Crime 925).

It is the prosecutor's responsibility to ensure proper disclosure of any material falling within the disclosure regime, including authorization material (*R v GS* [2005] EWCA Crim 887). If the prosecutor recognizes contentious issues regarding the authorization process, a redacted version of the authority should be disclosed and an unedited version supplied to the judge for determination that the defendant is not vulnerable to a miscarriage arising from non-disclosure (*R v Hardy and Hardy* [2002] EWCA Crim 3012). The defence cannot go on fishing trips and if seeking to challenge admissibility and a ruling under s 78 PACE, must have convincing reasons for doing so (*R v GS* [2005] EWCA Crim 887). Where the defence declares specific issues with the authorization process, as in *R v Grant* [2005] EWCA Crim 1089, full disclosure of all documentation related to a covert investigation authorization may be ordered. Although in cases involving *intrusive* surveillance a court may rely on the approval forms signed by the Surveillance Commissioner as evidence of lawful authorization (*R v GS* [2005] EWCA Crim 887), in matters concerning *directed* surveillance the court may wish to inspect the authorization documentation for itself. Whether these principles will be extended by analogy to the deployment of CHISs, the deployment of relevant sources, and to long-term authorizations, time will tell as and when courts are invited to consider such issues.

In *R v Harmes* [2006] EWCA Crim 928, the court considered the authorization documentation in detail, noting (at para 22) that renewals of the authorization had failed to detail either changes in circumstances or changes in planned police activity, and concluding (at para 42) that 'there were serious breaches of the Act and the Code in the process of authorization'.

The failure properly to disclose relevant material in relation to the undercover deployment of PC Mark Kennedy (operating under the alias of Mark Stone) led directly to the quashing of multiple convictions. Chairing the Appeal Court bench, the Lord Chief Justice opined:

> It is a case which has given rise to a great deal of justifiable public disquiet, which we share. Something went seriously wrong with the trial. The prosecution's duties in relation to disclosure were not fulfilled. The result was that the appellants were convicted following a trial in which elementary principles that underpin the fairness of our trial system were ignored. The jury were ignorant of evidence helpful to the defence which was in the possession of the prosecution but which was never revealed. As a result justice miscarried.
>
> (*R v Barkshire & others* [2011] EWCA Crim 1885 at 1)

In addition to this instance, the convictions of a further twenty-nine persons were quashed on 21 January 2014, once again because the details of Mark Kennedy's deployment and precise involvement in their case were not disclosed (<http://www.theguardian.com/uk-news/2014/jan/21/drax-protesters-convictions-quashed-police-spy-mark-kennedy>, accessed 5 August 2015).

12.20 Good Practice in Light of the Case Law

The importance of *precise and detailed documentation* in relation to CHIS conduct cannot be overemphasized, particularly given the absence of specific statutory reference concerning infiltration and participation in otherwise criminal conduct.

Where it is necessary to conduct directed surveillance of an individual to evaluate the potential benefit and risks involved in their deployment as a CHIS, it may be necessary to authorize such conduct if the circumstances of the case coincide with the statutory grounds for which authorization is required. Regardless of whether authorization is required in the circumstances or not, the surveillance will be an infringement of Article 8(1) ECHR and must therefore be capable of justification under Article 8(2) (see CHIS Code, para 3.23).

Corroboration of information provided by a CHIS is crucial. For undercover or test purchase investigators, this can be achieved through technical means (where it is safe for the investigator to wear a tape-recorder or point-of-view video device) or through other appropriately authorized surveillance as required. In relation to informers reporting on their encounters with criminal associates, there will rarely be the opportunity to corroborate conversations during such interaction, and so their intelligence must be assessed accordingly and actions arising therefrom suitably risk-managed.

Similarly, the debriefing of CHISs should be fully documented and adjustments made to their risk assessment or conduct authorization as required.

The role and conduct of undercover officers must be revealed to the prosecutor so that a fully informed decision can be made about what should be disclosed to the defence.

12.21 **Deploying a CHIS in Scotland and Overseas**

Except where the investigation is concerned with the national security or the economic well-being of the UK; or where conduct has been authorized by virtue of s 48(4) RIPA2000; or where a public authority listed in s 46(3) RIPA2000 and the Regulation of Investigatory Powers (Authorisations Extending to Scotland) Order 2000 (SI 2000/2418); CHIS conduct that is required to be authorized and which will take place in Scotland should be authorized pursuant to the Regulation of Investigatory Powers (Scotland) Act 2000 (accessible at <http://www.legislation.gov.uk/asp/2000/11/contents>, accessed 5 August 2015; see also CHIS Code, paras 4.25–4.26).

Paragraphs 4.27–4.31 of the CHIS Code deal briefly with circumstances in which a UK CHIS might be deployed in a foreign jurisdiction and in which a foreign CHIS might be deployed in the UK. With increasing reliance upon biometric border security controls, management of such deployments is increasingly complex, and advice from the international expertise within the National Crime Agency should be sought.

KEY POINTS ON PROPORTIONALITY

(1) A test purchase investigator must not act as an *agent provocateur*. This means they must not incite or procure a person, or through that person anybody else, to commit an offence, or an offence of a more serious character, which that person would not otherwise have committed.

(2) However, a test purchase officer is entitled to join a conspiracy which is already in being or an offence which is already laid on, or, for example, where a person has made an offer to supply goods, including drugs, which involves the commission of a criminal offence.

(3) If, during the course of an investigation into an offence or series of offences, a person involved suggests the commission of, or offers to commit, a further similar offence, a test purchase officer is entitled to participate in the proposed offence. The investigator must not incite such an offence.

(4) It is proper for the test purchase investigator to show interest in, and enthusiasm for, proposals made even though they are unlawful, but in doing so they must try to tread the difficult line between showing the necessary interest and enthusiasm to keep their cover (and pursue their investigation) and actually becoming an *agent provocateur*. Invariably this means the investigator will enter a criminal conspiracy or become part of a pre-arranged criminal offence.

---

(5) Test purchase investigators must obtain confirmation that the information they are acting on is accurate and reliable before becoming involved in operations.

(6) Test purchase investigators must bear in mind that, by virtue of s 78 PACE, a judge may take into account the circumstances in which evidence was obtained in considering its adverse effect on the fairness of proceedings in court.

(7) Police officers must be fully conversant with Article 6 ECHR (right to fair trial) and Article 8 (right to respect for private and family life).

Checklist of key issues when considering whether or not to deploy a CHIS

- What evidence or intelligence is being sought?

- How is it relevant to the operation under consideration?

- What is the least intrusive means of securing such evidence or information?

- Has the least intrusive means of securing the evidence or information been attempted? If not, why not?

- What is the likelihood of collateral intrusion against the privacy of persons not being investigated? How will collateral intrusion be prevented (or if not, minimized) and how will the product of collateral intrusion be managed?

- What are the risks to the organization of such tactics? (Chapter 4)

- What are the risks to the organization's staff, especially the CHIS, of such tactics? (Chapter 4)

- What are the risks of the CHIS being compromised by another person? (Chapter 4)

- What are the risks of the CHIS compromising him or herself? (Chapter 4)

- If the CHIS has compromised him or herself, how are the additional risks going to be managed? (Chapter 4)

- What are the risks to the public or specific third parties, including the family and friends of the CHIS, when such tactics are deployed? (Chapter 4)

- What are the risks to the subject of the investigation? (Chapter 4)

- Will such methods breach Article 8(1)? (Chapter 2.2)

- Is there justification for doing so provided by Article 8(2)? (Chapter 2.2)

- How is the legality test met? (Chapter 2.2.3)

- How is the legitimacy test met? (Chapter 2.2.4)

- How is the necessity test met? (Chapter 2.2.5)

- How is the proportionality test met? (Chapter 2.2.5)

- Is the proposed CHIS a juvenile? If so, have the appropriate safeguards been put in place? (CHIS Code, para 4.24)

- Is the proposed CHIS a vulnerable person? If so, have the appropriate safeguards been put in place? (CHIS Code, para 4.23)

- Has the CHIS been properly trained as an undercover investigator?

- Has the CHIS been properly assessed, evaluated, briefed, and debriefed as a (paid) informer?

- Is the CHIS prepared to enter into the witness protection scheme if necessary?

- Is the organization prepared to provide the resources necessary to place the CHIS on the witness protection scheme?

- Are the arguments justifying the application to use covert investigation based on reliable information/intelligence, or has the applicant adopted a 'tick-the-box' approach to completing the application without giving full consideration to the facts of the case and the issues arising?

- Have the arguments justifying the granting of authorization to use covert investigation been fully articulated, or has the authorizing officer merely paid lip service to the pro forma authorization template via which authority is granted?

- How will the product of the surveillance be managed? (Chapter 5)

- When should this authority be reviewed? What circumstances will or may arise that will necessitate review before then?

- How are the methods by which the evidence/intelligence will be obtained to be protected at trial?

Planning covert investigation actions

Remember to include the PLAN for covert investigation tactics in all investigation policy-book entries relating to covert investigation considerations and decisions.

P Proportionality

Why is it proportionate to obtain the intended product of this surveillance in the manner proposed? (Chapter 2.2.5)

L Legitimacy

What is the legitimate purpose of the proposed action: the prevention of disorder or crime; the interests of national security; the interests of public safety;

the interests of the economic well-being of the country; the protection of health or morals; the protection of the rights and freedoms of others? (Chapter 2.2.4)

A Authority to Undertake Proposed Action

What is the lawful foundation and authority for the proposed action? From whom must authorization be sought? (Chapter 2.2.3)

N Necessity of Proposed Action

Why is the proposed action necessary? (Chapter 2.2.5)

13

Covert Investigation Abroad

13.1 **Introduction**

Criminals have always utilized jurisdiction borders as a means of evading prosecution or disrupting investigation. In the final quarter of the twentieth century, as global communications and transport networks became accessible to ever more people, it became easier to escape from a jurisdiction and easier to commit crime on a transnational scale, for instance the trafficking of illicit commodities from source countries to criminal markets overseas. With local community policing in the UK increasingly incorporating transnational communities with links in the UK and overseas, for instance in the EU or the Indian sub-continent, it is possible that a covert investigation otherwise contained within a single local English police force may nevertheless have transnational actions associated with it. A surveillance team from anywhere in the UK could quite conceivably find that their subject travels through the Channel Tunnel in the space of twenty-five minutes to meet criminal associates in France or Belgium, before returning to the UK the same day.

To counter transnational criminality and aid its investigation a corpus of instruments and conventions has been created to facilitate mutual legal assistance and international law enforcement cooperation: these are the means by which domestic investigators can secure help as required in their own investigations where evidence or the suspect is located outside their own jurisdiction.

Further information and reading

This is an area of increasing activity for investigators and lawyers alike. For legal commentary (together with the reproduction of some key legal instruments), see D McClean, *International Judicial Assistance* (Clarendon Press, Oxford, 1992); C Murray and L Harris, *Mutual Assistance in Criminal Matters* (Sweet & Maxwell, London, 2000); A Jones and A Doobay, *Jones and Doobay on Extradition and Mutual Assistance* (Sweet & Maxwell, London, 2005), 362–377. For a collection of key legal instruments, C Van den Wyngaert (ed), *International Criminal Law: A Collection of International and European Instruments* (3rd revd edn, Martinus Nijhoff, Leiden, 2005).

The term *transnational* (cross-border) is preferred here to *international* (between states) because the latter term is used to qualify specific behaviours, instruments, and institutions in relation to international law that do not apply to the cross-border investigation of crimes proscribed in domestic jurisdictions. The International Criminal Court has permissive jurisdiction only over genocide, crimes against humanity, war crimes, and international aggression, not domestic crimes committed on a transnational scale (Statute of the International Court, Article 5 (Rome, 17 July 1998, UN Doc A/CONF 183/9) *International Legal Materials* 1998, 999; alternatively, Van den Wyngaert, *International Criminal Law*, 139, 130).

In the absence of an international or supranational criminal code, different domestic jurisdictions have to be able to work alongside each other in cooperation when criminality crosses their mutual border. This is the *raison d'être* of mutual legal assistance treaty law and the premise underpinning the philosophy of mutual recognition promoted within the EU by the UK (*Hansard* HL (series 6) vol 411, col 973 (2 December 2003)) until Brexit.

13.2 Which Public Authorities May Conduct Covert Investigation Abroad?

Section 27(3) RIPA2000 prescribes that surveillance authorized under s 26 can include 'conduct outside the United Kingdom'. In respect of directed or intrusive surveillance and the deployment of CHISs, those authorities empowered to conduct such investigations within the UK can also conduct such authorized activity abroad without offending UK law.

Part III PA97 limits the area of lawful authorization in relation to property interference to the relevant area overseen by the authorizing officer and, as appropriate, adjacent UK territorial waters (s 93).

Section 15(4) of IPA2016 makes provision for mutual assistance in relation to incoming and outgoing requests for the interception of communications, to the extent that such requests are compliant with an appropriate international mutual assistance agreement. Section 85 of IPA2016 provides that overseas telecommunications and postal operates can also be subject to requests for communications data, with s 85(4) detailing considerations for the practicability of such requests.

Therefore relevant empowered investigators are as described in Chapters 6, 10, 11, and 12.

13.3 What Powers Does the Law Provide in Relation to Covert Investigation Abroad?

Section 27(3) RIPA2000 prescribes that surveillance authorized under s 26 can include 'conduct outside the United Kingdom'. In respect of directed or intrusive surveillance and the deployment of CHISs, conduct that can be authorized within the UK can also be authorized to take place in a foreign jurisdiction without offending UK law. However, such activity may breach the domestic law of the foreign jurisdiction in which it is proposed to conduct surveillance. In effect, authorizations for conduct outside the UK simply validate the conduct for the purposes of UK law (CSPI Code, para 1.20; CHIS Code, para 4.27). The HRA is taken to apply to the actions of public authorities in overseas territories within the jurisdiction of the UK, such as embassies and military bases. The

Regulation of Investigatory Powers Ordinance 2012 extends the authority of the Chief Surveillance Commissioner to sovereign bases overseas.

Part III PA97 limits the area of lawful authorization in relation to property interference to the relevant area overseen by the authorizing officer and, as appropriate, adjacent UK territorial waters (s 93).

Therefore relevant investigation powers are as described in Chapters 6 and 13, taking into account the provisions of the foreign jurisdiction in which it is proposed to conduct the covert investigation.

Two international instruments make provision for international law enforcement covert investigation cooperation within the EU: the Schengen Convention 1990 (International Legal Materials 1991, 84) and the EU Convention on Mutual Assistance in Criminal Matters 2000, 29 May 2000 Brussels, OJ 2000/C 197/1. The latter supplements the 1959 Convention on Mutual Assistance in Criminal Matters, which is open to Member States of the Council of Europe and not just EU members but which contains no specific provisions for covert investigation (European Treaty Series 30, done Strasbourg 20 April 1959).

Article 40 of the Schengen Convention provides for 'cross-border surveillance', where a person under surveillance and presumed to have taken part in a criminal offence to which extradition may apply (Article 40(7)) crosses the mutual border of two contracting parties to the Convention. If investigators in the requesting state have prior authorization to do so from the requested state which the suspect enters during the course of the surveillance, Article 40(1) permits the original investigators to continue their surveillance in the territory of the requested state, subject to any request to the requested state to assume responsibility for the surveillance. In spontaneous circumstances where it was not possible to seek prior authorization, surveillance may be continued for up to five hours in the territory of the requested state whilst authorization to continue the surveillance is sought from the requested state. Article 40(3)(f) expressly prohibits the domestic surveillance team operating in a foreign territory pursuant to this article from challenging or arresting the subject under surveillance whilst in the jurisdiction of another state. The UK entered into this Article of the Schengen Convention on 22 December 2004 (*Mutual Legal Assistance Newsletter 19*, UK Central Authority, February 2005), the obligations being given domestic effect in s 83 Crime (International Co-operation) Act 2003 which creates new s 76A RIPA2000.

Article 40 can only be applied by police and customs investigators engaged on a criminal investigation. Although the government had repeatedly asserted that SOCA was not a police force (*Hansard* HC Standing Committee D, cols 9 and 34 (11 January 2005); see also cols 32, 33, 35, 38 and 43), the National Crime Agency has been designated as such to enable its staff to utilize Article 40. (Authorities designated for the purposes of Article 40 are listed in the *Schengen Handbook on Cross-Border Police Co-operation*, OJL 239, 408, 22 September 2000.)

This provision is not to be confused with 'hot pursuit' permitted by Article 41 Schengen Convention, which is restricted to uniformed officers (or plain-clothes officers clearly displaying visible insignia identifying them as police officers) pursuing a suspect fleeing the scene of a crime or escaping from custody across a land border. As the UK and Eire have not entered into this part of the Schengen Convention, hot pursuit is not permitted across the UK's only EU land border. Contracting parties and the law enforcement agencies permitted to use Articles 40 and 41 are listed in the Schengen Handbook.

Other covert investigation tactics may be permitted under Article 13 of the EU Mutual Legal Assistance Convention subject to the agreement of the requesting and requested states. Under this provision it is for the requested state to decide whether or not to implement the request for covert investigation put to it, having 'due regard to its national law and procedures'. The domestic law of the state in which the covert investigation takes place shall apply to the activities undertaken.

Article 13 EU Mutual Legal Assistance Convention makes provision for the establishment of multi-national joint investigation teams (JITs), members of which could apply for any such domestic covert or coercive measures within their own jurisdictions without recourse to mutual legal assistance procedures. Diplomatic negotiation is required to establish a JIT and advice should be sought from the Home Office Judicial Co-operation Unit (Home Office Circulars 53/2002 and 26/2004 refer).

Further information and reading

Joint investigation teams are given a liability framework by ss 103 and 104 Police Reform Act 2002 and a statutory powers framework by ss 16(2)(b), 16(4)(b), 18(2), and 27(1) Crime (International Co-operation) Act 2003. See also the EU Council Framework Decision of 13 June 2002 on Joint Investigation Teams (2002/465/JHA) OJ 2002/L 162/1 and the EU Commission Recommendation for a Model Agreement for setting up Joint Investigation Teams, 7 April 2003, CRIMORG 17, 7061/0. For UK government guidance on JITs, see Home Office Circulars 53/2002 and 26/2004.

There are an increasing number of studies into the effectiveness and practicalities of joint investigation teams. See, for instance, L Block, *From Politics to Policing: The Rationality Gap in EU Council Policy-Making* (2011, Eleven, The Hague, chapter 7); also C Rijken, 'Joint Investigation Teams: principles, practice and problems. Lessons learnt from the first efforts to establish a JIT' *Utrecht Law Review* 2(2) (2006), 99.

In relation to non-EU states, the capability to request covert investigation assistance abroad will depend upon the nature of any mutual legal assistance treaty in force between the UK and the other state in question. On existing mutual legal assistance treaties and their provisions, advice should be sought from the UK Central Authority.

Further information and reading

The UK Central Authority is the single point of contact in England and Wales by which international letters of request (also known as *Commissions Rogatoires*) are transmitted and received. Information about the UK Central Authority and mutual legal assistance is available at <http://www.homeoffice. gov.uk/police/mutual-legal-assistance/> (accessed December 2011).

UK accession to the EU Mutual Legal Assistance Convention meant that provision had to be made for providing assistance in respect of communication interception notwithstanding the general prohibition on the use of intercepted communications as evidence in UK criminal trials (s 17 RIPA2000).

Section 1(4) RIPA2000 permits UK investigators to request foreign interception of communications when three conditions are met: (1) where the UK is party to a designated international agreement which has come into force; (2) where the interception is being carried out for the purposes of a criminal investigation; and (3) where the investigation is being carried out in the territory of a state party to the designated agreement. The EU Mutual Legal Assistance Convention is the only such designated agreement at the time of writing. (See Regulation of Investigatory Powers (Conditions for the Lawful Interception of Persons outside the UK) Regulations 2004 (SI 2004/157); Regulation of Investigatory Powers (Designation of an International Agreement) Order 2004 (SI 2004/158).)

Such requested intercepted communications could not be used in evidence in the UK by virtue of the prohibition in s 17 RIPA2000.

The reciprocal arrangement is provided under s 5(1)(c). The Secretary of State is able to stipulate that any communications intercepted in the UK and provided to foreign authorities should not be used in evidence abroad.

Further information and reading

It is useful to read the official record of parliamentary debates on these issues to understand the Government's position. See Caroline Flint, Parliamentary Under-Secretary of State for the Home Department (*Hansard* HC, Standing Committee D, col 219 (18 January 2005)). The whole issue of interception evidence was debated during consideration of the Serious Organised Crime Bill (*Hansard* HC, Standing Committee D, cols 205–224 (18 January 2005)). It was previously debated at length during the RIP Bill debates (*Hansard* HL (series 5) vol 613, cols 1307–1344 (12 June 2000)).

13.4 **What Authority Regime Is Required for Covert Investigation Abroad?**

The authority provided by s 27(3) RIPA2000 is constrained by mutual legal assistance treaty law. An investigator cannot simply operate abroad on the basis of this RIPA2000 subsection alone.

Thus *in addition* to the authority regimes for directed and intrusive surveillance and the deployment of CHISs described in Chapters 6 and 13, *permission must be sought* from the foreign authorities in whose jurisdiction the surveillance is going to take place.

With the exception of circumstances provided for by Article 40 Schengen Convention, covert investigation abroad will normally be conducted on behalf of English investigators by the authorities in the requested state. This fact does not negate the need for a RIPA2000 authority to be in place authorizing the covert investigation to take place.

Where the evidence required and to be obtained by English covert investigation teams operating overseas is to be relied upon by the prosecution, in any cases of doubt about the need for a surveillance authority it is good practice to have a surveillance authority in place. Evidence derived from unauthorized covert investigation is vulnerable to exclusion from trial under s 78 PACE (arguments for which could be based on Articles 6 or 8 ECHR, as well as English case law).

Where a vehicle-tracking device is deployed and it is anticipated that the vehicle will travel through multiple national jurisdictions, a single authorization naming the different jurisdictions will suffice rather than a different authorization for each jurisdiction.

Where the work of a JIT will lead to trial in the UK and reliance therein on evidence from covert investigations undertaken by the JIT, the appropriate surveillance authority for the covert investigation will be required no matter where it took place. The establishment of a JIT may offer a mutual legal assistance shortcut, but it does not negate the necessity of obtaining the appropriate surveillance authorities.

Where the subject of the covert investigation is neither a UK national nor likely to be the subject of criminal proceedings in the UK, and the conduct under investigation would neither affect a UK national nor give rise to material likely to be used in evidence before a UK court, it would appear in these specific circumstances (which might arise from a JIT investigation) that a RIPA2000 authority would not be required (CSPI Code, paras 1.20–1.23 and CHIS Code, paras 4.27–4.31).

In respect of interception of communications, the powers and authority regime (Secretary of State's warrant) are stipulated in s 1(4) RIPA2000.

13.5 What Significant Case Law Has Been Decided in Relation to Covert Investigation Abroad?

> **Further information and reading**
>
> For illuminating discussions of the various issues that can arise from gathering evidence abroad, including by means of covert investigation, see C Gane and M Mackarel, 'The admissibility of evidence obtained from abroad into criminal proceedings: the interpretation of mutual legal assistance treaties and use of evidence irregularly obtained', *European Journal of Crime, Criminal Law and Criminal Justice*, 4 (1996), 98–119.
>
> Although it pre-dates RIPA2000, it nevertheless contains much pertinent consideration and comparative study of covert investigation principles within the context of mutual legal assistance.
>
> Where foreign agencies undertake covert investigation in their own jurisdiction, either on behalf of UK authorities or pursuant to their own investigations being prepared to share the product with UK authorities, consideration must be given to whether the foreign product has been obtained in a manner that might lead to it being excluded from trial in England because foreign agencies may lawfully act in ways that UK authorities cannot. See, for example, C Harfield, 'The governance of covert investigation', *Melbourne University Law Review*, 34(3) (2010), 773–804, specifically p 803; also C Harfield, 'Managing human rights and covert methods in transnational criminal investigations', in S Hufnagel, C Harfield, and S Bronitt (eds), *Cross-Border Law Enforcement: Regional Law Enforcement Cooperation—European, Australian and Asia-Pacific Perspectives* (Routledge, London, 2011) pp 231–242.

The fact that evidence for use in an English trial has been obtained from abroad with the aid of a mutual legal assistance treaty does not guarantee its admissibility nor preclude any procedural challenge by the defence. The evidence may be subject to restrictions placed on its use by the requested state and cannot be used for any other purpose than was specified in the original request for assistance (s 9 Crime (International Co-operation) Act 2003). Where evidence is relied upon both to secure a conviction and subsequently confiscate assets, both purposes should be articulated in the international letter of request (*R v Gooch (No. 1)* [1999] 1 Cr App R (S) 283).

Investigators must also beware of how evidence is perceived and used abroad when supplying covert investigation material gathered within the UK to requesting foreign jurisdictions. Criminal intelligence material supplied to foreign jurisdictions on an 'intelligence only' basis has, nevertheless and within the context of foreign evidential laws, legitimately been disclosed to the defendant (and in some cases also the press) before trial. Hence, for instance, 'evidence is unlimited in French law, when acts discovered by foreign judicial or police authorities are used in a French case, they are considered as information and are therefore subject to discussion during the arguments in the trial as to the facts of the case' (*Kamal Jain*, Appeal Court of Aix en Provence 4 May 1992, confirmed by the Cour de Cassation, Paris, 7 October 1993, case no. M92–83.707 D). Information that might normally and successfully be protected from disclosure at trial through PII applications in the UK may not be so protected abroad. In some jurisdictions, if it exists, it must be used at trial.

Further information and reading

For comparative studies on criminal procedure, including rules of evidence, in Belgium, England, France, Germany, and Italy, see M Delmas-Marty and J Spencer (eds), *European Criminal Procedures* (Cambridge University Press, Cambridge, 2002).

Whether or not the contents of an international letter of request are disclosable is debatable. Confidentiality cannot be relied upon in mutual legal assistance. See Jones and Doobay, *Jones and Doobay on Extradition and Mutual Assistance*, 402. See also Murray and Harris, *Mutual Assistance in Criminal Matters*, 47.

Similarly, CPIA disclosure issues can be complicated further when evidence from a foreign jurisdiction is relied upon. With careful investigation planning and prior consultation with the appropriate prosecutor, such issues need not be prohibitively problematic.

Other case law guidance suggests that the discretion permitted the court under s 78 PACE extends to evidence sought to be adduced from abroad. Indeed, some authorities argue such discretion affords investigators the opportunity to engage in 'forum shopping' or 'process laundering'. Certainly the courts have held that violation of Article 8 ECHR will not automatically result in exclusion of the evidence obtained as a result, but investigators and the prosecution cannot rely upon that discretion as a means of bypassing prescribed procedure (*R v Governor of Pentonville Prison, ex p Chinoy* [1992] 1 All ER 317, following *R v Sang* [1979] 2 All ER 1222; *Khan v UK* (2001) 31 EHRR 45 supporting *R v Khan* [1997] AC 558). 'Fishing expeditions' have been criticized by courts and requests for covert investigation should be specific and closely founded upon the chain of evidence, although it is accepted that not all evidence obtained through mutual legal assistance will necessarily be relied on in court (*R v Secretary of State ex p Fininvest SpA* [1997] 1 WLR 743).

R v Aujla [1998] 2 Cr App R 16 highlights an anomaly in respect of intercepted communications evidence and mutual legal assistance. It was held that intercept products by a foreign jurisdiction that had already been adduced at trial in the Netherlands were admissible in an English trial because the prohibition on the use of intercept products as evidence in the UK (at the time prohibited under s 9 Interception of Communications Act 1985; a restriction subsequently preserved under s 56 IPA2016) applied only to intercept products obtained in the

UK. The prohibition on evidential use thus does not apply to intercept products obtained abroad by foreign authorities for their own purposes. This reasoning was affirmed by the House of Lords in *R v P (Telephone intercepts: Admissibility of Evidence)* [2001] 2 WLR 463.

13.6 Sources of Advice

Once it is clear that an investigation is likely to necessitate evidence or intelligence-gathering abroad and that such needs are likely to require the use of covert investigation methods, investigators will need to engage with a number of different agencies in order to achieve a successful outcome.

Failure to follow protocols in transnational investigation can lead to any or all of the following consequences: loss of or inability to access evidence; abandonment of investigation or prosecution; or, where investigators have operated unilaterally and without permission overseas, the arrest, conviction, and imprisonment abroad of the investigators concerned.

The numerous sources of specialist advice are listed in Table 13.1.

Table 13.1 Sources of guidance for investigators planning (covert) investigations abroad

Mutual legal assistance law	RIPA2000 and IPA2016 Codes of Practice; Legislative Explanatory Notes
	Crown Prosecution Service (or equivalent prosecution authority)
	UK Central Authority, Home Office
Non-evidential foreign assistance	Europol (EU only)
	Interpol
Planning an international request	Crown Prosecution Service
	Eurojust
	European Judicial Network
	UK Central Authority
Drafting an international request	Crown Prosecution Service
	Eurojust
	UK Central Authority
Request transmission procedures	Crown Prosecution Service
	UK Central Authority
Joint investigation teams	Judicial Co-Operation Unit, Home Office Eurojust

Further information and reading

The UK Central Authority is based in the Home Office and is the single point of contact in England and Wales by which international letters of request (also known as *Commissions Rogatoires*) are transmitted and received. There is limited scope for direct transmission of requests with the EU. The latest list of states allowing direct transmission is held by the UK Central Authority. Home Office advice on mutual legal assistance (both for UK authorities seeking assistance from abroad and for foreign authorities seeking assistance from the UK) is available online at <http://www.homeoffice.gov.uk/police/mutual-legal-assistance/> (accessed December 2011).

The UK National Central Bureau of Interpol is co-located with the UK Europol Bureau within the National Crime Agency.

International considerations are also discussed in the CSPI Code, paras 1.20–1.23; the CHIS Code, paras 4.26–4.30; the Interception Code, para 2.1; and the Communications Data Code, paras 7.11–7.21.

The first source of advice should be the prosecutor: is covert investigation abroad vital in achieving a successful conviction? The question is as much practical as legal.

For instance, some foreign jurisdictions do not permit their surveillance personnel to testify in court. Their evidence is adduced in the inquisitorial trial system by way of third-party report, a method prohibited by the hearsay rules in the adversarial court process. How foreign surveillance evidence might be adduced in an English court must inform the operational planning of the surveillance, as such practicalities may limit the surveillance options available, although with UK adoption of Article 40 Schengen Convention this has become less of a problem for English investigators within the EU. Prosecutors (supported by Eurojust) will be able to resolve such practicalities.

There are other factors for consideration. Is there a realistic prospect of conviction without the foreign evidence? Would a conviction for a different charge (which did not require foreign surveillance evidence) achieve the same reduction in harm? As the person whose role it is to present the evidence and case at court, the prosecutor is often as well positioned as an investigator, if not better positioned, to make such a determination.

Once the decision has been made in conjunction with a prosecutor to proceed with a request for covert surveillance to be conducted abroad, the advice of the other authorities listed in Table 13.1 should be sought. Because the prosecutor is pivotal in the management of investigations in many foreign jurisdictions, British investigators may find that foreign authorities will expect to deal with a British prosecutor rather than a British investigator.

Further information and reading

On foreign investigators conducting covert investigation in the UK see CSPI Code, paras 1.23, 5.19–5.21 and CHIS Code, paras 4.27–4.31.

Checklist of key considerations when planning covert investigation abroad

- What evidence or intelligence is being sought?
- How is it relevant to the operation under consideration?
- Is it absolutely necessary, in order to secure a conviction, to conduct covert investigation abroad?
- Would an alternative charge, not dependent upon foreign evidence, secure the same reduction in harm upon conviction (eg the same length of prison sentence as a conviction that relied upon the foreign evidence)?
- What is the advice of the prosecutor?
- What is the advice, if applicable, of Eurojust?
- What is the advice, if applicable, of Europol or Interpol?
- What is the least intrusive means of securing such evidence or information?
- What are the risks to the organization of such tactics? (Chapter 4)
- What are the risks to the organization's staff of such tactics? (Chapter 4)
- What are the risks to the British public, the foreign public, or specific third parties when such tactics are deployed? (Chapter 4)
- What are the political/diplomatic risks arising from this operation? (Chapter 4)
- What are the risks to the subject of the investigation? (Chapter 4)
- Will such methods breach Article 8(1)? (Chapter 2.2)
- Is there justification for doing so provided by Article 8(2)? (Chapter 2.2)
- How is the legality test met? (Chapter 2.2.3)
- How is the legitimacy test met? (Chapter 2.2.4)
- How is the necessity test met? (Chapter 2.2.5)
- How is the proportionality test met? (Chapter 2.2.5)
- Are the arguments justifying the application to use covert investigation based on reliable information/intelligence, or has the applicant adopted a 'tick-the-box' approach to completing the application without giving full consideration to the facts of the case and the issues arising?
- Have the arguments justifying the granting of authorization to use covert investigation been fully articulated, or has the authorizing officer merely paid lip service to the pro forma authorization template via which authority is granted?
- How are the methods by which the evidence/intelligence will be obtained to be protected at trial in the UK?
- If covert investigation product from the UK is to be used in a trial abroad, how are the methods by which the evidence/intelligence will be obtained to be protected at trial overseas?
- What are the consequences of foreign authorities disclosing confidential intelligence or unused material supplied by British authorities?
- What risk management plan is in place to address these consequences?

Planning covert investigation actions

Remember to include the PLAN for covert investigation tactics in all investigation policy-book entries relating to covert investigation considerations and decisions.

P Proportionality

Why is it proportionate to obtain the intended product of this surveillance in the manner proposed? (Chapter 2.2.5)

L Legitimacy

What is the legitimate purpose of the proposed action: the prevention of disorder or crime; the interests of national security; the interests of public safety; the interests of the economic well-being of the country; the protection of health or morals; the protection of the rights and freedoms of others? (Chapter 2.2.4)

A Authority to Undertake Proposed Action

What is the lawful foundation and authority for the proposed action? From whom must authorization be sought? (Chapter 2.2.3)

N Necessity of Proposed Action

Why is the proposed action necessary? (Chapter 2.2.5)

Note: at time of publication the UK is an EU Member State. How UK law enforcement cooperation with EU states will work post-Brexit is still under consideration.

What Does Good Covert Investigation Look Like?

Community confidence and trust in public authorities is corroded by the exposure of wrongdoing that ought to have been held to account but which has been veiled behind secrecy provisions. In such circumstances the suspicion inevitably arises that secrecy has been employed to shield what was a purposeful and intentional misuse of power rather than an unwitting error. The value of secrecy is debased when it is improperly or inappropriately relied upon. It is to be hoped that debate will be anchored by objectivity rather than swayed by sensationalism. But disclosures of undercover officers' morally harmful conduct, revelations about mass surveillance, and exposure of unlawful hacking for commercial profit (facilitated by police corrupt practices) have all tainted the profession of covert investigation. If the community is to tolerate and consent to such methods, trust must be repaired.

A portfolio of reviews and reports (see further reading box below) is informing the current reform debate and it is impossible to predict at the time of writing what might be the eventual outcome. Although the IPA2016 is clearly a significant step in recent reforms, it does not address all the issues currently being debated and is itself, not uncontroversial in its measures. (Proposed reform that was being discussed in government at the time the first edition was published thirteen years ago has yet to be agreed upon, let alone articulated into legislation.)

Further reading and information

House of Lords Library Note LLN-2015-0018, *Reports Into Investigatory Powers*, published 8 July 2015 and accessible online at <http://researchbriefings.parliament.uk/ResearchBriefing/Summary/LLN-2015-0018> (accessed July 2015), presents a summary of recent inquiries into investigation powers:

David Anderson QC, the government's Independent Reviewer of Terrorism Legislation, *A Question of Trust: Report of the Investigatory Powers Review* (June 2015).

The Intelligence and Security Committee of Parliament, *Privacy and Security: A Modern and Transparent Legal Framework*, House of Commons paper HC1075 (March 2015).

The Annual Report of the Chief Surveillance Commissioner (September 2014).

The Annual Report of the Intelligence Services Commissioner (June 2015).

The Report by the Prime Minister's Special Envoy on Intelligence and Law Enforcement Data Sharing, Sir Nigel Sheinwald (June 2015).

During a House of Commons debate on these reports on 25 June 2015, the Home Secretary, Theresa May, said that taken together they constitute a 'substantial Independent Review' on the use of investigatory powers and the arrangements for their oversight. Although the reports differ in some of their conclusions, both the Government's Independent Reviewer of Terrorism Legislation and the Intelligence and Security Committee of Parliament have recommended for the overhaul of the current legislative framework for the use of investigatory powers and the replacement of legislation such as the Regulation of Investigatory Powers Act 2000.

The Library Note in its electronic form contains web links to each of these reports or a summary of them.

The Library Note quoted above should be read in conjunction with another Library Note published six days earlier:

Human Rights and Civil Liberties in the United Kingdom, LLN-2015-0016 (2 July 2015), accessible online at <http://researchbriefings.parliament.uk/ResearchBriefing/Summary/LLN-2015-0016> (accessed January 2018).

Innovation and reform must be evidence-based, and not merely a political reaction:

vague appeals to national security and the war on terror, though cloaked in the language of proportionality, are frequently misused when employed to justify warrantless wire-taping, enhanced interrogation techniques and extraordinary renditions.

John Kleinig, 'The ethical perils of knowledge acquisition', *Criminal Justice Ethics* 28(2) (2009), 201–222, at 204.

The work of the ongoing Undercover Policing Inquiry is documented on its website at <https://www.ucpi.org.uk> (accessed January 2018).

A generic strategic framework presents itself.

In the first place, there must be consensus about the role of covert investigation within society and what effect on society it is likely to have: to what conduct in their name will the community consent? Taken together, a variety of different technologies have created the capability not just to prevent, prosecute, and punish, but to pre-empt. That latter capability redefines policing (in its widest sense). At the moment the criminal justice system exists to restore order where it has been disturbed, and the police exist as a constituent element of that system, gathering the information that other criminal justice system actors need to arrive independently at the most accurate possible decisions in a manner that is fair to those who are adversely affected by the decisions. A pre-emptive capability has the potential to enable public authorities to bypass the criminal justice system, to disturb the current balance, and redefine the current relationship between the executive and judicial processes. The debate is of wider significance than simply tackling terrorism or organized crime. How national security is preserved in part defines national security and the consequences for those being secured. Does covert investigation sit within the context of community safety (safety enhanced through respect for individual dignity made manifest in human rights protection) or does it sit within the context of national—or regime—security (behind which individual and human rights can be argued to take second place)? (See also Kleinig, 2009, 208–210.)

Secondly, moral justification (the 'why') must underpin the ethics (the 'how') of covert investigation. This foundation has three aspects:

- any given law must be morally sound;
- the general purpose to which public authorities put any given law must be morally sound; and
- the manner in which the provisions of the law are executed by individual state agents must, in every instance, be morally sound.

There is much work yet to be done to explore and define the ethical boundaries of morally justified covert investigation, both as a process and as a portfolio of specific techniques (each of which present their own profiles of morally problematic issues). Response to the systemic issues raised by the SDS history there must be, but legislative overreaction may cause damage of as much significance to legitimate community interests and moral claims, as the significant damage caused to the legitimate interests and moral claims of individuals directly affected by the relationships they had with SDS undercover officers. We have explored very briefly in Chapter 1 a strategic overview of the moral issues, and have proposed a series of basic tests intended, as much as anything, to trigger further dialogue and to encourage those who use covert investigation to think about the implications of doing so in ways that we did not encounter during our service.

Thirdly, once there is agreement on the values that the community wishes to concrete as societal norms, law (defining the 'what', the 'when', and the 'where' of statutory coercive powers) must be devised and drafted in such a way as to be accessible and understandable both by those who are to use it, and those against whom the law might be used (law that does not meet the latter criteria will not deter those on the fringes of criminality and misconduct who might be amenable to deterrence). Law and morality are not the same thing, but a law that is morally sound is a first step towards achieving agency legitimacy from the foundation of lawfulness.

Further information and reading

A parallel debate is underway about whether individual persons have legally enforceable rights derived as an intrinsic element of their personhood or humanity (the status quo), or whether (in what might be viewed as a statutory social contract exchange) rights are some form of state-sponsored privilege to be conferred upon legally defined/confirmed 'citizens' who have demonstrably executed specified responsibilities towards the state and/or community (a possible outcome of proposals currently under consideration).

See House of Lords Library Note, *Human Rights and Civil Liberties in the United Kingdom*, LLN-2015-0016 (2 July 2015), accessible online at <http://researchbriefings.parliament.uk/ResearchBriefing/Summary/LLN-2015-0016> (accessed January 2018).

Fourthly, the community being served by covert investigation laws and users is entitled to hold accountable those so empowered. Just because conduct is being undertaken covertly does not exempt public authorities and their agents from appropriate forms of scrutiny. It is useful here to reiterate the principles of governance and regulation outlined in Chapter 3. Documented governance must serve to demonstrate that:

- information gathered as evidence to sustain a prosecution (or other enforcement action) or intelligence to facilitate investigation management has been obtained in a manner that preserves the integrity of the criminal justice or administrative systems and their actors;
- the statutory rights of the person(s) being investigated have not been infringed except where there is statutory provision to do so;
- the rights and privacy of other citizens not suspected of criminal involvement or regulatory misconduct have been protected and collateral harm as a consequence of covert investigation has been minimized through effective investigation management; and
- the professional integrity of investigators has been demonstrated or, if necessary, its absence exposed.

Compliance with these principles is demonstrated in a two-stage process: pre-deployment authorization of intended action ('front-end accountability', to borrow a phrase from Simon Bronitt's speech to the Brisbane Current Legal Issues Seminar, 6 August 2015); and post-deployment documented record of what took place ('back-end accountability'), the documentation from both these stages being made available for independent audit.

Fifthly, covert investigation should only be conducted when investigators have the fullest possible understanding of the operating environment and the direct and indirect implications of utilizing proposed methodologies. The operating environment, we have suggested (Chapter 4), is four-dimensional and multi-faceted. Experience suggests that investigators, their managers, and the organization executive leadership may not always fully appreciate how complex the environment is when they embark on covert operations.

Further information and reading

Executive virtues such as efficiency and economy need to be coupled with the values of fairness, respect and the consideration of others' legitimate interests if they are not to be corrupted in significant ways.

John Kleinig, 'The ethical perils of knowledge acquisition', *Criminal Justice Ethics* 28(2) (2009), 201–222, at 202.

Finally, those empowered to use covert methods must use such powers with diligence and discretion. The law and accountability mechanisms must meticulously and rigorously be complied with (because of the imbalance of power in the criminal justice process and the need to preserve the integrity of the criminal justice system if it is to serve the common interest and not appear to serve just the interests of a sociopolitical elite), without forgetting that there is no requirement that public authorities must use such methods.

Just because investigators can does not mean that investigators should.

Index

Please note that page references to Tables will be followed by the letter 't'